Experimentation for Engineers

Experimentation for Engineers

FROM A/B TESTING
TO BAYESIAN OPTIMIZATION

DAVID SWEET

MANNING

SHELTER ISLAND

For online information and ordering of this and other Manning books, please visit www.manning.com. The publisher offers discounts on this book when ordered in quantity. For more information, please contact

> Special Sales Department
> Manning Publications Co.
> 20 Baldwin Road
> PO Box 761
> Shelter Island, NY 11964
> Email: orders@manning.com

Manning Publications Co.
20 Baldwin Road
PO Box 761
Shelter Island, NY 11964

Development editors:	Karen Miller and Katherine Olstein
Technical development editor:	Alain Couniot
Review editor:	Mihaela Batinić
Production editor:	Kathleen Rossland
Copy editor:	Carrie Andrews
Proofreader:	Jason Everett
Technical proofreader:	Ninoslav Čerkez
Typesetter:	Dennis Dalinnik
Cover designer:	Marija Tudor

ISBN: 9781617298158
Printed and bound by CPI Group (UK) Ltd, Croydon, CR0 4YY

To B and Iz.

brief contents

contents

preface

When I first entered the industry, I had the training of a theoretician but was presented with the tasks of an engineer. As a theoretician, I had worked with models using pen-and-paper or simulation. Where the model had a parameter, I—the theoretician—would try to understand how the model would behave with different values of it. But now I—the engineer—had to commit to a single value: the one to use in a production system. How could I know what value to choose?

The short answer I received from more experienced practitioners was, "Just try something." In other words, experiment. This set me off on a course of study of experimentation and experimental methods, with a focus on optimizing engineered systems.

Over the years, the methods applied by the teams I have been on, and by engineers in trading and technology generally, have become ever more precise and efficient. They have been used to optimize the execution of stock trades, market making, web search, online advertising, social media, online news, low-latency infrastructure, and more. As a result, trade execution has become cheaper and more fairly priced. Users regularly claim that web search and social media recommendations are so good that they worry their phones might be eavesdropping on them (they're not).

Statistics-based experimental methods have a relatively short history. Sir R. A. Fisher published the seminal work, *The Design of Experiments*, in 1935—less than a century ago. In it he discussed the class of experimental methods in which we'd place an A/B test (chapter 2). In 1941, H. Hotelling wrote the paper "Experimental determination of the maximum of a function," in which he discussed the modeling of a response surface (chapter 4). Response surface methodology was further explored by G. Box and K. P. Wilson. In 1947, A. Wald published the book *Sequential Analysis*, which studies the idea of analyzing experimental data measurement by measurement (chapter 3), rather than waiting until all measurements are available (as you would in an A/B test).

While this research was being done, the methods were being applied in industry: first in agriculture (Fisher's methods), then in chemical and process industries (response surface methods). Later (from the 1950s to the 1980s) experimentation merged with statistical process control to give us the quality movements in manufacturing, exemplified by Toyota's Total Quality Management, and later, popularized by Six Sigma.

From the 1990s onward, internet companies have experienced an explosion of opportunity for experimentation as users have generated views, clicks, purchases, likes—countless interactions—that could be easily modified and measured with software on centralized web servers. In 2005, C.-C. Wang and S. R. Kulkarni wrote "Bandit problems with side observations," which combined sequential analysis and supervised learning into a method now called a *contextual bandit* (chapter 5).

In 1975, J. Mockus wrote "On the Bayes methods for seeking the extremal point," the foundation for Bayesian optimization (chapter 6), which takes an alternative approach to modeling a response surface and combines it with ideas from sequential analysis. This method was developed over the decades since by many researchers, including D. Jones et al., who wrote "Efficient global optimization of expensive black-box functions," which, in 1998, applied some modern ideas to the method, making it look much more like the approach presented in this book.

In 2017, Vasant Dhar asked me to talk to his Trading Strategies and Systems class about high-frequency trading (HFT). He was gracious enough to allow me to focus specifically on the experimental optimization of HFT strategies. This was valuable to me because it gave me an opportunity to organize my thoughts and understanding of the topic—to pull together the various bits and pieces that I'd collected over the years. Slowly, those notes have grown into this book.

I hope this book saves you some time by putting all the bits and pieces I've collected in one place and stitching them together into a single, coherent unit.

acknowledgments

I am grateful to so many people for their hard work, for their support, and for their faith that this book could be brought into existence.

Thanks to Andrew Waldron, my acquisitions editor, for taking a chance on my proposal and on me. And thanks to Marjan Bace for giving it the thumbs-up.

Thanks to Katherine Olstein, my first development editor, for tirelessly reading and rereading my drafts and providing invaluable feedback and instruction.

Thank you to Karen Miller, my second development editor, and to Alain Couniot for technical editing. Thank you to Bert Bates for great high-level advice on writing a technical book, and to my technical proofreader, Ninoslav Čerkez. Thanks also to Matko Hrvatin, MEAP coordinator; Melissa Ice, development administrative support; Rebecca Rinehart, development manager; Mihaela Batinić, review editor; and Rejhana Markanovic, development support.

Thanks to Professor Dhar for entrusting his students to me and my new material. Thanks to Andy Catlin for believing that I could teach a brand-new class based on an incomplete book. And thank you to my students for being gracious beta testers and providing valuable, as-you're-learning feedback that I couldn't have found anywhere else.

Several people sat with me for interviews. I appreciate the time and support of P.B., B.S., M.M., and Yan Wu (of Bond).

Thank you to the many Manning Early Access Program (MEAP) participants who bought the book before it was finished, asked great questions, located errors, and made helpful suggestions.

To all the reviewers: Achim Domma, Al Krinker, Amaresh Rajasekharan, Andrei Paleyes, Chris Heneghan, Dan Sheikh, Dimitrios Kouzis-Loukas, Eric Platon, Guillermo Alcantara Gonzalez, Ikechukwu Okonkwo, Ioannis Atsonios, Jeremy Chen, John Wood, Kim Falk, Luis Henrique Imagiire, Marc-Anthony Taylor, Matthew Macarty, Matthew Sarmiento, Maxim Volgin, Michael Kareev, Mike Jensen, Nick Vazquez, Oliver Korten, Patrick Goetz, Richard Tobias, Richard Vaughan, Roger Le, Satej Kumar Sahu, Sergio Govoni, Simone Sguazza, Steven Smith, William Jamir Silva, and Xiangbo Mao; your suggestions helped make this a better book.

about this book

Experimentation for Engineers teaches readers how to improve engineered systems using experimental methods. Experiments are run on live production systems, so they need to be done efficiently and with care. This book shows how.

Who should read this book

If you want to build things, you should also know how to evaluate them. This book is for machine learning engineers, quantitative traders, and software engineers looking to measure and improve the performance of whatever they're building. Performance of the systems they build may be gauged by user behavior, revenue, speed, or similar metrics.

You might already be working with an experimentation system at a tech or finance company and want to understand it more deeply. You might be planning or aspiring to work with or build such a system. Students entering industry might find that this book is an ideal introduction to industry practices.

A reader should be comfortable with Python, NumPy, and undergraduate math (including basic linear algebra).

How this book is organized: A road map

Experimentation for Engineers is loosely organized into three pieces: an introduction (chapter 1), experimental methods (chapters 2–6), and information that applies to all methods (chapters 7 and 8).

- Chapter 1 motivates experimentation, describes how it fits in with other engineering practices, and introduces business metrics.

- Chapter 2 explains A/B testing and the fundamentals of experimentation.
- Chapter 3 shows how to speed up A/B testing with multi-armed bandits.
- Chapter 4 focuses on systems with numerical parameters and introduces the idea of a response surface.
- Chapter 5 uses a multi-armed bandit to optimize many parameters in the special case where metrics can be measured very frequently.
- Chapter 6 combines the concepts of a response surface and multi-armed bandits into a single method called Bayesian optimization.
- Chapter 7 talks more deeply about business metrics.
- Chapter 8 warns the reader about common pitfalls in experimentation and discusses mitigations.

About the code

This book contains many examples of source code both in numbered listings and in line with normal text. In both cases, source code is formatted in a `fixed-width font like this` to separate it from ordinary text. Sometimes code is also **in bold** to highlight code that has changed from previous steps in the chapter, such as when a new feature adds to an existing line of code. In many cases, the original source code has been reformatted; we've added line breaks and reworked indentation to accommodate the available page space in the book. In rare cases, even this was not enough, and listings include line-continuation markers (➡). Additionally, comments in the source code have often been removed from the listings when the code is described in the text. Code annotations accompany many of the listings, highlighting important concepts.

You can get executable snippets of code from the liveBook (online) version of this book at https://livebook.manning.com/book/experimentation-for-engineers. The source code for all listings as well as generated figures is available on GitHub (https://github.com/dsweet99/e4e) inside Jupyter notebooks. You can always find your way there from the book's web page at www.manning.com/books/experimentation-for-engineers. The code is written to Python 3.6.3, NumPy 1.21.2, and Jupyter 5.4.0.

liveBook discussion forum

Purchase of *Experimentation for Engineers* includes free access to liveBook, Manning's online reading platform. Using liveBook's exclusive discussion features, you can attach comments to the book globally or to specific sections or paragraphs. It's a snap to make notes for yourself, ask and answer technical questions, and receive help from the author and other users. To access the forum, go to https://livebook.manning.com/book/experimentation-for-engineers/discussion. You can also learn more about Manning's forums and the rules of conduct at https://livebook.manning.com/discussion.

Manning's commitment to our readers is to provide a venue where a meaningful dialogue between individual readers and between readers and the author can take place. It is not a commitment to any specific amount of participation on the part of the author, whose contribution to the forum remains voluntary (and unpaid). We suggest you try asking the author some challenging questions lest his interest stray! The forum and the archives of previous discussions will be accessible from the publisher's website as long as the book is in print.

about the author

DAVID SWEET worked as a quantitative trader at GETCO and a machine learning engineer at Instagram, where he used experimental methods to optimize trading systems and recommender systems. This book is an extension of his lectures on quantitative trading systems given at NYU Stern. It also forms the basis for the course Experimental Optimization, a course that he teaches in the AI and data science master's programs at Yeshiva University. Before working in industry, he received a PhD in physics, publishing research in *Physical Review Letters* and *Nature*. The latter publication—an experiment demonstrating chaos in geometrical optics—has become a source of inspiration for computer graphics artists, a tool for undergraduate physics instruction, and an exhibit called "TetraSphere" at the Museum of Mathematics in New York City.

about the cover illustration

The figure on the cover of *Experimentation for Engineers* is "Homme Sicilien," or "Sicilian," taken from a collection by Jacques Grasset de Saint-Sauveur, published in 1788. Each illustration is finely drawn and colored by hand.

In those days, it was easy to identify where people lived and what their trade or station in life was just by their dress. Manning celebrates the inventiveness and initiative of the computer business with book covers based on the rich diversity of regional culture centuries ago, brought back to life by pictures from collections such as this one.

Optimizing systems by experiment

The past 20 years have seen a surge in interest in the development of experimental methods used to measure and improve engineered systems, such as web products, automated trading systems, and software infrastructure. Experimental methods have become more automated and more efficient. They have scaled up to large systems like search engines or social media sites. These methods generate continuous, automated performance improvement of live production systems.

Using these experimental methods, engineers measure the business impact of the changes they make to their systems and determine the optimal settings under which to run them. We call this process *experimental optimization*.

This book teaches several experimental optimization methods used by engineers working in trading and technology. We'll discuss systems built by three specific types of engineers:

- Machine learning engineers
- Quantitative traders ("quants")
- Software engineers

Machine learning engineers often work on web products like search engines, recommender systems, and ad placement systems. Quants build automated trading systems. Software engineers build infrastructure and tooling such as web servers, compilers, and event processing systems.

These engineers follow a common process, or workflow, that is an endless loop of steady system improvement. Figure 1.1 shows this common workflow.

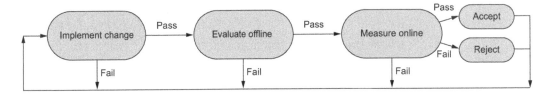

Figure 1.1   Common engineering workflow. (1) A new idea is first implemented as a code change to the system. (2) Typically, some offline evaluation is performed that rejects ideas that are expected to negatively impact business metrics. (3) The change is pushed into the production system, and business metrics are measured there, online. Accepted changes become permanent parts of the system. The whole workflow repeats, creating reliable, continuous improvement of the system.

The common workflow creates progressive improvement of an engineered system. An individual or a team generates ideas that they expect will improve the system, and they pass each idea through the workflow. Good ideas are accepted into the system, and bad ideas are rejected:

1 *Implement change*—First, an engineer implements an idea as a code change, an update to the system's software. In this stage, the code is subjected to typical software engineering quality controls, like code review and unit testing. If it passes all tests, it moves on to the next stage.

2 *Evaluate offline*—The business impact of the code change is evaluated offline, away from the production system. This evaluation typically uses data previously logged by the production system to produce rough estimates of *business metrics* such as revenue or the expected number of clicks on an advertisement. If these estimates show that applying this code change to the production system would worsen business metrics, then the code change is rejected. Otherwise, it is passed to the final stage.

3 *Measure online*—The change is pushed into production, where its impact on business metrics is measured. The code change might require some configuration—the setting of numerical parameters or Boolean flags. If so, the engineer will measure business metrics for multiple configurations to determine which is best. If no improvements to business metrics can be made by applying (and configuring) this code change, then the code change is rejected. Otherwise, the change is made permanent and the system improves.

This book deals with the final stage, "measure online." In this stage, you run an experiment on the live production system. Experimentation is valuable because it produces a measurement from the real system, which is information you couldn't get any other way. But experimentation on a live system takes time. Some experiments take days or weeks to run. And it is not without risk. When you run an experiment, you may lose money, alienate users, or generate bad press or social media chatter as users notice and complain about the changes you're making to your system. Therefore, you need to take measurements as quickly and precisely as possible to minimize the ill effects of ideas—call them *costs* for brevity—that don't work and to take maximal advantage of ones that do.

To extract the most value from a new bit of code, you need to configure it optimally. You could liken the process of finding the best configuration to tuning an old AM or FM radio or tuning a guitar string. You typically turn a knob up and down and listen to see whether you're getting good results. Set the knob too high or too low and your radio will be noisy, or your guitar will be sharp or flat. So it is with code configuration parameters (often referred to as *knobs* in code your author has read). You want them set to just the right values to give maximal business impact—whether that's revenue or clicks or some other metric. Note that the need to run costly experiments is what specifies *experimental* optimization methods as a subset of optimization methods more generally.

In this chapter, we'll discuss engineering workflows for each of the engineer types listed earlier—machine learning engineer (MLE), quant, and software engineer (SWE). We'll see what kinds of systems they work on, the business metrics they measure, and how each stage of the generic workflow is implemented.

In your organization, you might hear of alternative ways of evaluating changes to a system. Common suggestions are domain knowledge, model-based estimates, and simulation. We'll discuss the reason why these tools, while valuable, can't substitute for an experimental measurement.

1.1 Examples of engineering workflows

While the engineers listed earlier may work in different domains, their overall workflows are similar. Their workflows can be seen as specific cases of the common engineering workflow we described in figure 1.1: implement change, evaluate offline, measure online. Let's look in detail at an example workflow for an MLE, for a quant, and for an SWE.

1.1.1 Machine learning engineer's workflow

Imagine an MLE who works on a web-based news site. Their workflow might look like figure 1.2.

The key machine learning (ML) component of the website is a predictor model that predicts which news articles a user will click on. The predictor might take as input many *features*, such as information about the user's demographics, the user's previous

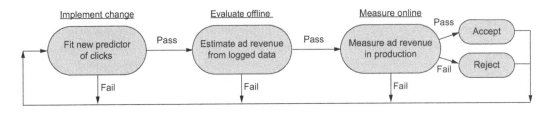

Figure 1.2 Example workflow for a machine learning engineer building a news-based website. The site contains an ML component that predicts clicks on news articles. (1) The MLE fits a new predictor. (2) An estimate of ad revenue from the new predictor is made using logs of user clicks and ad rates. (3) The new predictor is deployed to production and actual ad revenue is measured. If it improves ad revenue, then it is accepted into the system.

activity on the website, and information about the news article's title or its content. The predictor's output will be an estimate of the probability that a specific user will click on a given news article. The website could use those predictions to rank and sort news articles on a headlines-summary page hoping to put more appealing news higher up on the page.

Figure 1.2 depicts the workflow for this system. When the MLE comes up with an idea to improve the predictor—a new feature or a new model type—the idea is subjected to the workflow:

1   *Implement change*—The MLE fits the new predictor to logged data. If it produces better predictions on the logged data than the previous predictor, it passes to the next stage.

2   *Evaluate offline*—The business goal is to increase revenue from ads that run on the website, not simply to improve click predictions. Translating improved predictions into improved revenue is not straightforward, but methods exist that give useful estimates for some systems. If the estimates do not look very bad, the predictor will pass on to the next stage.

3   *Measure online*—The MLE deploys the predictor to production, and real users see their headlines ranked with it. The MLE measures the ad revenue and compares it to the ad revenue produced by the old predictor. If the new predictor improves ad revenue, then it is accepted into the system.

A news-based website may have many other components besides a click predictor. Each of those components would be exposed to the same workflow as the predictor, ensuring that the system steadily produces more ad revenue.

MLEs work on many kinds of systems. Sorting news headlines by click probability is an example of a broader class of system called a *recommender system*. Recommender systems are used to rank videos, music, social media posts, consumer goods, and more. Search engines are a similar ML system, in that they may rank search results specifically for the user. Targeted advertising, which chooses ads specifically for the user, is another type of MLE system. Now let's turn to finance and see how quants follow the same workflow pattern.

1.1.2 Quantitative trader's workflow

A quant's workflow is very similar to the MLE's workflow. Only the details change. There's a different prediction to be made, for example. See figure 1.3.

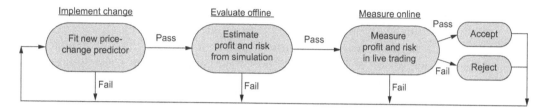

Figure 1.3 Example workflow for a quant designing an automated trading strategy. The strategy contains a price-change predictor. (1) The quant produces a new predictor. (2) Profit and risk estimates come from a simulation using historical market data. (3) Live trading measures the true profit and risk. If the new predictor increases profit and/or reduces risk, then it is accepted into the system.

This quant is building an automated trading strategy. It is a piece of software that issues BUY and SELL orders to an exchange hoping to, as they say, buy low and sell high. A key component is a model that predicts change in the price of the financial instrument (e.g., a stock) being traded. If the price is predicted to increase, it's a good time to issue a BUY order. Similarly, if the price is predicted to decrease, it's a good time to SELL. The business metric for this system is profit. But it's also risk. Quants want both higher profit *and* lower risk. It is not uncommon (in practice, it's the norm) to be concerned with more than one business metric when optimizing a system. Chapter 7, section 3 will discuss this important practical point in detail.

Figure 1.3 shows the quant's workflow. Changes to the trading strategy pass through these stages:

1 *Implement change*—The quant fits the new price-change predictor to historical market data and verifies that it produces better predictions than the previous predictor.

2 *Evaluate offline*—Better price predictions do not guarantee higher profits (or lower risk). The full trading strategy—predictor, BUY/SELL orders, and so on—is run through a simulation (also called a *backtest*) on historical market data. The simulation generates predictions and mimics buying and selling to estimate profit and risk. Sufficient improvement in the strategy will allow the predictor to pass to the next stage.

3 *Measure online*—The predictor is deployed to live trading, where orders are placed and money and stock shares change hands. Only live trading can tell the

true profit and risk of the strategy. The change to the predictor will be reverted if it worsens the strategy's profit or risk.

Quants typically work on one of two types of trading systems: *principal* or *agency*. A principal strategy trades directly for the profit of the operator (the quant, or the company employing the quant). An agency strategy trades on behalf of customers as a service, helping customers reduce their trading costs.

There are many variations to these two types of strategies. They may trade stocks, futures contracts, options, or many other financial products. Each product type typically has multiple exchanges around the world on which to trade.

Also, a key defining component of a strategy is its timescale. A principal strategy owns a stock (or other instrument) for some amount of time before selling it. That amount of time may be on the order of minutes, hours, days, or weeks. Sometimes even as long as months or as short as seconds. Each timescale requires a different predictor and a different understanding of risk.

The MLE and quant workflows are similar because their systems are similar. They typically consist of a predictive model fit on data and some decision-making code that determines how the prediction is used. A software engineer's workflow is somewhat different and is the next topic.

1.1.3   *Software engineer's workflow*

SWEs work on a broad range of systems. In this text, we'll define SWE problems as those that do not involve building models from data (thus differentiating them from MLEs and quants). SWEs build compilers, caching systems, web servers, trading system infrastructure (on which trading strategies run), and much more.

As an example, let's consider the problem of improving the response time of a search engine with the goal of lowering the "bounce rate," which is the probability that a user will navigate away from a website after seeing just one page. Figure 1.4 shows the SWE's workflow.

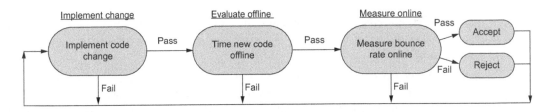

Figure 1.4   Example workflow for a software engineer building a search engine server. The server queries, aggregates, and transforms relevant data before sending the user a response. (1) The SWE changes the transformation portion of the code. (2) They time the code offline, verifying that it takes less time than the old code to transform several test data sets. (3) Running in production, the SWE measures whether the use of this new code results in a lower bounce rate, the business-relevant metric. If so, the new code is accepted as a permanent part of the system.

This SWE has built a search engine. It is a web server that responds to a user's request by querying internal sources for a data set, transforming that data set, and delivering a formatted response to the user. Users are very sensitive to the time it takes for a web server to respond. If it takes too long, a user may navigate away from the web page before the response is delivered.

While there are many ways to slow down a web server's response (slow browser, slow network, cache misses, etc.), this SWE has a hypothesis that it's the data transformation step that is too slow. To fix the problem, they subject their hypothesis to the workflow:

1 *Implement change*—The SWE implements a code change that they expect to speed up the transformation step.
2 *Evaluate offline*—This code is run and timed offline on many samples of the internal data sets that resulted from previous user requests. If it proves to be faster, it passes to the next stage.
3 *Measure online*—The code change is deployed to production where responses are served to real users. The SWE measures the bounce rate and compares it to the bounce rate before the code change. If the new code lowers the bounce rate, it is accepted as a permanent part of the system.

Engineering teams tend to generate many creative ideas for improving the system they work on. If these ideas are the raw material, the workflow is the factory that processes them—steadily and reliably—into system improvements.

Each pass through the workflow ends with an online measurement of business metrics. That measurement is taken via an experiment on a live production system.

1.2 Measuring by experiment

The engineered systems encountered in trading and technology are complex. This complexity can make it difficult to measure the impact of changes made to them. Consider a website that sells a product. A useful business metric might be daily revenue, the total number of dollars paid to the company by customers each day. That number depends on the quality of the product, its competition, how many people know about the product, how many people have already bought it, whether people are more inclined to shop on a given day (e.g., is it a weekend? Is it Black Friday?), how easy it is to navigate and understand the website, and so on. Many, many factors affect daily revenue, and many of them are not under the control of the company.

If you were to make a change to this website and record a day's revenue, how could you say whether the change improved that revenue? Would you have made more or less on the day you measured if you hadn't made the change? More importantly, would you expect to make more or less in the future if you left the change in or took it out? These questions can be answered by running experiments.

1.2.1 *Experimental methods*

Experimental methods ignore all the other factors that affect a business metric and tease out just the impact of the change you made to the system. Surprisingly, satisfyingly, experiments even account for the impact of the factors that are unknown to you, the engineer (chapter 2 discusses this in detail). It's this ability to isolate the impact of your system change and ignore everything else that makes an experiment the right tool for the job of measuring business impact.

Experiments are indeed valuable, but that value comes at a cost. Experiments take time to run, and they risk generating suboptimal system performance (e.g., if the change the engineer just implemented makes things worse instead of better) or damaging it (e.g., due to a bug in the new code). To get the most out of experimentation, we'll try to minimize these costs. Chapter 2 presents the idea of experiment design, where we minimize the amount of time an experiment will take to run while still giving the results we need. The subsequent chapters on experimental methods, chapters 3 through 6, all discuss ways to reduce these costs further in specific situations. Chapters 3 and 5, which cover bandit algorithms, make the experiment design adaptive, so that while the experiment is running and collecting measurements, the design steadily improves.

Recall that some system changes require the measurement of business metrics for multiple configurations to discover which is best. This induces a high measurement cost. The methods of chapters 4 and 6—response surface methodology and Bayesian optimization, respectively—use statistical inference to make good guesses about which system configurations are most promising, thus reducing the total number of measurements needed to find the best configuration.

These methods have been used in industry anywhere from 10 to 70 years (depending on the method) and are popular in the fields in which I work—quantitative trading and social media. What makes trading and technology so amenable to experimentation is that systems in these industries have many interactions with the world. Trading systems can send thousands or tens of thousands of orders per day. Websites may have from thousands to billions (for the largest websites) of requests per day. Each interaction provides an opportunity to experiment.

Drawing on personal experience, discussions with colleagues, and interviews specifically for the preparation of this book, I have tried to limit the material to a set of methods proven to work well in practice. Along with explanations of methods and real-world examples, I've also collected practical problems and pitfalls.

1.2.2 *Practical problems and pitfalls*

All these experimental methods assume you know your business metric. Chapter 7 discusses how to define one and how there's usually more than one to consider. It also looks more closely at how to interpret experiment results and how that may be complicated when there are multiple metrics and multiple decision-makers involved.

Finally, chapter 8 lists ways in which real-world data can deviate from the assumptions made in the development of the experimental methods and common sources of error in interpretation of results.

One practical problem worth addressing before even getting into the details of experimentation is the question of whether you should experiment at all. It takes time and effort to build the tools needed to design, measure, and analyze changes to your system. You should get something in return for all that work. The next section discusses some common arguments against experimentation and presents counterarguments.

1.3 Why are experiments necessary?

Any SWE is likely familiar with the admonition, attributed to Donald Knuth, that "premature optimization is the root of all evil"—that is, rather than implement ideas that you expect will make your code run faster (or better in some other way) at the outset, first write simple code to solve the problem, devise a way to time the code, then test your ideas one at a time to see which ones actually speed things up. It's too difficult to reason about everything that could affect speed—the whole code base, the computer architecture, the operating system, and so on—all at once, so you rely on a test.

Similar reasoning applies to improving business metrics. There are too many factors that could affect business metrics for a web product, including all the software engineering factors listed above, as well as data quality, model quality, changes in user sentiment, changes in browser technology, news of the day, and much more. This is the case for any engineered system: many factors affect business metrics, and they do so in complicated ways. Experimentation is necessary to accurately measure the impact on business metrics of a change to the system.

There are other tools available to assess the business-metric impact of a system change. Some examples are

- Domain knowledge
- Offline model quality
- Simulation

These tools are discussed in detail below. You'll see that they have two things in common: (1) they are cheaper (less resource-intensive) to use, and (2) they are less accurate than an experimental result. These tools may be useful supplements to your decision-making, but they can't replace experiments.

1.3.1 Domain knowledge

Domain knowledge is the specialized knowledge of a field, a market, or a business that people acquire through education and experience. You might think this kind of knowledge would make people good at predicting which new ideas will make a positive business impact. But for the past 10 years, I've given an informal survey to my quant coworkers. I've asked, "Of the ideas you've implemented and tested, how many have actually worked?" The answer *every single time* has been 1 in 10. And it's always been said with a chuckle and an air of resignation. That survey isn't exactly scientific, but similar stories come from elsewhere, too. Microsoft reports that only one-third of experiments improve metrics. Amazon reports a success rate below 50%. Netflix says only 10% (see http://mng.bz/Xao6). Even though the people generating the ideas had domain knowledge, most experiments failed to produce the expected results. There seem to be aspects of the world that keep most good ideas from working.

One aspect is complexity. Your system is likely made up of many components: hardware components like computers and network switches, software components (both in-house and third-party), and human elements—operators, suppliers, customers. These components interact with each other, with the physical environment, and with society at large. Computers interact via networks. Humans interact with each other online and in person. They also interact with your servers through a browser or an API.

The physical environment includes the temperature of a data center—which, when too high, adversely impacts computer performance or causes failure. It also includes the weather, which affects people's behavior. When the weather's bad, do people use your product more because they can't engage in outdoor activities? Do their posts or comments reflect their mood, which is in turn affected by the weather? There is evidence (D. Hirshleifer, T. Shumway, "Good Day Sunshine: Stock Returns and the Weather," at www.jstor.org/stable/3094570) that sunshine in the morning in New York City is correlated with increased stock returns on that day on the New York Stock Exchange. The proposed causal mechanism is that sunshine makes the traders more optimistic. No engineer—or anyone, for that matter—could be expected to anticipate effects like this just from experience or reasoning.

To put a finer point on it, if you have N components in your system, you have $\sim N^2$ pair-wise interactions. In other words, if your system has many components, then it has a huge number of interactions. That's too much for a person to consider when trying to guess the impact a system change will have on business metrics.

Generally, we'll ignore most of that complexity when reasoning about a system in order to make things more manageable. We'll create a mental model or even a mathematical model. In either case, the model of how your system operates contains the information about the system that you deemed important enough to include. In some models, this information might be called the *signal*. You leave out irrelevant details, which you might call *noise*. There's a third category of things that affect your system's performance: the things you didn't even consider, because you don't know about them. The "unknown unknowns," they're sometimes called (perhaps Donald Rumsfeld said it best: https://papers.rumsfeld.com/about/page/authors-note). These things could affect experimental results by any amount, either positively or negatively. You won't anticipate them or have intuition about them because they're missing from your model.

It's plausible that the "unknown unknowns" of your system might include its most valuable aspects. A *Harvard Business Review* article (http://mng.bz/yaAq) tells the story of a proposed change to Microsoft's Bing search engine. A domain knowledge–based decision made the change a low priority for implementation, but when it was finally coded up and put into production, it had a tremendous positive impact on revenue (over $100 million per year). It was simply the case that no one could understand the system—the code, the design, the users, and so on—completely enough to predict the dramatic impact of that change. Not because they weren't smart. Not because they weren't knowledgeable. Just because Bing, the user base, and the world they interact with are collectively just too complex.

If your company is competitive and surviving, there's a good chance your "unknown unknowns" overlap with your competitors'. (My reasoning for this claim is that if your competitor discovered something valuable enough, it would either find its way into your product, too, or your company would be competed away.) If that's the case, then to do something novel—to find value where your competitors haven't—you'll need to make changes to your system that you can't evaluate with your existing domain knowledge. You'll need to run experiments instead.

Domain knowledge is valuable. It will help you generate ideas and prioritize them—to make good bets. But domain knowledge won't tell you outcomes. To understand impact on business metrics, you need to take experimental measurements. In addition, I posit that the most valuable changes you make to your system may come as surprises, creating impact unpredicted by domain knowledge.

1.3.2 Offline model quality

It is common practice among MLEs to include a prediction model (e.g., a classifier) as a component in a system. It is not an uncommon experience to improve a model's fit-quality metric (e.g., cross-entropy) and yet not see the business metric improve when the model is deployed.

Let's say you build a model that predicts whether a user will click on news articles about sports. You gather a data set from production logs. It contains examples of sports articles that were presented to a user along with a record of which articles the user clicked on. Your model analyzes each article's headline and predicts clicks very well. When you're done building your model, you test it on out-of-sample data—data that wasn't used in the fitting process—just to be sure you didn't overfit. The model works great.

Next you put your model into production like this: Every time a user loads the sports news page, you sort the articles by your model's prediction, hoping to show the articles the user is more interested in nearer to the top of the list. You find that the user isn't more likely to click on the articles near the top. In fact, your model no longer seems to predict clicks very well. The model wasn't overfit. You checked for that. It's something different. The data used to fit your model was missing *counterfactuals*— events that happen in your system after you deploy a change but that didn't happen before deployment.

The historical data you used to fit the model was generated by the system *without your model in it*. The articles were sorted some other way (perhaps sorted by date, or maybe using a different click-prediction model). When you fit your model, you were teaching it how users responded to that old system, the one with the old sorting method. Users responded differently to the new sorting method. It is difficult, if not impossible, to predict exactly how users will respond to the deployment of a new model.

The same experience might be had by a quant. They could build a new price-change prediction model using a regression, find that it has a higher R^2 (a common measure of the quality of a fit) than their old model, and works well out-of-sample, but still, when deployed, the profit of the strategy does not improve. The market is made up of traders—some algorithmic, some human—and they will respond differently to the new model's presence in the market than they did to the old model's. In this case, during fitting, the quant taught the new model about the old market, the one in which the new model was not a participant.

This is such a common experience that most quants and MLEs will (eventually) be familiar with it. The *Facebook ML Field Guide*, episode 6 (http://mng.bz/M07n) refers to this problem as the "online-offline gap." The only way to be sure you've improved the system is to run the final stage of the workflow, the online measurement.

1.3.3 *Simulation*

Simulations are tools that estimate a system's business metrics offline. They might combine logged data, models of users or markets, scientific models, or heuristics. They can vary considerably in their form from domain to domain.

Simulations differ from the simple fitting metrics (cross-entropy or R^2) discussed in the previous section. Simulations typically account for all components of a system and aim to produce numbers like revenue or user engagement that may be compared to the numbers that come from experimental measurements.

For example, a standard quant's tool is a trading simulation. Offline, it runs historical market data—trades and quotes—through the same trading strategy code that is used in production. When that strategy asks to execute a trade, the simulator mimics the behavior of the market using heuristics or a model of the market. From this simulation, a quant can estimate profit, risk, shares traded, and other useful business metrics.

Simulations can give more precise answers—meaning numbers with smaller error bars—than experiments because they can use much more data. For example, a single simulation might process 1 month to 10 years of data, depending on the timescale over which the strategy trades, in a single run. This simulation might take minutes to hours to run, depending on the complexity of the strategy. An experiment, on the other hand, that takes a measurement with 1 month of data needs to run for *1 month*. Want 10 years of experimental data? You'll wait 10 years.

Simulations may also be run multiple times on the same data set. Each run could try slight variations on the same strategy and allow the quant to choose the best one—the one with the best profit-to-risk tradeoff, for example—to trade in production.

With experiments multiple runs are impossible. You can't trade for a month, say, then "rewind" real life and trade again with a different strategy. There are effective ways to compare different strategies experimentally, but the process is orders of magnitude faster in simulation.

Simulations may be more precise and faster, but experiments are more accurate. Simulations might be biased (inaccurate) because of missing counterfactuals, just like prediction models. What happens, for example, when a trading strategy sends an order to an exchange? It might show up in the market, and other traders will see and respond to it. This changes future market data, which is then seen by the trading strategy and used for its decisions, and so on. Other traders' real responses to our actions simply don't exist in simulation.

MLEs use simulation, too. Engineers working on Facebook Feed use a simulator that replays logged data through the Feed code that estimates users' responses. In "Combining online and offline tests to improve News Feed ranking" (http://mng.bz/aPgB), they note that their offline simulations are biased. While the simulation results are related to real results, they don't match exactly and the relationship between them is nontrivial. (The blog post goes on to design a model-based mapping from simulation results to experimental results.)

Researchers who study a field called *evolutionary robotics* design robot controllers—pieces of code that take in sensor information and output commands to a robot's actuators—using algorithms inspired by evolution. The evolutionary algorithms search for controller parameters that optimize the performance of the robot as measured by a simulation. The researchers notice so often that controllers designed in simulation don't work on real robots that they have coined a term for this effect: the *reality gap*.

In a live-streamed event, Tesla Autonomy Day (https://youtu.be/Ucp0TTmvqOE, 2:02:00–2:06:00), CEO Elon Musk is asked why Tesla relies so much on data collected from real drivers instead of training their autonomous driving controller via simulation. He says that they *do* use simulation, but that since they "don't know what they don't know"—and all of what they don't know would be missing from the simulation—they invest effort and money into collecting lots of real data. In the same video, AI director Andrej Karpathy gives several examples of rare, unanticipated images from around the world that need to be interpreted by their vision system. Without appealing to real-world data, their system would never learn to deal with these images.

Simulation is a powerful offline design tool. Simulations can be used in the second stage of the workflow to generate estimates of business metrics. Because they tend to be biased, and you can never know exactly how, it is always necessary to test changes to your system with an experiment.

Summary

- Experimental optimization is the process of improving an engineered system using measurement-based design decisions.
- Experimental methods minimize the time and risk associated with experimental measurements.
- Experiments are the most accurate way to measure the impact on business metrics of changes to an engineered system.
- Domain knowledge, prediction models, and simulation are powerful supplements to experiments but are not replacements for them.

A/B testing: Evaluating
a modification to
your system

In chapter 1, you saw that the final step in the engineer's workflow is to measure how business metrics are impacted by a modification of your system. You do this by running an experiment on the modified production system. Experiments are the most accurate way to measure changes in business metrics.

In this chapter, you'll learn how to run an A/B test, the simplest and most widely used type of experiment. An A/B test measures the business metric for each of version A and B. If you find that B has a better business metric, you make the modification permanent; otherwise you leave the system as is.

An A/B test has three stages (figure 2.1):

- *Design*—You prepare for the experiment by determining how many measurements to take. Taking multiple measurements, called *replication*, reduces

15

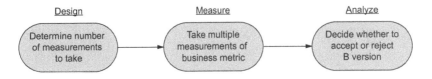

Figure 2.1   Three stages of an A/B test: Design, Measure, and Analyze.

natural variation in your final estimate of the business metric for A and B (see section 2.2).

- *Measure*—When you measure the business metric, you'll take care to measure only the effect of switching from version A to version B by using a technique called *randomization*. Without randomization, it's easy to inadvertently include the impact of other factors that affect your business metric—time of day, user demographics, location of a data center, and so on.
- *Analyze*—Finally, you'll compare the business metric estimates for A and B and decide whether to switch to B or not.

There's a saying in engineering circles: "In God we trust. All others bring data." It means that you should make decisions based on measurements of business metrics rather than on intuition or other soft criteria. An A/B test is the gold standard for acquiring the data you need to make good-quality decisions. By the end of this chapter, you should be able to execute the three stages of an A/B test—design, measure, and analyze—to decide whether to modify your system.

2.1   *Take an ad hoc measurement*

To understand A/B testing, we need to first understand the problems it solves. One way to do that is to, for a moment, ignore A/B testing methods and, instead, proceed simply and intuitively and see what problems we run into. Specifically, let's reconfigure a trading system and see if that reduces trading costs.

Imagine you're a quant, and you're developing an agency trading system. The system takes in customer orders like "Buy 1,000 shares of AAPL stock over the next hour," and after buying the shares on behalf of the customer, it reports the cost of executing the trade. Customers, of course, prefer lower costs, so you use execution cost as your business metric. Your job as a quant is to find ways to modify the trading system that result in lower execution cost.

A simple change you can make to the system is to buy the shares on a different exchange. An *exchange* is a third-party service that facilitates anonymous trading between any two trading systems. Your system sends trading commands to the exchange's server. A command might be "Buy 100 shares of AAPL right now." If, for example, it sends that command ten times over the course of an hour, it will have purchased 1,000 shares of AAPL stock for one of your customers.

At present, your system trades on an exchange run by a company called ASDAQ (version A of your system). You suspect it might be cheaper to trade on the exchange BYSE (version B of your system). You'll measure execution cost on each exchange and compare to see if your suspicion is correct.

First, we need to take a brief detour. In this section, we're discussing the idea of taking measurements on a trading system that doesn't actually exist. For the purpose of exposition and teaching in this book, we'll create a *simulator* and take measurements on it. The simulator is a stand-in for the real trading system.

We'll write a Python function that returns a simulated execution cost for each exchange. We'll take measurements on that function and treat them as if they were measurements on the trading system. Let's build the simulator, then move on to the measurements.

2.1.1 Simulate the trading system

A simulation is a bit of code that mimics the behavior of some real-world system. The following listing simulates a measurement on your trading system. It returns the execution cost for a single trade.

Listing 2.1 Simulate the trading system

```
def trading_system(exchange):
    if exchange == "ASDAQ":
        execution_cost = 12
    elif exchange == "BYSE":
        execution_cost = 10
    execution_cost += np.random.normal()
    return execution_cost
```

The cost varies randomly from trade to trade.

The function takes an exchange name as an argument so that we can measure the cost of trading on each exchange and compare. Notice that the cost varies randomly from trade to trade. The randomness is meant to represent all the factors that might change from trade to trade: the stock being traded, the number of shares, the direction (i.e., buy or sell), natural market costs induced by the set of traders who happen to be in the market at the same time as you, and so on.

As a rule, let's not look too closely at what's going on inside our simulator. In a real-life situation, you won't know in detail the process that generates your business metric values. The business metric will be a result of the interactions between your trading system, the exchanges, the other traders, and your customers—each of which is complex in its own right. When we don't know what's happening inside a function, and we just know its inputs (here, exchange) and outputs (here, execution_cost), we say the function is a *black box*. This simulator—and any real-life system you work on as an engineer—may be treated as a black box. Try out the simulator:

```
np.random.seed(17)
trading_system("ASDAQ")
12.28
```

You just ran a simulated trade on ASDAQ and measured the execution cost to be 12.28 mips. (Trading costs may be measured in various units, most with silly-sounding names. We'll call ours mips for the sake of conversation.)

Note that the first line—np.random.seed(17)—is there so that when you run the code, you get the same answer as is written above (i.e., 12.28). Without it (or with an argument other than 17), the call to np.random.normal() will return a different value, and thus trading_system() will return a different value. Feel free to run without a call to seed() or with a different seed argument. The seed is there to make it possible to discuss the behavior of the code in precise terms. You'll see calls to seed() appear throughout the book for that reason. Now let's get to the work of comparing the costs of trading on the two exchanges.

2.1.2   *Compare execution costs*

Your task is to compare the execution cost of trades on ASDAQ to that of trades on BYSE. You'll start with the simple, intuitive approach of executing one trade on each exchange, recording the cost of each, and comparing:

```
np.random.seed(17)
print (trading_system("ASDAQ"))
print (trading_system("BYSE"))
12.28
8.14
```

The trade on ASDAQ cost 12.28 mips, and the trade on BYSE cost 8.14 mips. It was cheaper to trade on BYSE. Try that again:

```
np.random.seed(18)
print (trading_system("ASDAQ"))
print (trading_system("BYSE"))
12.08
12.19
```

This time it was cheaper to trade on ASDAQ, which contradicts your first measurement. The measured value varies from measurement to measurement.

VARIATION

If you keep running measurements, you'll find that sometimes ASDAQ will be cheaper and sometimes BYSE will be. Figure 2.2 shows a histogram of 1,000 measurements on each exchange.

This sort of variation from measurement to measurement is typical, and it makes your decision about which exchange to use unreliable. A/B testing uses a technique called

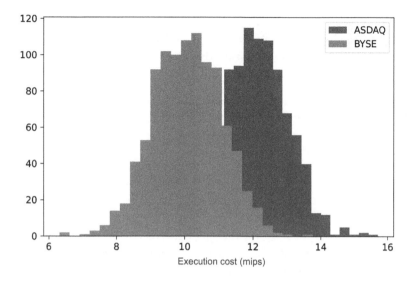

Figure 2.2   Execution costs of 1,000 trades on ASDAQ and 1,000 trades on BYSE. BYSE is usually cheaper to trade on than ASDAQ.

replication—averaging over multiple measurements—to increase the reliability of your decision. To get a feel for how this works, let's take an average over 100 measurements:

```
np.random.seed(17)
print(np.array([trading_system("ASDAQ")
        for _ in range(100)]).mean())
print(np.array([trading_system("BYSE")
        for _ in range(100)]).mean())
12.11
10.01
```

This measurement reports ASDAQ's average execution cost as 12.11 and BYSE's as 10.01, indicating that BYSE is the better choice. Try that again:

```
print(np.array([trading_system("ASDAQ")
        for _ in range(100)]).mean())
print(np.array([trading_system("BYSE")
        for _ in range(100)]).mean())
11.88
10.00
```

Again, the average-of-measurements approach suggests that BYSE is the better choice. If you repeat this procedure, you'll find that BYSE is reliably measured to have lower execution cost than ASDAQ.

BIAS

Since you need to take many measurements, you'll need to do a little planning to get them all done. You'll take all the BYSE measurements in the morning, go get lunch, then take the ASDAQ measurements in the afternoon. What you aren't aware of is the fact that all trading—regardless of exchange—is cheaper in the afternoon (for reasons that have to do with natural market dynamics). The following listing simulates this effect; let's call it the *time-of-day effect.*

Listing 2.2 **A simulator that accounts for time of day**

```
def trading_system_tod(exchange, time_of_day):
    if time_of_day == "morning":
        bias = 2.5
    elif time_of_day == "afternoon":
        bias = 0
    return bias + trading_system(exchange)
```

Cost is still a function of exchange.

Cost is lower in the afternoon.

This simulator captures the effect of switching between exchanges by calling `trading_system()`, but it adds an extra cost in the morning, making all trading more expensive in the morning (cheaper in the afternoon). This extra cost is called a *bias*. Specifically, it's a *sampling bias*, indicating that taking a measurement (also called *sampling*) under different conditions will consistently yield different results. For example, let's measure a single exchange—ASDAQ—many times in the morning and many times in the afternoon. (Notice that we're taking many measurements to combat variation.)

```
np.random.seed(17)
print(np.array([trading_system_tod("ASDAQ", "morning")
        for _ in range(100)]).mean())
print(np.array([trading_system_tod("ASDAQ", "afternoon")
        for _ in range(100)]).mean())
14.61
12.01
```

This measurement says that ASDAQ is cheaper to trade in the afternoon. If we repeat it, we'll get the same qualitative result: cheaper in the afternoon. Now, if we follow the proposed plan of measuring BYSE before lunch and ASDAQ after, we'll get a result like

```
np.random.seed(17)
print(np.array([trading_system_tod("BYSE", "morning")
        for _ in range(100)]).mean())
print(np.array([trading_system_tod("ASDAQ", "afternoon")
        for _ in range(100)]).mean())
12.61
12.01
```

If we were unaware of the time-of-day effect, we would conclude from this measurement that ASDAQ's trading costs were lower than BYSE's. This is the opposite result of the previous section, and it is wrong. Also, it persists. If you rerun this measurement, you'll usually get the result that ASDAQ is cheaper.

This incorrect result comes from applying the time-of-day bias differently—and consistently—to ASDAQ than to BYSE. When a bias is applied differently and consistently (to the two versions of the system being compared) like this, it's called *confounder bias.* Confounder bias can lead to incorrect decisions about whether to make changes to your system.

A simple trick to remove confounder bias is *randomization.* You still run your experiment in both morning and afternoon, as you planned, but every time your system makes a trade, it should flip a coin. If the coin comes up heads, send the orders to ASDAQ. If it comes up tails, send them to BYSE. You'll find that about half of your ASDAQ orders happen in the morning and half happen in the afternoon. The same will hold true for BYSE. The following listing shows how to do this explicitly.

Listing 2.3   A randomized measurement

```
def randomized_measurement():
    asdaq_measurement = []
    byse_measurement = []
    for tod in ["morning", "afternoon"]:        ◁─── Measure before and after lunch.
        for _ in range(100):                    ┌─── Flip a coin to choose the exchange.
            if np.random.randint(2) == 0:       ◁─┘
                asdaq_measurement.append(trading_system_tod("ASDAQ", tod))
            else:
                byse_measurement.append(trading_system_tod("BYSE", tod))
    return (np.array(asdaq_measurement).mean(),
            np.array(byse_measurement).mean())
```

Take 100 measures in each time period.

Note that `np.random.randint(2)` evaluates to zero 50% of the time and to one 50% of the time, similar to a coin flip coming up heads 50% of the time and tails 50% of the time.

Running `randomized_measurement()` produces the result

```
np.random.seed(17)
randomized_measurement()
(13.39588870623852, 11.259639285763223)
```

These measurements show that ASDAQ is more expensive than BYSE, which is correct. If you run `randomized_measurement()` again, you'll find that ASDAQ is more expensive. Randomization removed the time-of-day bias from your measurement.

The amazing thing is that you don't have to know about the time-of-day effect to remove it from your measurements. Put another way, the randomization logic (i.e., flipping a coin) does not use any information about the biases in your system. Randomization removes all confounder biases without you having to know they even exist. But beware, they *do* exist, and if you don't randomize, you'll often end up making bad decisions about how to improve your trading system.

Variation and bias are the two problems that experiments aim to solve. Variation causes measurements to be sometimes too high and sometimes too low, although on average they'll be correct. Bias causes measurements to be consistently too high or too low, no matter how many measurements you average over.

A/B testing uses replication to reduce variation and randomization to remove bias. In section 2.2, we'll look a little more closely at replication.

2.2   Take a precise measurement

Variation is both unpredictable and out of your control, but that doesn't mean you can't make a meaningful decision about which exchange to trade on. The key point to understand is that once you make that decision, you'll trade on that exchange over and over—perhaps thousands of times per day for months or maybe years. (You will only stop if you come up with an even better way to trade.) If you were to trade on ASDAQ for that whole time, you'd usually achieve lower execution costs than if you traded on BYSE. Even though *sometimes* BYSE would have been a better choice, *usually* ASDAQ is.

A concept that captures this idea is *expectation*. The expectation of the execution cost of ASDAQ is 12 mips. You can see in figure 2.2 that the dark histogram is centered on 12 mips and varies about that number. The tendency of execution costs to always be around 12 mips is what makes measurements useful. Your measurements now—during experimentation—will lie near the expectation, and your measurements in the future—during normal system operation—will also lie near the expectation.

The expectation is predictable, even if the variation is not. It's this predictability that makes experiments useful. It enables you to imagine that your measurement of expectation will hold in the future, after the experiment is over. Variation just gets in the way. We'll see in the next section how A/B testing copes with variation in measurements.

2.2.1   Mitigate measurement variation with replication

You saw in the previous section that simply taking a measurement of execution cost on each exchange and comparing them wasn't sufficient to enable you to make a good decision about which exchange to trade on. You tried this method twice and got two different answers, which is unacceptable. You'd prefer to use a procedure that produces reliably good decisions. Since your decisions are based on your measurements, you need to take reliably good measurements. The solution is to take many measurements and average them. Comparing averages is more reliable than comparing single measurements. We know a few facts about expectation:

- Measurements of a business metric are reliably near their expectation.
- Future system performance is measured by expectation.
- Expectation is predictable.

Here's one more useful fact: an average over multiple measurements is typically closer to the expectation than is any single measurement. Putting these facts together yields an improved procedure for deciding which exchange to trade on:

1 Take multiple measurements of execution cost on each exchange.
2 Take an average of the measurements for each exchange.
3 Use whichever exchange has a lower average cost.

The process of taking multiple measurements is called *replication* in experimentation parlance.

> **NOTE** To make our discussion clearer, I'm going to refer to a single measurement of execution cost as an *individual measurement* and an average over multiple individual measurements as an *aggregate measurement*. This is not standard terminology, but standard terminology may refer to each of them as "measurements," which can get confusing. You may also see individual measurements referred to as observations or samples in other texts. In these new terms, we'll say that the procedure is to compare aggregate measurements of execution cost to decide whether to use exchange ASDAQ or BYSE.

To see how aggregate measurements are closer to the expectation, focus, for a moment, on ASDAQ. Take three measurements:

```
np.random.seed(17)
measurements = np.array([trading_system("ASDAQ") for _ in range(3)])
print(measurements)
[[12.27626589 10.14537192 12.62390111]
```

These values are all near the expectation, 12 mips. Now take the average (the mean):

```
measurements.mean()
11.681846307513723
```

The mean, 11.68, is closer to 12 (the expectation) than two of the three values in the array c. We can quantify how much closer by computing *deviations* from the expectation for all the individual measurements

```
print (measurements - 12)
[ 0.27626589 -1.85462808  0.62390111]
```

and similarly for the aggregate measurement

```
measurements.mean() - 12
-0.3181536924862769
```

The mean is only about .32 from expectation, whereas the individual measurements are as far as 1.85 away.

We normally describe the size of deviations by the *standard deviation*: `SD=np.sqrt(((measurements - 12)**2).mean())`. In this special situation where we have a simulator available, we can simply read from `trading_system()` (listing 2.1) that the expected cost is 12 mips, so we can compute deviations from that. When dealing with real-life data—from a black box system—we won't know the expectation. Instead we'll estimate the expectation by the mean and write `sd=np.sqrt(((measurements - measurements.mean())**2).mean())`.

You can simplify all that by using NumPy's built-in standard deviation function: `sd=measurements.std()`. The standard deviation of the individual measurements is about `sd=1.1`.

If we repeat this little three-measurement experiment multiple times, we'll get multiple answers, but the mean will in general be closer to the expectation than an individual measurement. Figure 2.3 shows 1,000 individual measurements and 1,000 aggregate measurements.

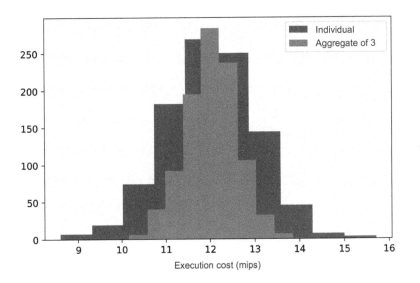

Figure 2.3   Histogram of 1,000 aggregate measurements of ASDAQ cost overlaid on histogram of 1,000 individual measurements. Notice that the aggregate measurement histogram is narrower.

Notice in figure 2.3 that the aggregate measurements are typically closer to the expectation than the individual measurements (i.e., the histogram of aggregate measurements is narrower). If we add more individual measurements to the aggregate, the histogram will get even narrower. See figure 2.4.

This is powerful. While the variation in an individual measurement is not controllable, the variation in an aggregate measurement is. If you want a single aggregate measurement to be closer to the expectation, you just need to add more individual measurements to it. We say that an aggregate measurement is more *precise* if the histogram of multiple aggregate measurements is narrower. Replication reduces the variation in—or, alternatively put, increases the precision of—the aggregate measurement.

To really appreciate the power of replication, recall that any system you experiment on is a black box, so you never get to know the expectation. (We knew it was

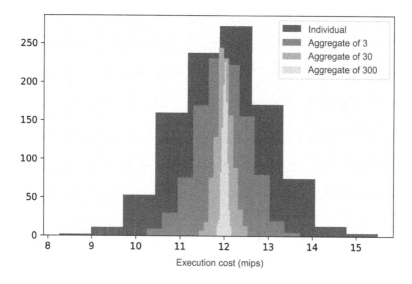

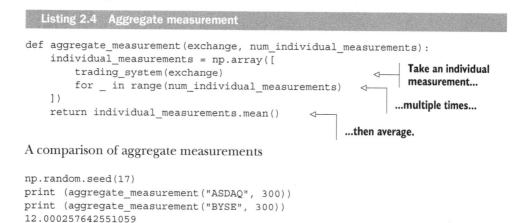

Figure 2.4   As more individual measurements are added to the aggregate, the aggregate measurements fall closer to the expectation of 12 mips (i.e., the histogram gets narrower as the number of individual measurements in the aggregate increases).

12 mips here only because we could read the code for trading_system(), and that code was very simple.) By replicating, you can take more precise measurements of the expectation, even though the true expectation is unknowable.

Back to your task of deciding between ASDAQ and BYSE. Compare measurements of execution cost again, but this time compare aggregate measurements of, say, 300 individual measurements each. The following listing shows a function that takes an aggregate measurement.

Listing 2.4   Aggregate measurement

```
def aggregate_measurement(exchange, num_individual_measurements):
    individual_measurements = np.array([
        trading_system(exchange)                          ◁─┐  Take an individual
        for _ in range(num_individual_measurements)       ◁─┘  measurement...
    ])
    return individual_measurements.mean()   ◁────────────────  ...multiple times...
                                                               ...then average.
```

A comparison of aggregate measurements

```
np.random.seed(17)
print (aggregate_measurement("ASDAQ", 300))
print (aggregate_measurement("BYSE", 300))
12.000257642551059
10.051095649188758
```

suggests that we use BYSE instead of ASDAQ. Trying again

```
print (aggregate_measurement("ASDAQ", 300))
print (aggregate_measurement("BYSE", 300))
11.987318214094266
10.021053044438455
```

results in the same decision—use BYSE.

Figure 2.5 repeats these aggregate measurements 1,000 times and displays them as histograms.

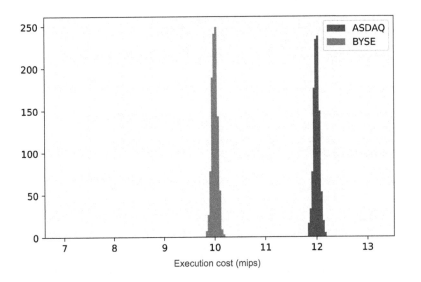

Figure 2.5   Aggregate measurements of execution costs incorporating 300 individual measurements each, repeated 1,000 times on ASDAQ and 1,000 times on BYSE. The aggregate measurements for BYSE are always lower (which is better) than those for ASDAQ.

If you were to compare any aggregate measurement from ASDAQ's histogram (the dark one) in figure 2.5 to any aggregate measurement from BYSE's histogram, you'd decide that ASDAQ was more expensive than BYSE. This shows that an aggregate of 300 individual measurements would produce a very reliable decision. Next up, we'll estimate the standard deviation in an aggregate measurement and call it the *standard error*.

STANDARD ERROR

We can see exactly how much replication reduces variation by calculating the standard deviation of the aggregate measurements, just like we did with the individual measurements. For example, we can collect 1,000 aggregate measurements consisting of three individual measurements each with

```
np.random.seed(17)
agg_3 = np.array([aggregate_measurement("ASDAQ", 3)
            for _ in range(1000)])
```

and similarly for aggregate measurements consisting of 30 or 300 individual measurements:

```
agg_30 = np.array([aggregate_measurement("ASDAQ", 30)
              for _ in range(1000)])
agg_300 = np.array([aggregate_measurement("ASDAQ", 300)
               for _ in range(1000)])
```

The standard deviation of each is

```
print (agg_3.std(), agg_30.std(), agg_300.std())
0.5721786019484487 0.18071680926647693 0.05808839858239513
```

You can see that the standard deviation—the width of the histograms in figure 2.4—decreases as the number of individual measurements in each aggregate measurement increases.

Note that we usually refer to the standard deviation of an aggregate measurement as the *standard error*. If we know the standard error, written *SE*, then we know how far, in some sense, the aggregate measurement could be from the true expectation of the business metric. When we run an experiment, the resultant aggregate measurement is a single number. In the preceding code, we generated 1,000 such numbers, and in the figures, we plotted those numbers as histograms. Imagine the following:

- The aggregate measurement produced by your experiment is a single value in a histogram.
- The center of the histogram is the expectation of the execution cost (the business metric).
- The width of the histogram is SE.

Based on this, it's reasonable to say that the expectation—the true execution cost—is probably within SE mips of your aggregate measurement's value.

The "catch" in all of this is that when you run an experiment, you produce only one aggregate measurement value (the average of many individual measurements). Since you can't calculate the standard deviation of a single value, you can't calculate the SE directly.

Fortunately, you can estimate SE. If you take `num_ind` individual measurements and collect them in an array, `costs`, then

- The aggregate measurement is `costs.mean()`.
- The standard deviation of the individual measurements is `sd_1 = costs.std()`.
- The standard error of the aggregate measurement is `se = sd_1/np.sqrt(num_ind)`.

We often denote the number of individual measurements as N and sd_1 as σ and write

$$SE = \sigma/\sqrt{N}$$

This suggests that a more complete aggregate measure might look like the following listing.

Listing 2.5   Aggregate measurement with SE

```
def aggregate_measurement_with_se(exchange, num_individual_measurements):
    individual_measurements = np.array(
        [trading_system(exchange) for _ in
        range(num_individual_measurements)]
    )
    aggregate_measurement = individual_measurements.mean()
    sd_1 = individual_measurements.std()
    se = sd_1 / np.sqrt(num_individual_measurements)
    return aggregate_measurement, se
```

Calculate aggregate measurement.

Collect individual measurement.

Calculate standard error.

This new function reports SE along with the aggregate measurement:

```
np.random.seed(17)
print (aggregate_measurement_with_se("ASDAQ", 300))
print (aggregate_measurement_with_se("BYSE", 300))
(12.000257642551059, 0.060254756364981225)
(10.051095649188758, 0.05714189794415452)
```

You can look at these numbers—from a single experiment, with no histograms available—and claim that BYSE is very likely the better choice by reasoning like this: BYSE's expectation might be higher than the aggregate measurement; perhaps it's $10.05 + 0.057 = 10.107$. Similarly, ASDAQ's expectation might be lower than the aggregate measurement; perhaps it's $12.00 - .060 = 11.94$ mips. Even if both of those were true, BYSE would still be cheaper than ASDAQ.

An aggregate measurement gives a more precise estimate of the expectation of a business metric than an individual measurement, which, in turn, produces a more reliable decision. Furthermore, you can increase precision (lower SE) by taking more individual measurements.

Standard error and $\sqrt{N}$

The standard deviation of the aggregate measurement, which we call the standard error, is

$$SE = \frac{\sigma}{\sqrt{N}}$$

While writing this book, I was asked where the $\sqrt{N}$ comes from.

First, recall that for random variables X and Y

i. $VAR(X) = STD^2(X)$

ii. $VAR(X + Y) = VAR(X) + VAR(Y)$

iii. For any number a, $VAR\left(\frac{X}{a}\right) = \frac{VAR(X)}{a^2}$

These properties follow directly from the definitions of variance (VAR) and standard deviation (STD).

Point ii only holds if X and Y are independent. We'll discuss this in some detail in chapter 8, section 8.1. For now, assume they're independent.

Let's say we take N individual measurements. Then the aggregate measurement is

$$agg = \frac{x_1 + x_2 + \cdots + x_N}{N}$$

The variance of the aggregate measurement is, by (ii) and (iii) (taking $a = N$), above

$$VAR(agg) = \frac{VAR(x_1) + VAR(x_2) + \cdots + VAR(x_N)}{N^2}$$

All the individual measurements are taken from the same system, so they all have the same standard deviation. Name it $\sigma = STD(X)$.

By (i), the variance is just the standard deviation squared, $VAR(X) = \sigma^2$. Substituting that into the previous equation gives

$$VAR(agg) = \frac{\sigma^2 + \sigma^2 + \cdots + \sigma^2}{N^2}$$

or

$$VAR(agg) = \frac{N\sigma^2}{N^2} = \frac{\sigma^2}{N}$$

"Standard error" (SE) is just another name for the standard deviation of the aggregate measurement, so by (i)

$$SE = \sqrt{VAR(agg)} = \frac{\sigma}{\sqrt{N}}$$

That's where the $\sqrt{N}$ comes from.

Your measurement procedure has improved a great deal by switching from individual measurements to aggregate measurements, but it can get even better. Since it takes time to collect individual measurements, it's in your interest to take no more of them than you really need to make a good decision.

There's a tradeoff, however. As you decrease the number of individual measurements, the standard error of the aggregate measurement will increase, which will make the histograms of ASDAQ's and BYSE's costs wider and, thus, more likely to overlap. Then it will be less clear which exchange has the lower cost. A/B test design determines the smallest number of individual measurements you can take without making your uncertainty about which exchange to choose too large. The next section explains this further.

2.3   *Run an A/B test*

You've seen how replication reduces variation, so you want to take multiple individual measurements of execution cost. But these measurements aren't free:

- The process (the measurement stage) will take some of your time. You might have to configure software, monitor the system for safety reasons, or even explain to customers or other members of your firm why system behavior is different than usual.
- When measuring both ASDAQ and BYSE, half of your trades are going to the one with the higher cost. The sooner you stop the experiment, the sooner you can send all trades to the better exchange.
- The less time a single experiment takes, the more experiments you can run. You have lots of ideas, and they each need to be A/B tested.

These are all *experimentation costs*. There's clearly motivation to limit the number of individual measurements, but if you take too few of them, your SEs will become so large that you won't be able to make a reliable decision about which exchange is better. There is a tradeoff between reducing experimentation costs and making reliable decisions.

To make this tradeoff successfully, it's helpful to "begin with the end in mind." First, understand how you'll analyze the measurements in the final stage of an A/B test (the analyze stage, shown in figure 2.6). Once you know that, you'll be able to determine—in the design stage, at the very start—the right number of individual measurements to take.

Figure 2.6   Begin with the end in mind. Understanding what happens in the analyze stage will help you to design an A/B test.

In section 2.3.1, we'll discuss the details of the analyze stage. Then, in section 2.3.2, we'll see how to use this new information to design an A/B test.

2.3.1 *Analyze your measurements*

When you reach the analyze stage, you'll have collected all the individual measurements. Your goal will be to decide whether future trades should be on ASDAQ or BYSE. Ideally, you'd know the true expected execution cost for each exchange and just choose the exchange with the lower expected cost. In practice you have, instead, some number of individual measurements with which to make the best decision you can.

The A/B testing approach to making this decision is to try to be "probably not wrong." We say "probably" instead of "definitely" because you don't know the expectations. Instead, you know a single aggregate measurement taken (randomly) from a histogram (or *distribution*) of potential values (figure 2.7).

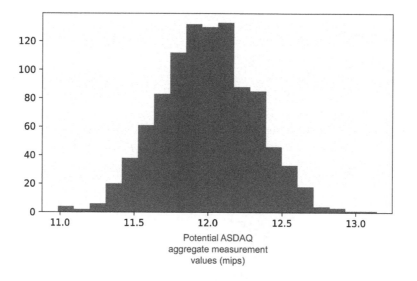

Figure 2.7 In an A/B test, you take and analyze a single aggregate measurement drawn from a histogram of potential values.

To make the analysis a little simpler, let's define a quantity delta, the difference between the aggregate measurement of BYSE and ASDAQ. Explicitly:

```
np.random.seed(17)
num_individual_measurements = 10
agg_asdaq, se_asdaq = aggregate_measurement_with_se("ASDAQ",
                    num_individual_measurements)
agg_byse, se_byse = aggregate_measurement_with_se("BYSE",
                    num_individual_measurements)
delta = agg_byse - agg_asdaq
se_delta = np.sqrt(se_byse**2 + se_asdaq**2)
```

Since delta = agg_byse - agg_asdaq, if we were to find that delta was positive, then we'd conclude that ASDAQ had a lower execution cost and that we should send all trades to ASDAQ. Notice that we can estimate the SE of delta with `se_delta = np.sqrt(se_byse**2 + se_asdaq**2)`. The quantity `delta` can also be thought of as being drawn randomly from a distribution of possible values, just like the BYSE and ASDAQ values. The A/B testing decision logic works like this:

1 Assume the true value—the expectation—of `delta` is zero. In other words, that BYSE and ASDAQ have the same expected execution costs.

2 If your measurement of `delta` is so far from zero that there's less than a 5% chance the statement in step 1 is right, then act as if step 1 was wrong and the true `delta` is not zero.

Step 2 says that you're going to *act as if* the true `delta` is not zero. That means that if you measure `delta` much lower than zero, you'll start sending all trades to BYSE. You'll never know for sure if this was the right decision, since you can't observe the true, expected value. What you'll be doing is taking a bet—with at most a 5% chance of being wrong—that BYSE is better.

For convenience, we usually work with z = `delta`/`se_delta`. This value, called the *z score*, is convenient because dividing by `se_delta` makes z's standard deviation equal to one. Following step 1, we assume z has an expectation of zero.

To make step 2 work, we need to be able to reason about the probability of `delta` taking on some value—equivalently, of z taking on some value. Figure 2.8 shows the intuition behind that.

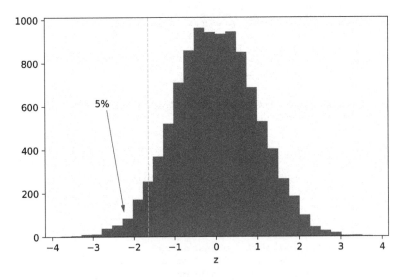

Figure 2.8   The distribution of z scores has mean zero (by assumption) and standard deviation one. The shaded area to the left of the vertical line is 5% of the total shaded area. The probability of a measurement of z having a value to the left of the vertical line is 5%.

Your aggregate measurement can now be represented as a single value drawn from the distribution plotted in figure 2.8. There is a 5% chance that value will fall to the left of the dashed vertical line. If it does, you should bet that your assumption in step 1 was incorrect. You should bet that the expectation of z is truly less than zero, which means that the expectation of `delta` is less than zero, which means that BYSE has lower costs than ASDAQ. When z is to the left of the vertical line, we say that the aggregate measurement is *statistically significant.*

When your bet is wrong—when z falls to the left of the vertical line, but the expectation of z isn't truly negative—we say that the A/B test has yielded a *false positive.* False positives will occur 5% of the time by design. Placement of the vertical line sets the rate of false positives at 5%. Move it to the right, and you'll get more false positives. Move it to the left, and you'll get fewer.

One more thing: the exact location of the vertical line in figure 2.8 is z = -1.64. We know this because the shape of the distribution of z is always normal (aka, Gaussian or "bell curve"), and for a normal distribution with mean zero and standard deviation one (a *unit normal*), 5% of the distribution falls below –1.64. (This number is available in any google-able cumulative unit normal distribution table.) We know that z is normal because that's guaranteed by the *central limit theorem.*

Okay, that's a lie. More accurately, a normal distribution becomes a better and better approximation of z (usually, but almost always) as we add more and more individual measurements to the aggregate measurement. The good news is that in practice, quants, SWEs, and ML engineers are usually working with enough measurements for this approximation to be a good one.

In other words, use `1.64` unless you have a good reason not to. And use it like this: If `z<-1.64`, act as if BYSE is better and start trading there. Otherwise, act as if BYSE isn't any better than ASDAQ and keep trading on ASDAQ. But always remember—in the back of your mind, at least—that you're really making a bet on which is better. There is no certainty in these decisions.

There's another consideration in your decision about whether ASDAQ or BYSE is better. It's not a statistical one, but a practical, business-oriented one: How big of a difference in execution costs do you actually care about? If your system were trading on ASDAQ before the A/B test and you found that BYSE were 1 mip cheaper than ASDAQ, would you bother to switch over to BYSE? Switching everything over to BYSE might take some effort. It might incur some risk. It might negatively impact your relationship with the ASDAQ exchange. Would 1 mip be enough to make the switch worthwhile? What about 0.1 mip? 0.01 mip? Surely at some small-enough number you'd answer, "No, it's not worth switching." That is the level we could call *practical significance*, which we'll denote `prac_sig`. For example, maybe `prac_sig` = 1.0 mip for your agency trading system. Even if a measurement is statistically significant, if you find that `-0.1 < delta < 0.0` (i.e., if `delta >= - prac_sig`), you should still act as if `delta = 0` and not change your system.

Now that you know how you'll use the measurements in the analysis stage, you are ready to make a good plan about what measurements to collect. You are ready to design an A/B test.

2.3.2   Design the A/B test

In an A/B test design (figure 2.9), you determine the number of individual measurements that you'll take in the measure stage. You want to take enough measurements so that if ASDAQ and BYSE have different execution costs, you'll be able to tell. More precisely, if the difference between execution costs is large enough to be practically significant, you want your aggregate measurement to be statistically significant.

Figure 2.9   In A/B test design, you determine the minimum number of individual measurements needed so that a practically significant difference in execution costs (the business metric) will also be statistically significant.

The phrase *statistically significant* means, as defined in the previous section, that `z <-1.64`. Starting from there, we can derive an expression for the required number of individual measurements, `num_ind`. Recall that `z = delta / se_delta` and `se_delta = np.sqrt(se_byse**2 + se_asdaq**2)`. Let's look more closely at `se_delta`.

The standard error of an aggregate measurement, generally, may be estimated by `se = sd_1/np.sqrt(num_ind)`, where `sd_1` is the standard deviation of the individual measurements. Similarly, we can write `se_delta = sd_1_delta / np.sqrt(num_ind)`, where `sd_1_delta = np.sqrt(sd_1_asdaq**2 + sd_1_byse**2)`. The variables `sd_1_asdaq` and `sd_1_byse` are the standard deviations of the individual measurements on their respective exchanges. We'll make this all more explicit in listing 2.6, but for now the point to focus on is that we can rewrite the statement `z = delta / se_delta` as

```
z = np.sqrt(num_ind) * delta / sd_1_delta
```

Finally, we rewrite `z < -1.64` as

```
np.sqrt(num_ind) * delta / sd_1_delta < -1.64
```

or, equivalently,

```
num_ind > (1.64 * sd_1_delta / delta)**2
```

This expression is the A/B test design. It says you must take at least this many individual measurements for your analysis stage to give a statistically significant result.

To be clear: this says that you'll make num_ind trades on BYSE and num_ind trades on ASDAQ; then you'll compute two averages, agg_byse and agg_asdaq, from which you'll compute delta = agg_byse - agg_asdaq. That means you're making 2*num_ind trades in total.

The problem with this expression is that, at design time, you don't know delta or sd_1_delta. They are summary statistics of the individual measurement that you have yet to take. The good news is that you can find good design-time substitutes for these numbers.

First, in place of delta, substitute your practical significance level, prac_sig. By doing this, you are saying that you want to be able to measure—to make statistically significant—delta values that are at least as large (in magnitude) as prac_sig. Since the value of prac_sig is based on business considerations, you may specify it at design time without taking any measurements. In the previous section, we decided that a difference of prac_sig = 1.0 mips would be large enough to warrant switching your trading from ASDAQ to BYSE. Next, you can estimate sd_1_delta in one of two ways:

1 Take the standard deviation of existing measurements of your business metric from logged data. For example, since your system was trading on ASDAQ before you had the idea to test BYSE, you will have ASDAQ cost data in your production logs. From that, you can calculate sd_1_asdaq directly. Then you can guess that sd_1_byse = sd_1_asdaq. Usually this is a good guess. When you are A/B testing a change to a production system, you'll usually find that the variation in a business metric doesn't change much from version A to version B. This is likely because you are changing only one isolated aspect of the system, and the business metric variations are due to *all* aspects of the system (plus variations in the market). You can approximate sd_1_delta = np.sqrt(sd_1_asdaq**2 + sd_1_byse**2) = np.sqrt(2*sd_1_asdaq**2).

2 Alternatively, in cases where you suspect that your change from version A to version B is dramatic enough to make the variations (the sd_1s) different, you can run a small-scale measurement just to measure sd_1. This is called a *pilot study*. You could estimate sd_1_asdaq and sd_1_byse directly from logged costs collected during a pilot study, then compute sd_1_delta from those estimates.

With these two substitutions—prac_sig for delta and an approximation for sd_1_delta—you can complete your A/B test design with a function like the following listing.

Listing 2.6 A/B test design

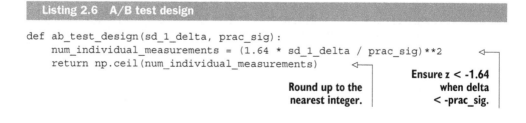

```
def ab_test_design(sd_1_delta, prac_sig):
    num_individual_measurements = (1.64 * sd_1_delta / prac_sig)**2      ⟵  Ensure z < -1.64
    return np.ceil(num_individual_measurements)      ⟵                      when delta
                                                                            < -prac_sig.
                              Round up to the
                              nearest integer.
```

To complete your design, you estimate sd_1_asdaq from 100 samples collected from your production logs:

```
np.random.seed(17)
sd_1_asdaq = np.array([trading_system("ASDAQ") for _ in range(100)]).std()
```

Then estimate sd_1_delta

```
sd_1_byse = sd_1_asdaq
sd_1_delta = np.sqrt(sd_1_asdaq**2 + sd_1_byse**2)
```

and specify prac_sig

```
prac_sig = 1
```

Finally, find the minimum number of individual measurements to take:

```
ab_test_design(sd_1_delta, prac_sig)
7.0
```

If you take seven individual measurements, you'll have a 5% chance of a false positive—of incorrectly acting as if BYSE is better than ASDAQ.

There's one more adjustment you need to make. What happens if BYSE really is better than ASDAQ, but you incorrectly conclude that it isn't, and so you don't switch your trading to BYSE? That's called a *false negative*. Contrast that with a false positive, defined in section 2.3.1, where BYSE *isn't* better, but you *do* switch. Just like you adjusted num_ind to limit the rate of false positives, you'd like a way to limit the rate of false negatives, too.

FALSE NEGATIVES

You just designed an A/B test that would limit the rate of false positive to 5%. You can use a similar approach to also limit the rate of false negatives. By convention, we usually limit false negative occurrences to 20% of the time. (We discuss why the limits are different in the sidebar.) We can adjust the number of individual measurements to account for the 20% limit on the false-negative rate.

Note that you may see the false-positive rate labeled as α and the false-negative rate as β. The convention is then expressed as $\alpha = 0.05$ and $\beta = 0.20$.

> ### Asymmetric limits on false positives and false negatives
> The conventional limit on the false-positive rate in A/B test design is 5%. The conventional limit on the false-negative rate is 20%. You aren't required to use these values, of course, but they've been accepted over time as good default values. Also, when you communicate results to other people, you might find that their intuition about A/B test results is calibrated to 5% and 20%.
>
> But why are they different?

When you run an A/B test, you start with a system running version A. If you make a false-positive error, you switch your system over to version B, even though B is worse than A. You have reduced the quality of your system. Your costs will go up or revenue will go down, or what have you. It's worse than having done nothing at all.

When you make a false-negative error, on the other hand, you leave the system running version A. You have done no harm. You've missed out on an opportunity to improve the system by switching to B—which is better than A in this case—but you haven't made the system any worse.

You might say that a false positive incurs an explicit cost and a false negative incurs an opportunity cost. Alternatively, you could say that a false positive damages the system, whereas a false negative does not.

The asymmetry in the false positive and false negative rates reflects a generally greater aversion to doing damage (a 5% limit) than to missing an opportunity (a 20% limit).

Assume that we run an A/B test and apply the rule developed in the previous section: "If z < -1.64, switch from ASDAQ to BYSE." We'd limit the false-positive rate to 5%. Let's extend that rule to also limit the false-negative rate to 20%. The approach is visualized in figure 2.10.

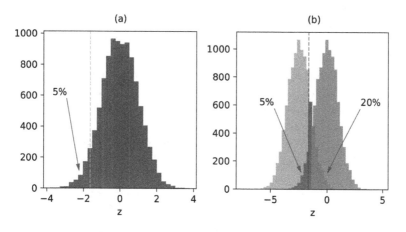

Figure 2.10   (a) The shaded area to the left of the vertical line contains 5% of the histogram. (b) The shaded area to the left of the vertical line contains 5% of the right-hand histogram. The shaded area to the right of the vertical line contains 20% of the left-hand histogram. A/B test design sets the location of the vertical line, which in turn determines the number of individual measurements.

The left panel, figure 2.10a, repeats figure 2.8 and depicts the rule for deciding whether an aggregate measurement is statistically significant, which limits false positives. In figure 2.10b, we simultaneously require that if the true distribution has a nonzero expectation—if BYSE really is cheaper than ASDAQ—that the probability of the z value falling to the right of the vertical line would be only 20%. If the z value were to fall to the right of the vertical line, we'd act as if delta = 0 and keep trading on ASDAQ, which would be the wrong decision. That would be a false negative.

Since z is normal and has standard deviation one, we can look up the fact that placing the vertical line at a distance of 0.84 from the expectation of z would leave 20% of the distribution to the right of the line. Call the expectation of z in this case -z0. (I'm saying that z0 > 0, so -z0, a negative number, is the center of the left-hand histogram in figure 2.10b.)

The two requirements on the vertical line—which we use to decide whether to switch to BYSE or stick with ASDAQ—are:

1 It must be at 1.64 to the left of z = 0, where z = 0 is the expectation of the hypothetical distribution where BYSE and ASDAQ have the same cost. This limits the false-positive rate to 5%.

2 It must be 0.84 to the right of -z0, where -z0 is the expectation of the hypothetical distribution where BYSE is cheaper than ASDAQ. This limits the false-negative rate to 20%.

For both statements to be true, we must have 0 - 1.64 = -z0 + .84 or z0 = 2.48. This is the design criterion.

To use the design criterion to specify the number of individual measurements, you need to express num_ind in terms of z0. First, recall that z = delta / se_delta. We can write z0, a specific value of z, in terms of delta0, a specific value of delta: z0 = delta0 / se_delta.

We choose delta0 to be the smallest difference in costs that we care to detect; the smallest difference where, if we erred and didn't switch to BYSE, we'd feel like we missed an opportunity. That difference is prac_sig = 1.0 mip, the practical significance level. Thus, delta0 <= - prac_sig. Since z0 = delta0 / se_delta, it's true that z0 <= - prac_sig / se_delta. Consideration of false-negative rates in this way, in A/B test design, is called *power analysis*.

Solving for num_ind

```
z0 <= - prac_sig / se_delta = np.sqrt(num_ind) * (-prac_sig) / sd_1_delta
```

and recalling that z0 = 2.48, and rewriting in terms of num_ind

```
np.sqrt(num_ind) * (-prac_sig) / sd_1_delta >= 2.48
```

yields a new A/B test design:

```
num_ind >= (2.48 * sd_1_delta / prac_sig)**2
```

This is shown in listing 2.7. Comparing to listing 2.6, you'll notice that we've simply changed the value 1.64 to 2.48.

Listing 2.7   A/B test design with power analysis

```
def ab_test_design_2(sd_1_delta, prac_sig):
    num_individual_measurements = (2.48 * sd_1_delta / prac_sig)**2    ◄─┐
    return np.ceil(num_individual_measurements)                          │
                                                           Use 2.48 instead
                                                                  of 1.64.
```

A new design, using `ab_test_design_2()`, demands more individual measurements to meet the additional requirement of a low false-positive rate:

```
np.random.seed(17)
sd_1_asdaq = np.array([trading_system("ASDAQ") for _ in range(100)]).std()
sd_1_byse = sd_1_asdaq
sd_1_delta = np.sqrt(sd_1_asdaq**2 + sd_1_byse**2)
prac_sig = 1.0
ab_test_design_2(sd_1_delta, prac_sig)
16.0
```

Your A/B test design is now complete. You need to take 16 individual measurements.

> **Number of individual measurements in practice**
>
> In a real agency trading system, the standard error of the cost of a single trade would be much higher, relative to the practical significance, than was used in the scenario in this chapter. Therefore, the number of individual measurements required to run an A/B test would be much larger. A real-world agency trading A/B test might take hundreds to thousands of individual measurements each day and take from 1 to 4 weeks to complete.

Now you can take the 16 individual measurements and analyze them.

2.3.3   Measure and analyze

You proceed to the measure stage (figure 2.11) and take at least 16 individual measurements of the execution cost of BYSE trades and at least 16 individual measurements of the execution cost of ASDAQ trades.

Figure 2.11   Take (at least) the number of individual measurements prescribed by the design stage. Randomize to remove bias.

You randomize to remove any biases from these measurements. See the following listing.

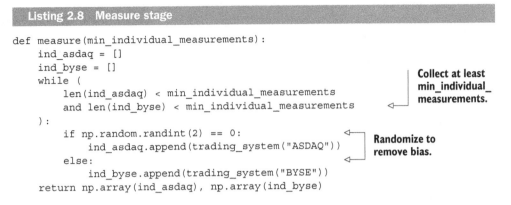

Listing 2.8 Measure stage

```
def measure(min_individual_measurements):
    ind_asdaq = []
    ind_byse = []
    while (                                                              Collect at least
        len(ind_asdaq) < min_individual_measurements                     min_individual_
        and len(ind_byse) < min_individual_measurements                  measurements.
    ):
        if np.random.randint(2) == 0:                      Randomize to
            ind_asdaq.append(trading_system("ASDAQ"))       remove bias.
        else:
            ind_byse.append(trading_system("BYSE"))
    return np.array(ind_asdaq), np.array(ind_byse)
```

The function `measure()` collects at least `min_individual_measurements` individual measurements for each of ASDAQ and BYSE. It randomly chooses which exchange to trade on (and to measure) as each new trading order arrives.

You can collect the measurements with

```
np.random.seed(17)
ind_asdaq, ind_byse = measure(16)
```

In the final stage, you analyze the measurements you've collected. First, you estimate the difference in estimated expected costs, the aggregate measurement:

```
ind_byse.mean() - ind_asdaq.mean()
-2.7483767796620846
```

BYSE was about 2.7 mips cheaper than ASDAQ in this experiment. That's a practically significant result, since its magnitude is greater than `prac_sig = 1.0` mip. BYSE has, so to speak, passed the first test. However, maybe that value is 2.7 mips because of variation in the aggregate measurements and BYSE is not actually cheaper than ASDAQ. In other words, maybe this is a false positive. You check for this error using the test for statistical significance discussed in section 2.3.1. You ask whether `z = delta / se_delta < -1.64`. See the following listing.

Listing 2.9 Analyze stage

```
                  def analyze(ind_asdaq, ind_byse):
aggregate      ┌──▷  agg_asdaq = ind_asdaq.mean()
measurements   │     se_asdaq = ind_asdaq.std() / np.sqrt(len(ind_asdaq))    ◁──┐ SE of
               └──▷  agg_byse = ind_byse.mean()                                 │ aggregate
                     se_byse = ind_byse.std() / np.sqrt(len(ind_byse))       ◁──┘ measurements

                     delta = agg_byse - agg_asdaq
                     se_delta = np.sqrt(se_asdaq**2 + se_byse**2)

                     z = delta / se_delta        ◁──┐ z score
                     return z
```

The function `analyze()` calculates and returns the z score:

```
analyze(ind_asdaq, ind_byse)
-6.353995237966593
```

Because `z` is well below the threshold of `-1.64`, this result is statistically significant. BYSE has passed the second test.

Since BYSE's aggregate measurement is both practically and statistically significantly lower than ASDAQ's, you decide to reconfigure your production trading system to direct all trades to BYSE. You're fairly confident this is a good idea, but you recognize that, unavoidably, there's still a 5% chance BYSE is not better than ASDAQ.

2.3.4 Recap of A/B test stages

In the scenario just presented, you aimed to decide whether to reconfigure your agency trading system to trade on BYSE instead of on ASDAQ. You compared them by their execution cost (your business metric), proceeding as follows:

- *Design*—You determined the minimum number of individual measurements needed to ensure that you could detect—with statistical significance—a difference between ASDAQ and BYSE as small as 1 mip, the smallest improvement that would be of practical significance to your business. That number was given by `(2.48 * sd_1_delta / prac_sig)**2`.
- *Measure*—You took the prescribed number of individual measurements, being sure to randomize between ASDQ and BYSE to remove confounder bias.
- *Analyze*—You asked whether the difference in costs between BYSE and ASDAQ was (1) practically significant (`delta < - prac_sig`) and (2) statistically significant (`delta / se_delta < -1.64`).

Ultimately, you measured lower execution costs on BYSE and reconfigured your system to trade there.

Summary

- The goal of an A/B test is to decide whether to switch from version A to version B.
- Replication of individual measurements increases the reliability of your final decision.
- Randomization removes confounder bias from your measurements.
- An A/B test design prescribes the minimum number of individual measurements to take.
- Switch to version B if its business metric is both practically and statistically significantly better than that of version A.

Multi-armed bandits: Maximizing business metrics while experimenting

This chapter covers
- Defining the multi-armed bandit (MAB) problem
- Modifying A/B testing's randomization procedure
- Extending epsilon-greedy to simultaneously evaluate multiple system changes
- Evaluating system changes even more quickly with Thompson sampling

In the previous chapter, we learned how to use A/B testing to evaluate changes to the system your engineering team is building. Once the tooling is in place to run A/B tests, the team should see a steady increase in the quality of the system as new changes follow the engineering workflow: implement a change candidate, evaluate it offline, and evaluate it online with an A/B test.

As the use of A/B testing increases, you'll spend more time evaluating "B" versions that underperform the current system, "A." (Recall from chapter 1 that most Bs underperform As.) Every time an underperforming B is measured, you pay a cost equal to the value of the business metric you would have achieved with A minus that achieved with B. If, for example, the business metric is revenue, then the cost of measuring B is "revenue of A – revenue of B." It will make sense to look for ways to reduce this cost. You can't just stop an A/B test early if it looks good because, although a shorter test would yield a lower cost, stopping early would produce false positives (see chapter 8, section 8.2).

We can, however, make A/B testing cheaper by reframing the problem just a bit. We can ask, "While evaluating a change candidate in production, how can we maximize the number of times we measure the better of A and B?" This question is the multi-armed bandit (MAB) problem. If, for example, A produced higher revenue than B, we'd like to measure A more often than B. The challenge is that we don't know at the outset which is better, A or B.

In this chapter, we'll first modify A/B testing to use summary statistics of individual measurements to better choose which change candidate to run. The resulting algorithm is called *epsilon-greedy*, and it solves the MAB problem. Then we'll see how, with a small tweak, epsilon-greedy enables us to evaluate multiple versions at once, which can make your workflow even faster. Finally, we'll see how using more detailed statistics of the measurements can create an even more efficient MAB algorithm called *Thompson sampling*.

3.1 Epsilon-greedy: Account for the impact of evaluation on business metrics

In industry, proposed system changes are likely to be rejected by an A/B test. This is not a quirk of A/B testing but rather is evidence that most of our good ideas simply don't improve complex engineered systems. Since an A/B test runs the A version half the time and the B version half the time, the overall system's business metric will lie halfway between that of A and that of B. If a B version underperforms the A version, then performance during an A/B test will be worse than just running A. Chapter 1, section 1.3.1 points out that B versions underperform the base system—the A version—as often as 90% of the time.

The good news is that the other 10% of the time B will be better, will be accepted into the system, and will produce value for a long time afterward. The "long time" improvement covers the cost of A/B testing.

In a mature system developed by a large enough team, we should expect to be running A/B tests all the time. "Mature" means that A/B tests may be run and analyzed effectively. By "large-enough," I mean a team that produces new versions quickly enough so that there's always something new that needs A/B testing. At this stage, the cost of A/B testing could be significant and worth investing some engineering effort to reduce. MAB algorithms help reduce that cost.

To help motivate and explain our first MAB algorithm, epsilon-greedy, we consider the following scenario: Imagine you're an ML engineer responsible for placing banner ads on a website. Each time a user arrives at your home page, your system queries an ML model for its estimates of the probability that the user will click on each of the ads in the ad inventory. Let's say the ad inventory contains 1,000 ads. The system serves the ad with the highest predicted click probability to the user. Figure 3.1 depicts

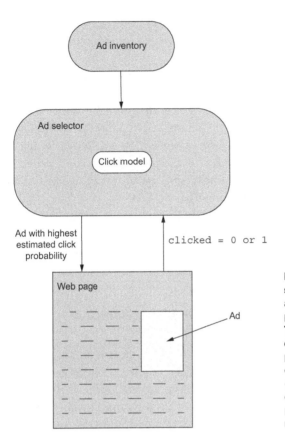

Figure 3.1   An ad-serving system. The ad selector pulls ads from the ad inventory, then asks the click model to estimate the probability that the user will click on each ad. The ad selector sends the ad with the highest estimated click probability to the user. The page tells the server whether the user clicked on the ad, shown here as a variable `clicked` **taking a value of either 0 (not clicked) or 1 (clicked). The rest of the web page is delivered to the user by a web server, not shown here.**

the system. We'll refer to the component of the system responsible for selecting which ad to serve as the *ad selector*.

If the user *does* click on the ad, your company will be paid $1, the cost per click (CPC), by the advertiser. Given that financial incentive, the A/B tests you run on this system measure the business metric called click-through rate (CTR):

$$CTR = \frac{\text{(number of clicks on ads)}}{\text{(number of ads shown)}}$$

The total revenue per day, which is the broader business concern, is CPC*CTR*[number of visitors to the home page]. You can let the ad-space salespeople try to increase the CPC from $1, and the marketing team can focus on getting more users to visit the home page. As the ad-serving ML engineer, you want to increase CTR by building an ML model that better estimates the probability a user will click on an ad. We'll call this the *click model*. In the following, you'll be comparing two click models: version A, the current click model, and version B, a new model you've just built.

3.1.1   A/B testing as a baseline

We developed A/B testing in chapter 2 with the goal of taking the fewest measurements possible under the constraints that the probability of a false positive stay below 0.05 and the probability of false negative stay below 0.20.

These limits—0.05 and 0.20—became standard values long ago in practical experiment design. They are convenient because, as probabilities, they are unitless—that is, they don't reference any domain-specific quantities like CTR, dollars of revenue, etc.—and so may be applied across experiments from a broad range of fields. Additionally, the standardization of these probability limits makes it easier to communicate results from one experimenter to another, as all experimenters build an intuition for the quality of results that is implied by 0.05 and 0.20.

When optimizing an engineered system, we want to increase a business metric, like CTR. An A/B test would increase CTR by

1   Determining via experiment whether version A of your click model has a better or worse CTR than version B does, then

2   Running the better version from now on

Step 2 produces a high CTR—the maximum of A's CTR and B's CTR. We won't change that.

Taking a measurement of version A or B (in step 1) means exposing real users to it and getting or losing their clicks, so what you choose to measure has real impact on your bottom line. Knowing that, let's modify step 1 so that during the experiment we more often measure whichever version (A or B) has a higher CTR. Our goal is to take as many measurements of the better version as we can while still taking *enough* measurements of the worse version to be sure it's worse.

To get started, let's create a simulation of the ad-selection system. We'll call the current version of the click model A (as usual) and simulate it so that the system produces a CTR of 0.005 (one half of 1%). According to the stats reported by LinkedIn (http://mng.bz/gRzE) for 2019, a CTR of 0.0050 for banner ads is a bit below the average of 0.0060 (0.60%). Knowing that, we propose a new click model, B, that we hope is better. For the purpose of presentation, we'll simulate the system with B so that it produces a CTR of 0.0070, above the industry average. See the following listing for the Python code that implements the simulation.

> **Listing 3.1   Simulate measurement of click on an ad**

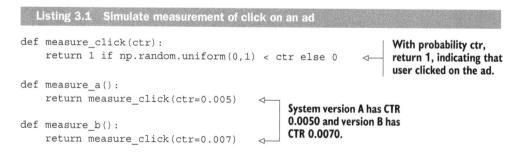

```
def measure_click(ctr):
    return 1 if np.random.uniform(0,1) < ctr else 0      ◁──  With probability ctr,
                                                               return 1, indicating that
                                                               user clicked on the ad.
def measure_a():
    return measure_click(ctr=0.005)    ◁─┐
                                         │  System version A has CTR
def measure_b():                         │  0.0050 and version B has
    return measure_click(ctr=0.007)    ◁─┘  CTR 0.0070.
```

The function `measure_click()` returns the value 1 to simulate the event "the user clicked on the ad" or the value 0 to simulate "the user didn't click on the ad." It returns 1 with probability ctr. The expectation of `measure_click(ctr)` is the value ctr—that is, if we could take the average of infinitely many return values of `measure_click(ctr)`, that average would be ctr. As such, the expected value of `measure_A()` is .0050 and the expected value of `measure_B()` is .0070. Or we could say, "The expected CTR of version A is .0050" (and similarly for B).

Next, let's simulate an A/B test following the steps summarized at the end of chapter 2, section 2.3.4:

1 Run a pilot study to measure sd_1_delta, which we'll abbreviate as sd_1 here.
2 Define a practical significance level, prac_sig.
3 Calculate the number of individual measurements to take, num_ind.

An individual measurement consists of displaying a single ad and recording whether it was clicked on. See the following listing for the A/B test design. Let's take prac_sig = 0.001. Given that 0.0050 is our current CTR, an improvement of 0.001 would mean 20% more revenue per day.

Listing 3.2   Design an A/B test

```
def design_ab_test():
    def pilot_study(num_pilot_measurements):
        clicked_pre_a = np.array([measure_a() for _ in
    range(num_pilot_measurements)])
        clicked_pre_b = np.array([measure_b() for _ in
    range(num_pilot_measurements)])
        sd_1 = np.sqrt( clicked_pre_a.std()**2 + clicked_pre_b.std()**2 )
        return sd_1

    sd_1 = pilot_study(1000)          # Run a pilot study to measure sd_1.
    prac_sig = 0.001                  # Define a practical significance level of .001 (.1%).
    num_ind = (2.48 * sd_1 / prac_sig) ** 2   # Calculate the number of individual measurements, num_ind.
    return int(num_ind)
```

The design of an A/B test comes down to the prescription of how many individual measurements to take. For this scenario, we need

```
np.random.seed(17)
num_ind = design_ab_test()
```

This produces num_ind = 91561, nearly 100,000, individual measurements. If you don't work in online advertising, that might seem like a lot of measurements, but consider that if 0.5% of 100,000 users clicked on an ad, your site would earn only $500. Since CTRs are small, you need to show lots of ads to sustain a business. For example, at a CTR of .0050 and a CPC of $1, to earn just $100,000 per year (a small amount of revenue for a big tech company), how many ads would you need to run?

$$\text{CTR} \times \text{CPC} \times \frac{\text{ads}}{\text{day}} \times \frac{\text{days}}{\text{year}} = [\$100,000 \text{ revenue}]$$

or

$$\frac{\$100,000}{.001 \times \$1 \times 365} \approx \frac{270,000 \text{ ads}}{\text{day}}$$

A business that could support itself through advertising would thus have many times the capacity needed to run this A/B test.

Simulating the A/B test is straightforward: For each individual measurement, we'll randomize between A and B. See listing 3.3 for the code. The randomization is taken care of by the condition `np.random.uniform(0,1) < 0.5`, where a random number chosen with uniform probability between 0 and 1 is less than 0.5 with probability 0.5. In other words, choose A half the time and choose B half the time.

Listing 3.3 Simulate a run of an A/B test

```
def run_ab_test(num_ind):
    clicked_a = []
    clicked_b = []
    for n in range(num_ind):
        # Randomize between A and B.
        if np.random.uniform(0,1) < 0.5:          ◁── Choose A or B with probability .5 each.
            clicked = measure_a()          ◁── Run A or B, taking an individual measurement.
            clicked_a.append(clicked)          ◁── Log the individual measurement for later analysis.
        else:
            clicked = measure_b()
            clicked_b.append(clicked)

    clicked_a = np.array(clicked_a)
    clicked_b = np.array(clicked_b)

    return clicked_a, clicked_b
```

Figure 3.2 depicts this same randomization logic in the ad-serving system. The probability of choosing model A is `p(A) = 0.5`, and similarly for B. Once the click model is chosen, it is applied to all the ads in the inventory, and the ad with the highest estimated click probability is served to the user. The response from the user, `clicked`, is returned to the ad selector in the figure to be logged for later analysis. Listing 3.3 simulates this logging by appending `clicked` to either `clicked_a` or `clicked_b`, depending on which model was used.

To complete the experiment, we would run an analysis like listing 3.4, where we compute the z score from the logged data, `clicked_a` and `clicked_b`.

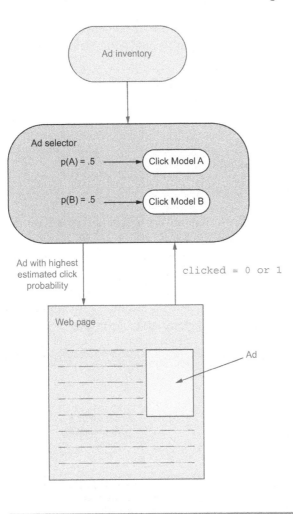

Figure 3.2   A/B testing click models in the ad-serving system. This figure focuses on the ad selector component from figure 3.1. To effect an A/B test, the ad selector first chooses randomly between click model A and click model B. The probability of choosing model A is 0.5, as indicated by `p(A) = 0.5`, and similarly for model B. Note that once the model is chosen, it is used to estimate click probabilities for the entire ad inventory before selecting an ad to serve. The individual measurement `clicked` is logged for later analysis.

Listing 3.4   Analyze the A/B test data

```
def analyze_a_b_test(clicked_a, clicked_b):
    mean_a = clicked_a.mean()
    mean_b = clicked_b.mean()
    std_a = clicked_a.std()
    std_b = clicked_b.std()
    m = mean_b - mean_a
    se = np.sqrt( (std_a**2 + std_b**2) / num_ind )
    z = m / se

    return z
```

Calculate the difference of mean click rates, m, and the standard error, se.

Calculate the z score, which determines whether we accept or reject version B.

The complete experiment—design, measure, and analysis—looks like

```
np.random.seed(17)
num_ind = design_ab_test()
clicked_a, clicked_b = run_ab_test(num_ind)
```

```
z = analyze_a_b_test(clicked _a, clicked _b)
print (num_ind, z)
91561 2.95
```

This yields z = 2.95. Since z > 1.64, we would accept the change and replace model A with model B.

Before the A/B test ran, the production system used model A, which produced a CTR of 0.0050. After the A/B test completed, the system would have used B, which produces CTR = 0.0070. During the A/B test, however, the system was randomizing between A and B, using each version half of the time. The CTR achieved by the system during the A/B test is, thus, just the average of A's and B's CTRs, or (0.0050 + 0.0070)/2 = 0.0060.

We couldn't have known B was better than A until after we ran the A/B test, but now that we know, we can look back and say that if we had run B instead of running an A/B test, we could have earned CTR = 0.0070 instead of the A/B test's CTR = 0.0060. The term used in multi-armed bandit literature to describe this lost opportunity is *regret*. We say that the A/B test produced a regret of

$$\text{CTR of model B} - \text{CTR of the A/B test} = 0.0070 - 0.0060 = 0.0010$$

We missed out on 0.0010 CTR by running the A/B test instead of running model B.

Let's delve deeper to understand how the CTR evolves while the A/B test is running. Listing 3.5 runs the A/B test again but instruments it to count the number of ads displayed and the number of ads that are clicked on. clicked_a and clicked_b have been removed in favor of counting the number of ads and clicks for A and B separately.

Listing 3.5 Trace the CTR as the A/B test runs

```
def ab_test(num_ind):
    sum_clicks = 0.0
    num_ads = 0.0
    sum_a = 0.0
    num_a = 0
    sum_b = 0.0
    num_b = 0

    ctr_vs_n = []
    ctr_a = []
    ctr_b = []
    for n in range(num_ind):
        if np.random.uniform(0,1) < 0.5:
            clicked = measure_a()
            sum_a += clicked
            num_a += 1
        else:
            clicked = measure_b()
            sum_b += clicked
            num_b += 1
```

Count ads and clicks separately for versions A and B.

Count the number of ads displayed.

```
sum_clicks += clicked          ◄──┐  Count the number
num_ads += 1                       │  of ads clicked.
if num_a > 0 and num_b > 0:
    ctr_a.append(sum_a/num_a)          ─┐  CTR so far for A,
    ctr_b.append(sum_b/num_b)           │  for B, and overall
    ctr_vs_n.append(sum_clicks/num_ads)─┘

return ctr_vs_n, ctr_a, ctr_b
```

This function's first output, `ctr_vs_n`, is the CTR achieved "so far"—up through the nth individual measurement. A plot of `ctr_vs_n` is shown in figure 3.3.

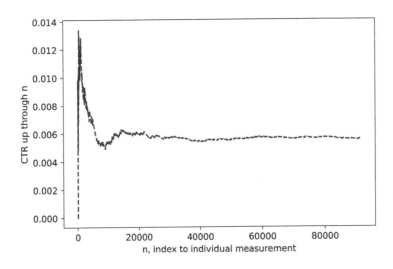

Figure 3.3   The CTR measured up through individual measurement `n` **in a simulated A/B test. The final CTR is** `0.0058`, **about halfway between the CTR of A (`0.0050`) and the CTR of B (`0.0070`).**

The trace of CTR in figure 3.3 fluctuates wildly initially—when fewer samples are included in it—then settles down to a final value of about `0.0058`, which is close to the expected value of `0.0060`. Running `ab_test()` 100 times produces final CTR values with mean `0.0060` and standard deviation `0.0002`. Figure 3.4 shows the mean and standard deviation of all 100 traces.

The second and third outputs for `ab_test()`—`ctr_a` and `ctr_b`—trace the CTR up through measurement n for A and B separately. For example, `ctr_a` traces the CTR only for ads selected using click model A, and similarly for `ctr_b`. These two traces, plotted in figure 3.5, let us see how each version's CTR measurement evolves over time and how they compare.

The dark line in figure 3.5, A's trace, appears above the light line, B's trace, early in the run. This indicates that the measured CTR for A was higher than that for B, even though B's expected CTR is better than A's. This can happen just due to the variation

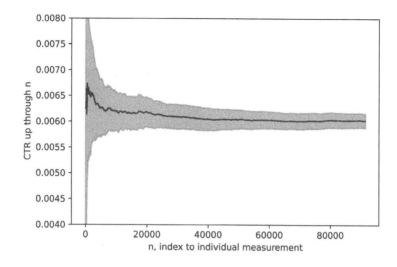

Figure 3.4   Distribution of 100 runs of `ab_test()`. The mean of all 100 traces is in black. The gray area is one standard deviation tall. The final mean is `0.0060`, which is the average of CTR A (`0.0050`) and CTR B (`0.0070`).

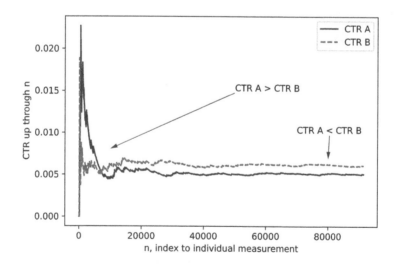

Figure 3.5   CTR for each of model A and model B. Early on, the dark line (A) is above the light line (CTR A > CTR B), but eventually it falls below (CTR A < CTR B) and stays there for the rest of the run.

in the individual measurements. Eventually, however, the lines settle down close to the expected CTRs, and it appears easy to tell that B outperforms A.

If I were running this A/B test and monitoring CTR A and CTR B, I might be tempted to stop around n = 100.000 or so. Seeing B consistently outperform A would make me want to accept B so that the system would earn B's CTR of `0.0070`, rather than the blended CTR of `0.0050` shown in figure 3.3. But I know stopping an A/B test early generates false positives (see chapter 8, section 8.2).

This tension between wanting to capitalize on the higher-performing B version as soon as possible and the desire to avoid a false-positive acceptance can be resolved by modifying A/B testing's randomization procedure to preferentially choose the better of A and B. This proposal is the epsilon-greedy algorithm, and it is one solution to the multi-armed bandit problem.

3.1.2 *The epsilon-greedy algorithm*

Instead of choosing between A and B with equal probability, `p(A)` = `p(B)` = `0.5`, epsilon-greedy assigns a higher probability to whichever version, A or B, has produced a higher CTR so far.

Epsilon-greedy works like this: With probability `1-epsilon`, use whichever version has a higher CTR so far. Otherwise, with probability `epsilon`, act like an A/B test and just choose between A and B with equal probability.

To convert A/B test logic to epsilon-greedy logic, we just need to change the randomization portion of `ab_test()` from

```
if np.random.uniform(0,1) < 0.5:
    # Run A
else:
    # Run B
```

to

```
if np.random.uniform(0,1) < 1-epsilon:
    # Run version with higher CTR so far
else:
    if np.random.uniform(0,1) < 0.5:
            # Run A
        else:
            # Run B
```

Notice that if we set `epsilon = 1`, then the first branch is never executed because `np.random.uniform(0,1)` is never less than `1 - epsilon = 0`. Similarly, if we set `epsilon = 0`, the second branch is never executed. The value of `epsilon` determines how strongly epsilon-greedy's randomization is biased toward the higher-CTR version of the system. In addition, `epsilon` is a parameter of the epsilon-greedy algorithm, not a parameter of the system itself. To make that distinction clear, we refer to `epsilon` as a metaparameter.

Figure 3.6 depicts the ad selector using the epsilon-greedy algorithm to decide between click models A and B. It now implements the epsilon-greedy algorithm rather than A/B test's randomization.

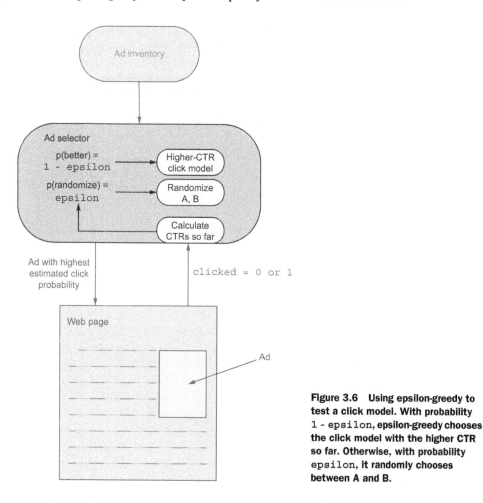

Figure 3.6 **Using epsilon-greedy to test a click model. With probability** 1 - epsilon, **epsilon-greedy chooses the click model with the higher CTR so far. Otherwise, with probability** epsilon, **it randomly chooses between A and B.**

The following listing shows an implementation of epsilon-greedy. Notice that if you were to pass in the argument epsilon = 1, this function would behave the same as ab_test().

Listing 3.6 The epsilon-greedy algorithm

```
def epsilon_greedy(num_ind, epsilon):
    sum_clicks = 0.0
    num_ads = 0.0
    sum_a = 0.0
    num_a = 0
    sum_b = 0.0
    num_b = 0
    ctr_vs_n = []                    ← Take num_ind
    used_b = []                        individual
    for _ in range(num_ind):           measurements.
        select = "Randomize"
```

```
if np.random.uniform(0,1) < 1-epsilon:          ◄───┐ Shows "with probability
    ctr_a = sum_a/num_a if num_a>0 else 0            │ 1-epsilon"
    ctr_b = sum_b/num_b if num_b>0 else 0
    if ctr_a > ctr_b:              ◄───┐ Calculate CTR up through this
        select = "A"                   │ measurement and collect in ctr_vs_n.
    elif ctr_b > ctr_a:            ◄───┘
        select = "B"
    # else, if they're equal, randomize

if select == "Randomize":          ◄───┐ Otherwise, if
    if np.random.uniform(0,1) < 0.5:    │ ctr_A == ctr_B,
        select = "A"                    │ just randomize.
    else:
        select = "B"

if select == "A":
    clicked = measure_a()
    sum_a += clicked
    num_a += 1
    used_b.append(False)
else:
    clicked = measure_b()
    sum_b += clicked
    num_b += 1
    used_b.append(True)
sum_clicks += clicked
num_ads += 1

ctr_vs_n.append(sum_clicks / num_ads)

return ctr_vs_n, used_b
```

As shown, epsilon_greedy() computes summary statistics—ctr_a and ctr_b—and uses them to make a better decision about which version, A or B, to use for each individual measurement. In this way, epsilon-greedy is adaptive (i.e., it modifies its decisions based on the data it has seen so far). In contrast, A/B testing does not adapt to the data. It always randomizes between A and B equally.

Compare a run of epsilon_greedy(num_ind, epsilon=0.10) to one of ab_test() in figure 3.7. Figure 3.7 shows a single trace of epsilon-greedy outperforming A/B testing in CTR by about 0.0067 - 0.0058 = 0.0009 and underperforming, by only 0.0003, the upper bound that would be achieved if we selected version B the entire time. In other words, the regret is 0.0003, which is smaller than the A/B test regret of 0.0010. Running epsilon_greedy() 100 times produces final CTR values with mean 0.0067 and standard deviation 0.0004. Figure 3.8 compares the distribution of 100 runs of ab_test() to that of 100 runs of epsilon_greedy()—epsilon_greedy() consistently achieves higher CTR.

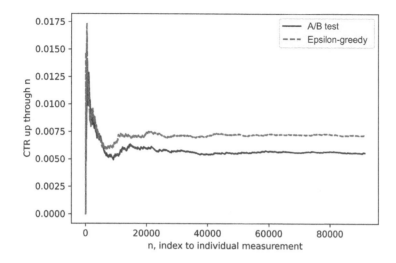

Figure 3.7   The epsilon-greedy algorithm achieves a higher CTR (about `.0067`) than an A/B test (about `.0058`) by using whichever version—A or B—has better realized performance 90% of the time and only 10% of time randomly choosing between A and B.

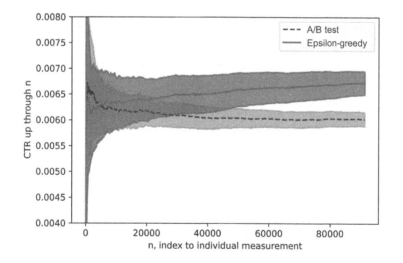

Figure 3.8   100 runs of `ab_test()` compared to 100 runs of `epsilon_greedy()`: `epsilon_greedy()` consistently achieves higher CTR. The final, mean CTR of `epsilon_greedy()` is `0.0068`, which is close to the maximum of `0.0070`, the CTR of B.

Figure 3.9 compares the percentage of the 100 runs in which B is selected for measurement to that in which A is selected.

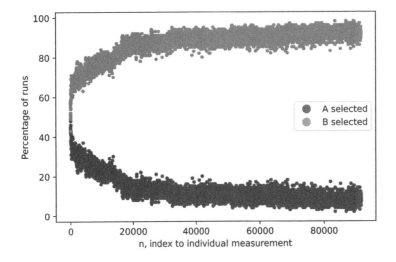

Figure 3.9 **Percentage of runs selecting B or A for each individual measurement. B is selected more and more frequently as the** `epsilon_greedy()` **runs progress.**

Following figure 3.9, we see that, at the beginning of a run, A and B are selected at equal rates—50% each, like an A/B test. By the end of a run, `epsilon_greedy()` chooses B with probability `1-epsilon = 0.90`. The steady increase in the rate of selecting B accounts for the steady increase in CTR that we observed in figure 3.8. To understand how the epsilon-greedy algorithm selects B more often over time, we need to think about how the standard errors of the aggregate measurements evolve over the course of the experiment.

First, note that `epsilon_greedy()` compares the aggregate measurements –ctr_a and `ctr_b` – at each iteration, n. Then it runs whichever version, A or B, has a higher measured CTR. Early in the experiment the standard errors (SEs) of `ctr_a` and `ctr_b` are large because few individual measurements have been taken.

When the SEs are large, we may measure `ctr_a` to be less than or greater than `ctr_b`, regardless of what the expectations (true values) of the CTRs are. As more individual measurements are collected, the SEs decrease, and it becomes more and more likely that if A's CTR is truly greater than B's, then we will measure `ctr_a > ctr_b`, and vice versa.

The *exploratory* measurements, taken 10% of the time, ensure that more individual measurements will be collected for both versions, regardless of which one has a better aggregate CTR right now. The *exploitative* measurements, taken 90% of the time, ensure that most of the experiment's measurements will be devoted to the version that is probably better.

The function `epsilon_greedy()` with `epsilon = 0.10` explores 10% of the time and exploits 90% of the time. An A/B test, by contrast, explores only for a predetermined `num_ind` measurements and exploits thereafter. We say that `epsilon_greedy()`

"balances exploration with exploitation" to achieve a good CTR during the course of an experiment.

3.1.3 Deciding when to stop

In our formulation of the epsilon-greedy algorithm so far, there is no prescription to stop exploring. In the preceding simulations, we chose num_ind, the number of measurements, using A/B test design so that we could compare A/B testing to epsilon-greedy. But if you chose to use epsilon-greedy in practice, there would be no natural point at which you'd make an acceptance/rejection decision. The A/B test-designed num_ind value doesn't apply here, because it was chosen to limit false positives and negatives. Instead, the goal with epsilon-greedy is to maximize a business metric, like CTR.

We can get epsilon-greedy to stop with a slight modification to the algorithm. Set epsilon at each iteration, n, to

$$epsilon = 2 \times c \times \frac{\left(\frac{\text{BM}_{\text{max}}}{\text{PS}}\right)^2}{n}$$

The value of BM_{max} is the largest plausible value of the business metric (CTR)—say 0.01. It's there to provide a scale for PS (the practical significance, prac_sig) so that epsilon remains unitless.

Since epsilon is proportional to $1/n$, it decays toward zero. You can stop the algorithm when epsilon is very small, say 0.01, at which point the algorithm is rarely exploring and, instead, usually running the system version it thinks is best. The sensitivity of epsilon-greedy's CTR to your choice of the stopping threshold is low, meaning that if you chose to stop at epsilon = 0.02 or epsilon = 0.005, you'd achieve a similar CTR. The lower the threshold, the longer the algorithm will run.

Whenever epsilon is 1 or larger, the epsilon-greedy code will randomly choose between A and B—it'll be doing pure exploration. Because epsilon decreases over time (i.e., as n increases), it will eventually fall below 1, and the algorithm will start exploiting, too. The metaparameter c controls the amount of time epsilon spends above 1, in pure exploration. Larger values of c will induce longer pure-exploration times. We'll use c = 5 throughout this text, but you should consider c to be a metaparameter of epsilon-greedy that may be different for different systems. Setting c too low will limit exploration, increasing the risk that epsilon-greedy will choose the wrong version (A or B). Setting c too high will just increase the running time with no benefit.

When the algorithm stops, if B has a higher mean CTR than A, you can accept B into the system. Otherwise, you can reject it. A modified version of epsilon_greedy(), with this new formula for epsilon, is in the following listing.

Listing 3.7 Epsilon-greedy with decaying epsilon

```
def epsilon_greedy_decay():
    bm_max = 0.01
    prac_sig = 0.001                    Set c, the new
    c = 5                               metaparameter.

    epsilon_0 = 2*c*(bm_max/prac_sig)**2    Implement the formula
    epsilon_stop = 0.01                     for decaying epsilon.

    sum_clicks = 0.0
    num_ads = 0.0
    sum_a = 0.0
    num_a = 0
    sum_b = 0.0
    num_b = 0
    ctr_vs_n = []
    epsilons = []

    n = 0                                       Since n starts
    selected = None                             counting from zero,
    while True:                                 divide by 1+n.
        epsilon = min(1.0, epsilon_0 / (1.0 + n))
        epsilons.append(epsilon)
        if epsilon < epsilon_stop:          Stop when epsilon
            break                           is very small.
        select = "Randomize"
        if np.random.uniform(0,1) < 1-epsilon:
            ctr_a = sum_a/num_a if num_a>0 else 0
            ctr_b = sum_b/num_b if num_b>0 else 0
            if ctr_a > ctr_b:
                select = "A"
                selected = "A"
            elif ctr_b > ctr_a:
                select = "B"
                selected = "B"
        if select == "Randomize":
            if np.random.uniform(0,1) < 0.5:
                select = "A"
            else:
                select = "B"

        if select == "A":
            clicked = measure_a()
            sum_a += clicked
            num_a += 1
        else:
            clicked = measure_b()
            sum_b += clicked
            num_b += 1
        sum_clicks += clicked
        num_ads += 1

        ctr_vs_n.append(sum_clicks / num_ads)
        n += 1
```

```
    if selected == "B":
        accept_reject = "Accept"
    else:
        accept_reject = "Reject"                         Return trace
    return ctr_vs_n, epsilons, accept_reject            of ctrs.
```

Figure 3.10 shows how `epsilon` decays during a single run. Note that the value of epsilon is unaffected by the individual measurements taken during the experiment. In the expression for `epsilon`

$$\text{epsilon} = 2 \times c \times \frac{\left(\frac{\text{BM}_{\text{max}}}{\text{PS}}\right)^2}{n}$$

all quantities (`2`, `c`, `BM`$_{\text{max}}$, `PS`) are constant except for `n`. Thus, epsilon decays on a fixed schedule regardless of the performance of A or B.

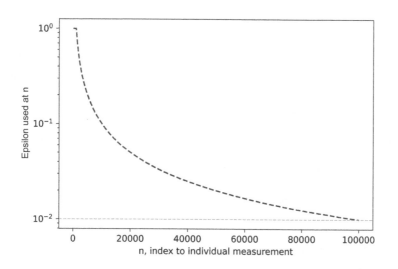

Figure 3.10   In a run of `epsilon_greedy_decay()`, `epsilon` **decays with time until it is below the threshold of** `0.01`, **at which point the algorithm stops. This algorithm takes fewer measurements than the comparable A/B test from figure 3.1.**

Note also that this run ends after only 100,000 measurements, which is fewer than the A/B test's recommendation of around 200,000.

   To make a fair comparison between `epsilon_greedy_decay()` and `epsilon_greedy()`, let's run `epsilon_greedy_decay()` until epsilon falls below `0.01`, then run B if it is accepted (or A if B is rejected) until the number of measurements equals that used in figures 3.3–3.5, 3.7, and 3.8. Running this 100 times gives the results shown in table 3.1, where they are compared to the A/B test and epsilon-greedy results from earlier in this section.

Table 3.1 `epsilon_greedy_decay()` **outperforms** `ab_test()` **in terms of the CTR obtained during the evaluation of a candidate system change. Its advantage over** `epsilon_greedy()` **is that it has a prescribed stopping time.**

Algorithm	Mean CTR	Std. Dev. CTR
`ab_test()`	0.0060	0.0002
`epsilon_greedy()`	0.0068	0.0002
`epsilon_greedy_decay()`	0.0068	0.0005

As table 3.1 shows, `epsilon_greedy_decay()` outperforms A/B testing in this system. In fact, `epsilon_greedy_decay()` is proven to have lower regret than both `ab_test()` and `epsilon_greedy()` over a broad range of systems.

> ## Optimal regret
> The algorithm `epsilon_greedy_decay()` has provably optimal asymptotic regret. In 1985, Lai and Robbins (see T. Lai and H. Robbins, "Asymptotically efficient adaptive allocation rules. *Adv. Appl. Math.*, vol. 6, pp. 4–22, 1985) proved that multi-armed bandit algorithms could at best have a regret that increases with $O(\log(n))$, where n is the number of measurements taken. In 2002, Auer, Cesa-Bianchi, and Fischer (see P. Auer, N. Cesa-Bianchi, and P. Fisher, "Finite-time analysis of the multiarmed bandit problem," Mach. Learn., vol. 47, 235–256, 2002) proved that `epsilon_greedy_decay()` achieves this best case regret. (In contrast, `epsilon_greedy()` and `ab_test()` have regret like $O(n)$, which is much worse). The "catch," if you will, is that to use `epsilon_greedy_decay()`, you need to tune c.

FALSE POSITIVES, FALSE NEGATIVES

Recall that A/B test design specifies a maximum false-positive rate of 5% and a maximum false-negative rate of 20%. This creates an asymmetry between A and B. It says staying with A when B is better (false negatives) is more acceptable (up to 20% of the time) than switching to B when A is better.

There's nothing like this in `epsilon_greedy_decay()`. In fact, there's nothing fundamental about this in A/B testing either. For example, you could set the false-positive and false-negative rate limits to be equal if you so desired, but the asymmetry is conventional, and likely wise: It biases the engineer away from making changes, accounting for the fact that change itself has a cost (a risk). Your business needs and subjectivity will determine how biased for or against change your decisions should be, but in order to implement that bias accurately, it's important to be aware that some bias is built into A/B testing in its standard form but is not built into epsilon-greedy.

In the runs in table 3.1, `epsilon_greedy_decay()` accepted version B 98% of the time, yielding a false-negative rate of 2%. Since this algorithm is symmetric with respect to A and B, it also has a false-positive rate of 2%. This rate will vary from system to system and with your choice of the metaparameter c, but it won't be controlled, like in an A/B test. Instead of controlling false positives and negatives, a multi-armed bandit algorithm tries to achieve the best business metric while evaluating the different versions of the system (A and B).

In summary, an epsilon-greedy experiment can be carried out by

- *Design*—Determine PS and BM$_{max}$ from business considerations, and set a value for c (e.g., c = 5).
- *Measure*—Select between versions A and B using epsilon-greedy's biased randomization, which "explores" with a rate

$$\text{epsilon} = 2 \times c \times \frac{\left(\frac{\text{BM}_{\text{max}}}{\text{PS}}\right)^2}{n}$$

Stop when `epsilon` falls below `0.01`.

- *Analyze*—Accept B if it has a higher realized business metric than A, or else reject it.

3.2 Evaluating multiple system changes simultaneously

So far in this book, we've learned how to evaluate a single system change candidate—that is, the "B" in "A/B test." Epsilon-greedy is preferable to A/B testing when we want to obtain a higher business metric during an evaluation of a change candidate.

In practice, you'll often need to evaluate multiple versions to make a single decision about how to improve the system. In the context of the ad-selection scenario, this need might result, for instance, from (1) competing click models, (2) tunable parameters, or (3) interactions between versions:

- *Competing click models*—It's possible for a team of engineers to produce multiple click models all with similar offline estimates of CTR. Since the models all have the same offline quality, you must evaluate them in production to determine which one actually produces the highest CTR (see chapter 5, section 5.2).
- *Tunable parameters*—The ad selector queries the click model for its estimate of the click probability for each of the ads in the inventory; then it serves the ad with the highest click probability. A realistic ad selector might also decide not to show any ad at all if all of the ads have a click probability below some threshold. Why clutter a page with an ad that the user very probably isn't interested in?

The user just gets a worse experience, and likely no revenue is earned anyway. The probability threshold used to make that decision is a parameter that needs to be tuned in production. You might tune it by postulating several values and evaluating each of them in production. A realistic system might have multiple "business logic" rules like this, and each one would have associated tunable parameters.

- *Interactions between versions*—Imagine two engineers work independently where one produces a new click model and one produces new business logic. In this case, you need to test three (not two) system versions: (1) the new click model, (2) the new business logic, and (3) the new model plus the new business logic. Case (3) is sometimes called an *interaction effect* or just an *interaction* if its CTR is not equal to the sum of the CTRs of (1) and (2).

  If this seems unintuitive, consider an example: The new business logic says, "Don't show a user the same ad two visits in a row." This change might show an improved CTR—case (2)—if users tend to not notice an ad they've just seen. The new click model might identify a small subset of great ads that users love so much that they click on them even if they've already seen them. That would improve CTR in case (1). These two improvements are not mutually exclusive because case (2) is a result of a small improvement for most ads, and case (1) is a large improvement for a small subset of ads.

The interaction happens when you run the new business logic and the new click model together and the business logic prevents the model from showing those few great ads too frequently. The CTR for case (3) would then be less than the sum of the CTRs for cases (1) and (2). The business logic might be damaging enough to make case (1) the right choice.

Let's modify epsilon-greedy to evaluate multiple system changes, like the ones just described. Recall how epsilon-greedy chooses between A and B for each individual measurement: *With probability epsilon, select A or B at random; otherwise, use whichever version has realized a higher business metric (e.g., CTR) so far.*

This can be straightforwardly modified to test multiple changes simultaneously. Let's call the versions B, C, D, and so on, then: With probability epsilon, select A or B or C or D or . . . at random; otherwise, use whichever version has realized the highest business metric (e.g., CTR) so far.

Recall (or notice in the preceding statement) that epsilon-greedy has no preference for A, the current system version. All of A, B, C, and so on are treated equally. As such, they are given a common name: *arms*. Each candidate version of the system (including A) is an *arm* in the multi-armed bandit problem.

Figure 3.11 depicts the ad selector testing multiple click models: A, B, C, . . . Little needs to be changed in the system or the testing logic to extend epsilon-greedy to more than two arms.

Multi-armed bandit nomenclature

An old-fashioned nickname for a slot machine is "one-armed bandit," so-called because (1) it is a tall rectangular box that has a long handle on the side that kind of looks like a torso with a single arm, and (2) it takes your money, like a bandit (a robber).

The MAB problem is imagined as a slot machine with multiple handles (or maybe just imagine multiple slot machines, each with one handle, it doesn't matter), where each handle results in a different probability of payout. Your goal is to make as much money (or lose as little money) as possible. Ideally, you'd just pull the highest-paying arm. But you don't know which arm that is, so you need a strategy to simultaneously learn which arm is best while maximizing your payout.

Recast in terms of experimental optimization: you want to simultaneously learn which change candidate (arm) is best while maximizing a business metric (payout).

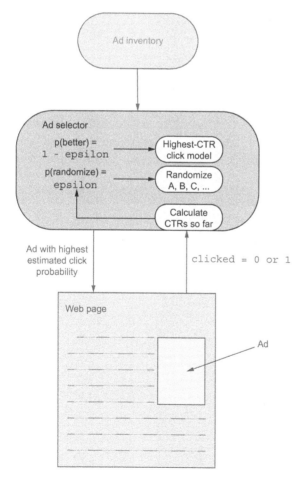

Figure 3.11 The ad selector testing multiple click models—or "arms"—using epsilon-greedy. With probability `1-epsilon`, the system chooses the model with the highest mean CTR so far. Otherwise (probability `epsilon`) the system chooses with equal probability from the available models.

Listing 3.7 modifies `epsilon_greedy_decay()` to handle more than two arms. Note that there is a small change to the expression for epsilon:

$$\text{Epsilon} = K \times c \times \frac{\left(\frac{BM_{max}}{PS}\right)^2}{n}$$

The variable `K` is the number of arms being evaluated. The previous version of this expression had a coefficient of 2 instead as we were evaluating two arms, A and B.

Note that the time needed to run the experiment grows linearly with `K`, the number of arms since the stopping time, n_{stop} is determined by the condition

$$\text{Epsilon} = 0.01 = K \times c \times \frac{\left(\frac{BM_{max}}{PS}\right)^2}{n_{stop}}$$

which yields

$$n_{stop} = K \times c \times \frac{\left(\frac{BM_{max}}{PS}\right)^2}{0.01}$$

For our scenario where BM_{max} = 0.01, PS = 0.001, c = 5, and K = 4, we get n_{stop} = 200,000. (Recall from section 3.1.3 that c is a metaparameter that controls the amount of time epsilon spends above 1, and that c = 5 was a reasonable choice.)

Listing 3.8   Epsilon-greedy with four arms

```
def epsilon_greedy_decay_multi():
    bm_max = 0.01
    prac_sig = 0.001          Run with
    k = 4            ◁——      four arms.
    c = 5

    epsilon_0 = k*c*(bm_max/prac_sig)**2
    epsilon_stop = 0.01

    sum_clicks = 0.0
    num_ads = 0.0
    sum_arm = [0.0]*k
    num_arm = [0.0]*k
    ctr_vs_n = []

    n = 0
    arms_selected = []
    while True:
        epsilon = min(1.0, epsilon_0 / (1.0 + n))
```

```
        if epsilon < epsilon_stop:
           break
        i_selected = None
        if np.random.uniform(0,1) < 1-epsilon:
            max_ctr = None
            for i in range(k):
                if num_arm[i] > 0:
                    ctr_arm = sum_arm[i] / num_arm[i]
                else:
                    ctr_arm = 0
                # break ties by randomizing
                ctr_arm += 1e-9 * np.random.normal()
                if max_ctr is None or ctr_arm > max_ctr:
                    max_ctr = ctr_arm
                    i_selected = i
            i_best_arm = i_selected
        else:
            i_selected = np.random.randint(k)

        arms_selected.append(i_selected)
        clicked = measure_arm(i_selected)
        sum_arm[i_selected] += clicked
        num_arm[i_selected] += 1
        sum_clicks += clicked
        num_ads += 1

        ctr_vs_n.append(sum_clicks / num_ads)
        n += 1

    return ctr_vs_n, arms_selected
```

Break ties randomly by adding a tiny, zero-center value. (annotation pointing to `ctr_arm += 1e-9 * np.random.normal()`)

Return a trace of the arms selected along with ctr_vs_n. (annotation pointing to `return ctr_vs_n, arms_selected`)

Also, we'll simulate a user's response to each arm's model with the function in the following listing.

Listing 3.9 Simulate several click models

```
def measure_arm(i_arm):
    return measure_click(ctr=.005 + i_arm*0.002)
```

This function models the arms' CTRs as linearly increasing in the index i_arm to make the presentation concrete and aid in discussion. However, there is no required relationship between the CTRs (or any business metric values) of the arms to use a multi-armed bandit algorithm.

We use epsilon_greedy_decay_multi() to simulate the simultaneous evaluation of K = 4 arms, where the best arm has CTR=.0050 + 3*0.0020 = 0.0110. Similarly, to the two-armed case in the last section, this algorithm produces a CTR close to that of the best arm—the mean of .0106 and standard deviation of .0006 over 100 runs—and selects the best arm 81% of the time. The trace of a single run is shown in figure 3.12.

Figure 3.13 shows the percentage of 100 runs selecting each of the four arms. At the beginning of a run, the arms are equally likely to be chosen—25% each—but as a run progresses, the best arm—arm 3—is increasingly preferred.

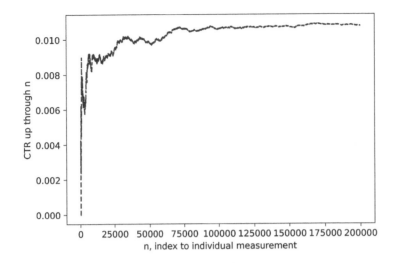

Figure 3.12   Epsilon-greedy evaluates $K = 4$ **arms, indexed 0, 1, 2, 3. It learns that arm 3 is the best while achieving a CTR of** 0.0108**, close to arm 3's CTR of** 0.0110.

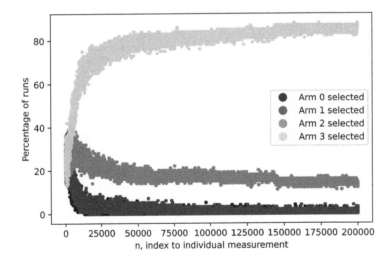

Figure 3.13   The percentage of 100 runs that selected each arm at each measurement, n. Arm 3 has the highest CTR, 0.0110**, so as n increases,** `epsilon_greedy_decay_multi()` **selects it increasingly more often.**

In this section, we extended epsilon-greedy to evaluate multiple candidate system changes, also called *arms*. The need to evaluate multiple arms in order to make a single system-change decision may arise due to competing models, parameters in business logic, and interactions between multiple simultaneously developed changes.

3.3   *Thompson sampling: A more efficient MAB algorithm*

Epsilon greedy is simple to implement, has optimal asymptotic regret, and does a good job of demonstrating the crux of the solution to the multi-armed bandit problem: the need to trade off exploration with exploitation.

But we can do better. With a little effort, we can construct an MAB algorithm that produces higher CTR while it runs, stops sooner, and doesn't have a system-dependent metaparameter like c.

Thompson sampling calculates the probability that each click model (each arm) will be the best one, call it p_{best}(arm). The rule of Thompson sampling is that when it's time to take an individual measurement, you randomize over the arms such that the probability of measuring an arm is equal to the probability that it is the best arm.

$$p_{measure}(arm) = p_{best}(arm)$$

This rule is a *randomized probability matching* rule. The choice of arm to measure is randomized (so that we explore), but better-seeming arms get run more often (so we also exploit). This is an elegant way to effect the exploration-exploitation tradeoff. Estimation of the probability that an arm is the best, p_{best}(arm), is the core calculation of Thompson sampling and is detailed in section 3.3.1. Randomized probability matching is discussed in section 3.3.2.

As more individual measurements are collected, the estimates of p_{best}(arm) become more certain (have lower error), and we become more likely to run the best arm. Put another way, Thompson sampling explores a lot at the beginning of an experiment, then transitions to exploiting a lot at the end—just like epsilon-greedy. Thompson sampling stops when any p_{best}(arm) is large enough, say larger than p_{stop} = 0.95 (a metaparameter).

Section 3.3.3 compares Thompson sampling to epsilon-greedy on our ad-selection system and shows that Thompson sampling achieves better CTR and stops experimenting sooner.

A NOTE ON METAPARAMETERS

Recall the metaparameter, c, from section 3.1.2. It affects both the initial rate of exploration and the stopping time of epsilon-greedy. The value of c that is optimal for the ad-selection system we're studying here might not be optimal for any other system you work with. The optimal c must be determined by trial and error. Unfortunately, I can give you no generic guidance for choosing the best value of this metaparameter.

This situation is quite different from A/B testing. Recall that an A/B test's stopping condition—the number of individual measurements to take, num_ind—was determined by limits on the probability of false positives (α) and false negatives (β). These probability limits are metaparameters, but they are easier to work with than c because they aren't system-dependent. No trial-and-error was required, for example, to choose a false-positive limit of 5% (i.e., α=0.05). Once this limit is chosen, an A/B test that respects it may be run on any system. Because these limits are not system-specific, we can learn useful values from our and others' experience experimenting on various systems. Indeed, we learned that the commonly used values α=0.05 and β=0.20 may be applied to any system we work on.

Thompson sampling's metaparameter, p_{stop}, is not system-dependent, so it may be set to the same value for many experiments on many systems. In that respect, it is more like α and β than it is like c, and thus an easier metaparameter to work with than c.

3.3.1   *Estimate the probability that an arm is the best*

The measure of quality of a click model is the CTR it produces when running in production. Epsilon-greedy used this metric to pick the best arm and run it with probability 1-epsilon. Thompson sampling, by contrast, will run each arm in proportion to p_{best}(arm). This section explains how to compute p_{best}(arm) using a technique called *bootstrap sampling*.

To start, recall the definition of CTR:

$$CTR = \frac{\text{(number of clicks on ads)}}{\text{(number of ads shown)}}$$

Or, equivalently

$$CTR = \text{mean}(I_{\text{clicked}})$$

where I_{clicked} is a vector with length equal to the number of ads shown. The ith element of I_{clicked} contains a 1 if the ith ad shown was clicked by a user and 0 if not.

CTR is an aggregate measurement. In chapter 2, we quantified the uncertainty of an aggregate measurement by the standard error:

$$SE = \frac{\text{stddev(CTR)}}{\sqrt{\text{num\_ind}}}$$

For example, let's say you collected 10 individual measurements:

$$\text{mean}(I_{\text{clicked}}) = [0, 0, 1, 0, 1, 1, 0, 0, 1, 0]$$

Then CTR = mean(I_{clicked}) = 4/10 = 0.4. In NumPy, we would write

```
I_clicked = np.array([0,0,1,0,1,1,0,0,1,0])
CTR = I_clicked.mean()
```

The SE is then

```
SE = I_clicked.std() / np.sqrt(len(I_clicked))
```

which has a value of about SE = 0.16.

Recall that SE estimates the standard deviation of the aggregate measurement, CTR. We can't calculate the standard deviation directly—with something like "CTR.std()"—because there is only one value for CTR. CTR is not a vector. We collect only one aggregate measurement value per experiment.

Now, if we ran, say, 30 experiments, collecting 10 individual measurements per experiment, then we could calculate 30 different CTR values. If we took the standard deviation of those 30 CTR values, it would be about equal to SE.

If we really ran 30 experiments, then we could also estimate the probability that an arm was best by

$$p_{\text{best}}(arm) = \frac{(\# \text{ of experiments where arm was best})}{30}$$

For example, if your new click model had higher CTR than the old model in 20 out of 30 of the experiments, we'd say that p_{best}(new model) = 20/30 = 0.66.

This is all fine to consider, but we don't want to really run 30 experiments. We just want to run one.

In the next section, we'll see how to generate (sort of) many experiments' worth of individual measurements using just the data from a single experiment. That way we can use the straightforward technique above to calculate p_{best}(arm) without having to run more than one experiment.

BOOTSTRAP SAMPLING

In the previous sections, we collected one set of 10 individual measurements, I_{clicked}, from which we computed the mean—the aggregate measurement, CTR—and the standard error. If we had many such sets—say 1,000 sets of 10 measurements each—we could compute the mean of each set, giving us 1,000 aggregate measurements. Having such a set of aggregate measurements in hand would be powerful. From that set, we could compute the probability that each arm is the best arm, p_{best}(arm), as we'll see in the next section. Bootstrap sampling generates synthetic measurement sets from a single, real measurement set—it makes a fake I_{clicked} vector from a real I_{clicked} vector.

As an introduction to bootstrap sampling, let's generate some synthetic measurement sets and compute the aggregate measurement, CTR, for each set. Here's how we generate the first set:

1 Choose a value at random from the 10 I_{clicked} values.
2 Choose a value at random from the 10 I_{clicked} values.
3 Choose a value at random from the 10 I_{clicked} values.
   ... ...
10 Choose a value at random from the 10 I_{clicked} values.

When you're done, you'll have a new data set with 10 values in it. Note that in each step, you are *sampling with replacement*—that is, each time you take a value from I_{clicked}, you "put it back." That means that some values may be chosen more than once, and some may be chosen not at all.

Since each value was drawn at random from $I_{clicked}$, the new data set has the same distribution as $I_{clicked}$. It looks almost as if you ran another experiment and measured 10 more $I_{clicked}$ values. You didn't, but you can pretend you did. If you don't like to pretend, say that you simulated another run of the experiment. See the following listing for a NumPy implementation of bootstrap sampling.

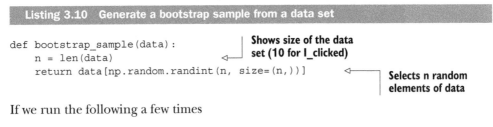

If we run the following a few times

```
np.random.seed(17)
print (bootstrap_sample(I_clicked))
print (bootstrap_sample(I_clicked))
print (bootstrap_sample(I_clicked))
```

we can get a feel for how the bootstrap-sampled data sets look:

```
[0 0 0 0 0 0 1 0 1 0]
[0 0 0 1 1 0 0 0 0 0]
[0 1 0 0 1 0 0 1 0 0]
```

Each bootstrap sample looks similar to the original data set in that there are mostly zeros and some ones. The bootstrap samples don't all have exactly four 1s in them, like $I_{clicked}$ did, but on average they do. As evidence, I've generated 1,000 bootstrap data sets and computed the CTR of each. A histogram is plotted in figure 3.14.

The mean of the CTRs is, as claimed, `0.40`, which was the CTR of the original data set, $I_{clicked}$. Also, the standard deviation of CTRs computed from these 1,000 bootstrap data sets is `0.16`, which matches the SE of the CTR of $I_{clicked}$. The histogram in figure 3.14, therefore, approximates the distribution of CTR measurements we might get if we ran an experiment consisting of 10 individual measurements 1,000 times. We can use these samples to estimate p_{best}. But first, a quick note about small samples.

WORKING WITH FEW INDIVIDUAL MEASUREMENTS

Recall from chapter 2, section 2.3.1 that the mean of a large number of individual measurements follows a normal distribution to good approximation. The more measurements you include in the mean (i.e., CTR), the better the approximation. Figure 3.15 shows bootstrap histograms like the one in 3.14, except in 3.15 we vary the number of individual measurements in $I_{clicked}$: First we use 10, then 100, then 1,000, then 10,000. The distribution looks more and more like a normal distribution (aka, gaussian distribution or "bell curve") as the number of individual measurement increases.

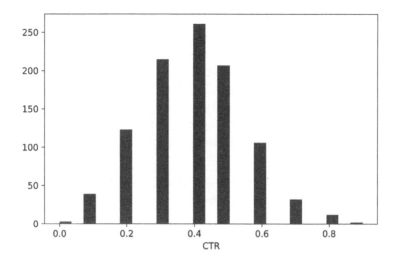

Figure 3.14 Histograms of CTR computed from 1,000 bootstrap data sets generated from $I_{clicked}$. The mean of these CTRs is 0.40, the CTR of $I_{clicked}$. The standard deviation is 0.16, which is the SE of the CTR of $I_{clicked}$.

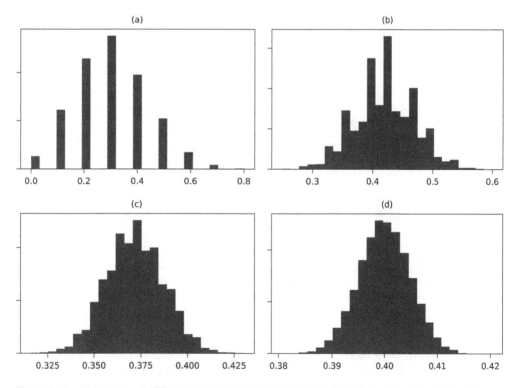

Figure 3.15 Histograms of CTR computed from the mean of 1,000 bootstrap data sets with varying numbers of individual measurements in $I_{clicked}$. (a) 10 measurements. (b) 100 measurements. (c) 1,000 measurements. (d) 10,000 measurements; this looks very much like a normal distribution.

We might be tempted to model the distribution of CTR by a normal distribution and avoid the extra work required to compute bootstrap samples. But when running an MAB (or any experiment, for that matter), we're trying to minimize the number of individual measurements we take. The fewer measurements the experiment takes, the lower the cost of running it. Certainly, when an MAB experiment is in its early stages, it will have fewer individual measurements and the aggregate measurement distribution will be non-normal. Creating a bootstrap sample lets us skip the step of modeling the distribution. Now, let's get back to the subject of p_{best}.

PROBABILITY OF BEING THE BEST ARM

Imagine again that we're comparing two click models—two arms—and for each arm we've collected 10,000 individual measurements:

```
I_clicked_1 = np.array([measure_click(ctr=.005) for _ in range(10000)])
I_clicked_2 = np.array([measure_click(ctr=.007) for _ in range(10000)])
```

The first arm has a CTR of `0.005` and the second has a CTR of `0.007`. The histograms of their bootstrap CTR estimates are shown in figure 3.16.

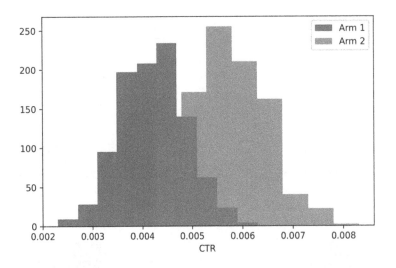

Figure 3.16 Histograms of bootstrap CTR estimates for two arms. Arm 1 has expected `CTR=0.0050`, and Arm 2 has expected `CTR=0.0070`. Because of the uncertainty in the measurements of CTR, it is not 100% certain from the data that Arm 2 is better than Arm 1.

From the data (CTRs, aggregate measurements) displayed in figure 3.16, it looks like Arm 2 is probably better than Arm 1. To quantify that intuition, define "the probability that Arm 2 is better than Arm 1"—that is, p_{best} (Arm 2), with the statement: If we ran a single experiment with 100 individual measurements, the estimated CTR of Arm 2 would be better than the CTR of Arm 1 with probability p_{best} (Arm 2). Equivalently, if we ran M experiments, about M × p_{best}(Arm 2) of them would show the CTR of Arm 2 being better than that of Arm 1. That definition is encoded in the following listing.

Listing 3.11   Estimate the probability of each arm being the better arm

```
def estimate_pbest(I_clicked_1, I_clicked_2):
    counts = [0, 0]                          ◁──┐  Count the number of times CTR of
                                                 │  I_clicked_1 is better and the number
    num_samples = 100                            │  of times CTR of I_clicked_2 is better.
    for _ in range(num_samples):
        ctr_1 = bootstrap_sample(I_clicked_1).mean()      ⊣  Each CTR is sampled
        ctr_2 = bootstrap_sample(I_clicked_2).mean()      │  from a distribution of
        if ctr_1 > ctr_2:                                 │  possible CTRs, as in
            counts[0] += 1                                │  figure 3.16.
        elif ctr_2 > ctr_1:
            counts[1] += 1
        else:
            pass

    p_best = np.array(counts)/ num_samples
    return p_best
```

Ignore cases where they are equal.

We see that `estimate_pbest()` returns `[pbest(Arm 1), pbest(Arm 2)]`—the probability that each arm is the better—estimated from 100 bootstrap samples. (Note: `estimate_pbest()` is comparing CTRs, the aggregate measurements. It is not comparing $I_{clicked}$ values, the individual measurements.)

The output of `np.random.seed(17); estimate_pbest(I_clicked_1, I_clicked_2)` is an array containing `[0.04, 0.95]`. The probability that Arm 2 is better than Arm 1 is `0.95`. The probability that Arm 1 is better is `0.04`. (These probabilities don't add to 1 because for a few of the samples, the measured CTRs were equal.) The logic in `estimate_pbest()` is extended to multiple arms in the following listing.

Listing 3.12   Estimate the probability that each arm is best

```
def estimate_pbest(I_clickeds):
    counts = [0] * len(I_clickeds)           ◁──┐  Count the number of
    num_samples = 100                            │  times each arm has the
    for _ in range(num_samples):                 │  best CTR.
        ctrs = [bootstrap_sample(I_clicked).mean()
                for I_clicked in I_clickeds]               ⊣  Each CTR is sampled
        ctrs = np.array(ctrs)                              │  from a distribution of
        i = np.where(ctrs == ctrs.max())[0]                │  possible CTRs, as in
        if len(i)==1:                                      │  figure 3.16.
            counts[i[0]] += 1

    return np.array(counts)/num_samples
```

Only count cases where there are no ties for best CTR.

Running `estimate_pbest()` on some sample data

```
np.random.seed(17)
I_clickeds = [None]*4
I_clickeds[0] = np.array([measure_click(ctr=.003) for _ in range(10000)])
```

```
I_clickeds[1] = np.array([measure_click(ctr=.005) for _ in range(10000)])
I_clickeds[2] = np.array([measure_click(ctr=.007) for _ in range(10000)])
I_clickeds[3] = np.array([measure_click(ctr=.009) for _ in range(10000)])
estimate_pbest(I_clickeds)
```

produces the probabilities [0, 0, 0.04, 0.94]. The estimate of the probability that Arm 4 has the best CTR is p_{best} (Arm 4) = 0.94.

We've defined the quantity p_{best}(arm) and developed a method of estimating it, the bootstrap, from both small and large numbers of individual measurements. We use p_{best}(arm) in Thompson sampling to decide when to stop and to choose which arm to run for an individual measurement. Thompson sampling stops when any arm's p_{best}(arm) > p_{stop}, where p_{stop} is a metaparameter(e.g., p_{stop} = 0.95). In the next section we'll see how p_{best}(arm) is used to choose which arm to run for an individual measurement.

3.3.2   *Randomized probability matching*

Imagine we're evaluating two click models—A and B—in production and it's time to decide which click model to use to serve an ad. Using estimate_pbest(), we might calculate p_{best} (A) = 0.75 and p_{best} (B) = 0.25. A/B testing would say to choose A or B at random (50% probability each). Epsilon-greedy would say to choose the one that has the better CTR so far with probability 1-epsilon (e.g., 1.0 - 0.10 = 0.90). An alternative lies somewhere in between: Run model A with probability 0.75 and model B with probability 0.25. This approach is called *randomized probability matching.*

In principle, since we have already learned to estimate p_{best}(arm), we are ready to try randomized probability matching. In practice, however, estimate_pbest() can be too slow to run effectively. It is slow because it needs to create and compute the means of many bootstrap samples. But if we just want to know which arm to use for the next randomization, there's a trick that makes it simple and efficient:

1 Create one bootstrap sample for each arm.
2 Estimate the CTR (i.e., the business metric) from each bootstrap sample.
3 Measure the arm with the highest estimated CTR.

The trick lies in the fact that the probability that an arm's bootstrap-estimated CTR is higher than the other arms' is just p_{best}(arm). This fact is what makes estimate_pbest() work, after all. Note that these three steps don't estimate p_{best}(arm). Rather, they just select an arm to measure in a way that obeys this rule:

$$p_{measure}(arm) = p_{best}(arm)$$

More-probably-better arms are more likely to be measured, exploiting their good CTR. Less-probably-better arms still get run sometimes (exploration), which improves the quality of our estimate of their p_{best}(arm), which improves the quality of future decisions about which arm to measure.

> **Bootstrap Thompson sampling**
>
> Randomized probability matching is what defines Thompson sampling. In this chapter, I'm presenting a specific type of Thompson sampling called *bootstrap Thompson sampling*. There are other, non-bootstrap, ways to compute p_{best}(arm), but I find the bootstrap to be robust and flexible in practice. (See this nice tutorial for other approaches to Thompson sampling: https://web.stanford.edu/~bvr/pubs/TS_Tutorial.pdf.)

Borrowing code from the inner loop of estimate_pbest(), we can write randomized probability matching as in the following listing.

Listing 3.13   Randomized probability matching

```
def rpm_select_arm(I_clickeds):
    ctrs = [bootstrap_sample(I_clicked).mean()
        for I_clicked in I_clickeds]
    ctrs = np.array(ctrs)
    i = np.where(ctrs == ctrs.max())[0]
    if len(i)!=1:
        return np.random.randint(len(I_clickeds))
    return i[0]
```

This code is borrowed from listing 3.12.

Only count cases where there are no ties for best CTR.

The function in listing 3.13 performs the required task of selecting an arm with probability proportional to p_{best} with only one call to bootstrap_sample() for each arm. That's much better than the 100 calls that would be needed if we used estimate_pbest().

However, rpm_select_arm() is still not as efficient as it could be. Each call to bootstrap_sample() accesses the entire collected data set. Since the function call happens on every arm-selection decision, and the data set grows linearly with these decisions, the running time of the algorithm will scale like [number of calls to rpm_select_arm()] x [data set size] = $O(T^2)$, where T counts the number of randomization decisions (which is proportional to time). That means that the longer the algorithm (your experiment) runs, the longer each additional decision will take. Eventually, randomization decisions will be too slow for production use. (Also, the simulations we're using in this book will take too long to run.)

ONLINE BOOTSTRAP

One solution is to construct an incremental (e.g., *online*) bootstrap sampler that doesn't need to access the entire data set but, instead, just accesses the latest measurement. It works like this: With probability ½, add each new measurement to a running sum. When you need to know the bootstrap mean, just divide that sum by the number of measurements added so far. The drawback is that we only have access to a single, fixed bootstrap sample. To remedy that, track B of these incremental bootstrap means. Then the running time decreases from $O(T^2)$ to $O(TB)$. The duration of a single randomization decision does not grow with time. (See https://arxiv.org/pdf/1410.4009.pdf.) Listing 3.14 implements this online bootstrap technique.

Listing 3.14 Online Bootstrap

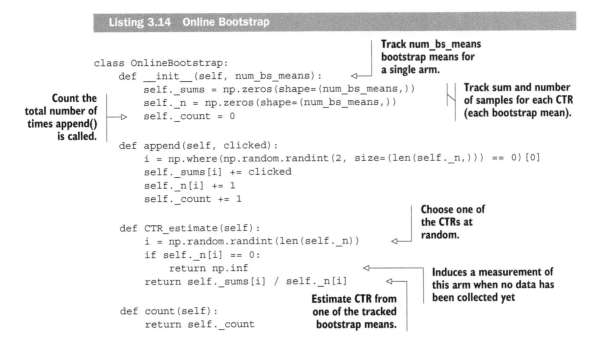

Track num_bs_means bootstrap means for a single arm.

Count the total number of times append() is called.

Track sum and number of samples for each CTR (each bootstrap mean).

```python
class OnlineBootstrap:
    def __init__(self, num_bs_means):
        self._sums = np.zeros(shape=(num_bs_means,))
        self._n = np.zeros(shape=(num_bs_means,))
        self._count = 0

    def append(self, clicked):
        i = np.where(np.random.randint(2, size=(len(self._n,))) == 0)[0]
        self._sums[i] += clicked
        self._n[i] += 1
        self._count += 1

    def CTR_estimate(self):
        i = np.random.randint(len(self._n))
        if self._n[i] == 0:
            return np.inf
        return self._sums[i] / self._n[i]

    def count(self):
        return self._count
```

Choose one of the CTRs at random.

Induces a measurement of this arm when no data has been collected yet

Estimate CTR from one of the tracked bootstrap means.

The functions rpm_select_arm() (listing 3.13) and estimate_pbest() (listing 3.11) are both made more efficient by use of OnlineBootstrap. See listings 3.15 and 3.16 for the online bootstrap versions.

Listing 3.15 Randomized probability matching with the online bootstrap

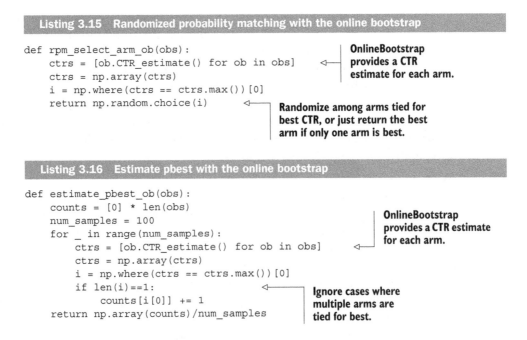

```python
def rpm_select_arm_ob(obs):
    ctrs = [ob.CTR_estimate() for ob in obs]
    ctrs = np.array(ctrs)
    i = np.where(ctrs == ctrs.max())[0]
    return np.random.choice(i)
```

OnlineBootstrap provides a CTR estimate for each arm.

Randomize among arms tied for best CTR, or just return the best arm if only one arm is best.

Listing 3.16 Estimate pbest with the online bootstrap

```python
def estimate_pbest_ob(obs):
    counts = [0] * len(obs)
    num_samples = 100
    for _ in range(num_samples):
        ctrs = [ob.CTR_estimate() for ob in obs]
        ctrs = np.array(ctrs)
        i = np.where(ctrs == ctrs.max())[0]
        if len(i)==1:
            counts[i[0]] += 1
    return np.array(counts)/num_samples
```

OnlineBootstrap provides a CTR estimate for each arm.

Ignore cases where multiple arms are tied for best.

Randomized probability matching is a method of selecting which arm to measure at each randomization decision in an experiment. It falls between the two extremes of A/B testing (select between arms A and B with equal probability) and epsilon-greedy (choose the best arm most of the time, with probability `1-epsilon`). Online bootstrap sampling is more computationally efficient than plain bootstrap sampling, and it prevents the time required to make a randomization decision from steadily growing throughout the lifetime of an experiment.

3.3.3 The complete algorithm

In the preceding sections, we explained all of the components of a Thompson sampling algorithm:

- `estimate_pbest_ob()`—A technique to calculate p_{best}(`arm`) efficiently
- `rpm_select_arm_ob()`—Randomized probability matching for arm selection, which uses p_{best}
- A stopping rule, which also uses p_{best}(`arm`)

To fully implement it, we need to clean up two more loose ends. First, there's the question of how many bootstrap means to collect in the online bootstrap. I have needed at least 100 in practice. There's a tradeoff when choosing this number: the larger that number is, the more exact (i.e., like a full bootstrap) the online bootstrap will be. But the smaller that number is, the faster the online bootstrap will be.

Finally, we need to ensure that our estimates of CTR are precise enough to detect differences at the level of practical significance. Please see the sidebar on discretization error.

Discretization error

Recall that CTR is estimated with

$$CTR = \text{mean}(I_{\text{clicked}})$$

where I_{clicked} is either 1 (user clicked on ad) or 0 (user didn't click).

Consider two CTR measurements based on n individual measurements of I_{clicked}:

$$CTR_A = \frac{0 + 1 + 1 + 0 + \cdots}{n}$$

and

$$CTR_B = \frac{0 + 1 + 1 + 0 + \cdots}{n}$$

(continued)

The least those two CTRs could differ is if a single $I_{clicked}$ was different. Let's say the first $I_{clicked}$ (it doesn't matter which one we choose) was 1 instead of 0 for CTR_B.

$$CTR_B = \frac{1 + 1 + 1 + 0 + \cdots}{n}$$

The smallest difference in the sums is 1, so the smallest difference between the two CTRs is

$$|CTR_A - CTR_B| = \frac{1}{n}$$

We'd like to have enough $I_{clicked}$ values in those means so that the smallest difference is no larger than PS:

$$|CTR_A - CTR_B| = \frac{1}{n} \leq PS$$

Or n = [smallest difference in sums]/PS=1/PS.

This source of imprecision—due to the discrete nature of the quantity being measured—is distinct from the natural variability that we quantified with SE. Both sources of imprecision need to be considered to take a good measurement.

The following listing puts this all together into the Thompson sampling algorithm.

Listing 3.17   Thompson sampling

```
def thompson_sampling():
    k = 4
    num_bs_means = 100
    p_stop = 0.95            ◄──  Stop when the probability
    smallest_sum_difference = 1    of an arm being best has
    prac_sig = 0.001                reached 0.95.

    min_samples_per_arm = smallest_sum_difference / prac_sig   ◄──

    obs = [OnlineBootstrap(num_bs_means) for _ in range(k)]    ◄──
    sum_clicks = 0.0
    num_ads = 0.0
    ctr_vs_n = []

    n = 0
    while True:
        num_samples_per_arm = [ob.count() for ob in obs]
        i_too_few = np.where(np.array(num_samples_per_arm) <
    min_samples_per_arm)[0]
```

Take enough samples to overcome imprecision due to discretization.

Create one OnlineBootstrap object for each arm.

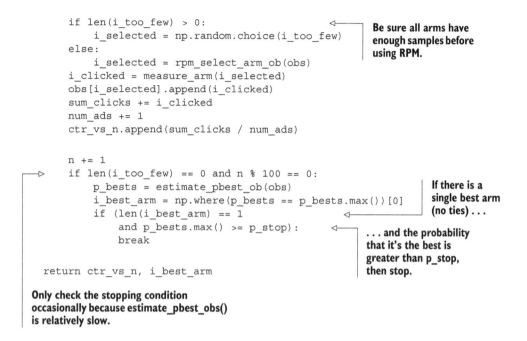

```
        if len(i_too_few) > 0:                          ⊲─────┐   Be sure all arms have
            i_selected = np.random.choice(i_too_few)          │   enough samples before
        else:                                                 │   using RPM.
            i_selected = rpm_select_arm_ob(obs)
        i_clicked = measure_arm(i_selected)
        obs[i_selected].append(i_clicked)
        sum_clicks += i_clicked
        num_ads += 1
        ctr_vs_n.append(sum_clicks / num_ads)


        n += 1
  ┌─⊳   if len(i_too_few) == 0 and n % 100 == 0:
  │         p_bests = estimate_pbest_ob(obs)                          If there is a
  │         i_best_arm = np.where(p_bests == p_bests.max())[0]        single best arm
  │         if (len(i_best_arm) == 1                    ⊲─────────┘   (no ties)...
  │             and p_bests.max() >= p_stop):    ⊲──────┐   ...and the probability
  │             break                                   │   that it's the best is
  │                                                      │   greater than p_stop,
  │     return ctr_vs_n, i_best_arm                      │   then stop.
  │
  └── Only check the stopping condition
      occasionally because estimate_pbest_obs()
      is relatively slow.
```

In listing 3.17, `estimate_pbest_obs()` is made more efficient by use of the online bootstrap, but it still takes much longer than the other parts of the inner loop because it generates 100 (online) bootstrap samples. To compensate for the relative slowness, `estimate_pbest_obs()` is called only once every 100 iterations. Figure 3.17 shows how Thompson sampling integrates into the ad selector.

The implementation of Thompson sampling in listing 3.17 evaluates K = 4 arms simultaneously, just like `epsilon_greedy_decay_multi()`. We'll compare the two algorithms, but please note that we didn't tune c for this simulated system, so the results for `epsilon_greedy_decay_multi()` are likely suboptimal.

> **Thompson sampling performance**
>
> Thompson sampling has a long history as a useful heuristic algorithm. It has been shown to have asymptotic optimal regret, just like epsilon-greedy. Also, Thompson sampling has shown empirical performance superior to epsilon-greedy and other MAB algorithms (O. Chapelle and L. Li, "An empirical evaluation of Thompson sampling," in Proc. 24th Int. Conf. on Neural Information Processing Systems, 2011, pp. 2249–2257).

The function `thompson_sampling()` completes much more quickly than `epsilon_greedy_decay_multi()`. While the latter takes 200,000 iterations for every run, `thompson_sampling()` takes on average 20,616 iterations and at most 103,500 over 100 runs.

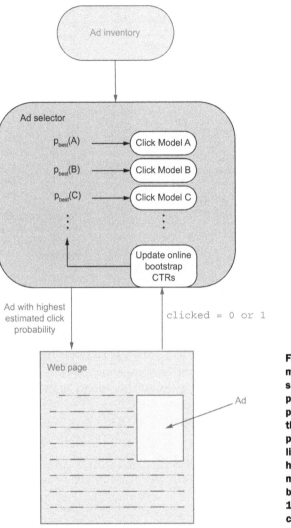

Figure 3.17   The ad selector testing multiple click models using Thompson sampling. The server chooses a click-probability model using randomized probability matching (listing 3.13)— that is, the selection with probability proportional to the probability (p_best, listing 3.16) that the model has the highest CTR. Randomized probability matching is made efficient by the online bootstrap (listing 3.15), which tracks 100 bootstrap-sampled CTRs for each click model.

The function thompson_sampling() accepted the correct arm 96% of the time, consistent with the stopping condition $p_{best} \geq 0.95$.

To make a fair comparison between thompsom_sampling() and epslion_greedy_decay_mutli(), I modified thompson_sampling() to switch to the best arm after completion and then continue until 200,000 iterations were complete. Figure 3.18 displays 100 runs of each of epsilon_greedy_decay() and thompson_sampling().

Table 3.2 summarizes the final values of the same 100 runs shows in figure 3.18— thompson_sampling() performs slightly better than epsilon_greedy_decay().

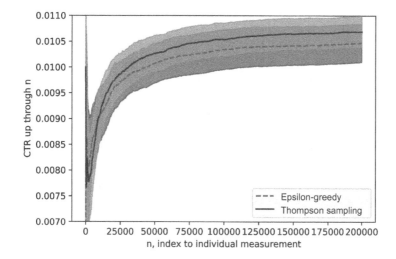

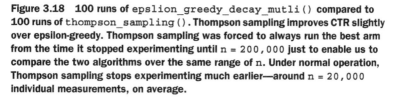

Figure 3.18 **100 runs of** `epslion_greedy_decay_mutli()` **compared to 100 runs of** `thompson_sampling()`. **Thompson sampling improves CTR slightly over epsilon-greedy. Thompson sampling was forced to always run the best arm from the time it stopped experimenting until** n = 200,000 **just to enable us to compare the two algorithms over the same range of n. Under normal operation, Thompson sampling stops experimenting much earlier—around** n = 20,000 **individual measurements, on average.**

Table 3.2 **On the example problem with** K = 4 **arms,** `thompson_sampling()` **performs similarly to** `epsilon_greedy_decay()` **but it completes much earlier on average and does not require one to tune the system-dependent parameter** c.

Algorithm	Mean CTR	Std. Dev. CTR
`epsilon_greedy_decay()`	0.0106	0.0006
`thompson_sampling()`	0.0107	0.0006

In summary, to evaluate multiple system versions (arms) with Thompson sampling, perform the following:

- *Design*—Choose a stopping threshold for p_{best} (arm)—for example, p_{stop} = 0.95.
- *Measure*—Use randomized probability matching to choose an arm at each randomization step. The online bootstrap makes this computationally efficient.
- *Analyze*—Accept the arm that has the highest p_{best} (arm).

Thompson sampling is an MAB algorithm that produces better business metrics while running than epsilon-greedy or A/B testing. It gets its advantage by computing and adapting to more detailed statistics (i.e., many online bootstrap means) than epsilon-greedy (a single mean) or A/B testing (none at all). It has no system-dependent metaparameter to tune, like epsilon-greedy.

Summary

- Multi-armed bandit algorithms reduce the cost of experimental optimization by trading off business metric improvement (exploitation) with evaluation of system versions (exploration).
- Epsilon-greedy is an MAB algorithm that is simple to implement and has optimal asymptotic regret but requires the engineer to tune a system-specific metaparameter.
- MAB algorithms make it easy to evaluate multiple versions—also called *arms*—simultaneously.
- Thompson sampling produces better business metrics during operation than epsilon-greedy and has no system-dependent metaparameter to tune.

Response surface
methodology: Optimizing
continuous parameters

This chapter covers

- Designing experiments to optimize continuous parameters
- Modeling your business metric as a function of system parameters
- Optimizing over the model
- Validating the optimal parameter settings

A/B tests are straightforward and reliable. They are the "gold standard" of experiments, but there is a cost—that is, the time, money, or risk involved in obtaining experimental results—to running them. Each of chapters 3–6 presents a method that aims to reduce that cost. For example, multi-armed bandits (MAB) adapt the experiment design continuously as new individual measurements are taken, and this reduces the time spent running the inferior version—A or B—of the system.

Response surface methodology (RSM) is specifically designed to optimize continuous parameters. RSM takes advantage of properties of continuous parameters to reduce experimentation cost compared to a more general method, like A/B testing. Both A/B testing and RSM help the engineer optimize a system by experimenting on it, but RSM has a narrower scope than A/B testing.

The RSM procedure requires the experimenter to make decisions based, in part, on visualization of the business metric. These visualizations help make the procedure more transparent. We believe that learning RSM will lay a solid foundation for understanding Bayesian optimization, which incorporates ideas from RSM.

In section 4.1, we'll discuss what's special about continuous parameters and how RSM takes advantage of their properties to improve efficiency. We'll also walk through the RSM procedure for optimizing a single parameter. RSM has the design, measure, and analyze stages familiar from A/B testing. Compared to A/B testing, though, RSM's analyze stage is more sophisticated.

In the analyze stage, you build a model that interpolates between measurements; then you optimize over that model to find good estimates of the optimal parameter settings. The optimal parameter settings are those at which your system achieves its best business metric. This process of optimizing over a model is the core innovation of RSM.

Section 4.2 presents another RSM walk-through, but this time for optimizing two parameters. Most stages in the RSM procedure require some modification to handle the extra parameter. The section also contains some discussion of how to extend RSM to more than two parameters. Let's get started and optimize a single continuous parameter.

4.1   *Optimize a single continuous parameter*

As a first step, you'll see how to optimize a single continuous parameter using RSM. An overview of the RSM procedure is shown in figure 4.1.

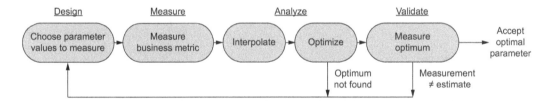

Figure 4.1   Overview of response surface methodology (RSM). RSM is an iterative process. First, in the design stage, we choose parameter values to measure. Next, we run the experiment to measure the business metric at those parameters. In the analyze stage, we use RSM techniques—interpolation and optimization—to estimate which parameter value is optimal. If the analysis fails, we return to the design stage. Otherwise, we validate the estimated optimal parameter value by measuring its business metric. If the measurement does not match the estimate, we return to the design stage. Otherwise, RSM has produced an optimal parameter value.

The RSM procedure is broken into four stages:

1 *Design*—The design stage is mainly concerned with choosing which values of the parameter to measure. We'll see how to choose these values using (1) prior knowledge of the system, and (2) and understanding of the requirements of the analyze stage. In the design stage, we'll apply knowledge from A/B testing to determine how many individual measurements to take at each parameter value.

2 *Measure*—Next, we measure the business metric at each parameter value by collecting the prescribed (by the design stage) number of individual measurements in production. This is the same as the measure stage of an A/B test (which we'll review in section 4.1.2).

3 *Analyze*—Analyzing RSM measurements takes two steps:
   - *Interpolate measurements*—First, we'll build a model, called a *surrogate function*, of the measurements that we can use to estimate the business metric at unmeasured values of the parameter. We say that the model *interpolates* between measured values. We can take many such estimates very quickly without running new experiments. In practice, estimating a business metric with a model could take a few milliseconds, whereas measuring it via experiment could take from hours to weeks.
   - *Optimize parameters*—We'll search through values of the parameter to find the one that gives the highest business metric, as estimated by the surrogate function. If the analysis fails to find an optimum, we'll restart the procedure and design a better experiment.

4 *Validate*—We run a final experimental measurement of the business metric of the optimal parameter to see whether it agrees with the estimate from the previous step. If so, we accept the optimal parameter as the new setting for the system. If not, we need to return to the design stage, adjusting for the new information we've gathered. Details on this appear in section 4.2.

Let's look at each stage in detail, starting with the design stage.

4.1.1 Design: Choose parameter values to measure

The RSM design stage uses both *domain knowledge* and an anticipation of the needs of the analyze stage to choose which parameter values to measure.

First, we'll see how to use domain knowledge to restrict the range of parameter values. Domain knowledge is any business or engineering knowledge you possess about your system. For example, you might know that the weights in your ML model must never be negative. As such, you would restrict the weights to only positive values in RSM experiments.

Next, we'll see how to determine where, exactly, inside the parameter range to measure the business metric. Choosing the right parameter values in this stage will lead to a good surrogate function in the analyze stage.

To get a feel for how to make use of domain knowledge, we'll consider the case of *optimizing* a proprietary trading strategy of the kind a quant might build at a bank or hedge fund.

As a quant trader at a hedge fund, you've been given the task of *optimizing* a proprietary strategy—or "prop" strategy. A prop strategy buys and sells shares of a stock in an automated way. The strategy makes its buy and sell decisions using something called a *signal*. A signal is a prediction of price changes of a stock and is a function of public market data. When the signal is positive (resp. negative), the stock price is expected to move up (resp. down).

Figure 4.2 shows this prop strategy containing a signal and connected to an exchange. The prop strategy sends BUY and SELL orders to the exchange, and the exchange sends *market data* (the term for all the public data emitted by an exchange) to the strategy. The strategy uses the market data to compute the signal that is the basis for making buy-or-sell decisions. When the signal is strong enough—when it crosses a threshold—the strategy will place an order to trade.

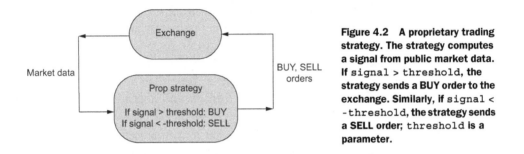

Figure 4.2 A proprietary trading strategy. The strategy computes a signal from public market data. If `signal > threshold`, the strategy sends a BUY order to the exchange. Similarly, if `signal < -threshold`, the strategy sends a SELL order; `threshold` is a parameter.

Your prop strategy buys low and sells high automatically, many times per day, in hopes of earning a profit. If, for example, it bought 100 shares of XYZ at $5.00/share and sold them at $7.00/share, your strategy's profit would be

100 shares * ($7.00/share – $5.00/share) = 100 shares * $2.00/share = $200

Each time the strategy trades, it pays a small cost per share, making the profit look more like

$$100 \text{ shares} * (\$7.00/\text{share} - \$5.00/\text{share}) - 100 \text{ shares} * \$.01/\text{share} =$$
$$100 \text{ shares} * \$1.99/\text{share} = \$199$$

if, for example, the cost was $.01/share. (The cost could be some combination of exchange fees, broker fees, the bid-ask spread, adverse selection, and market impact.)

To find the setting of threshold that maximizes profit, we could use A/B testing. We could call one value of `threshold` "A" and one value "B" and use an A/B test to compare their profitability. But we'd be left wondering whether we'd found the best value of `threshold`. How should we proceed? Using a process of haphazard guessing might produce a lucky result or might not.

We could be more systematic and test many closely spaced values of `threshold`—for example, `0.0, 0.01, 0.02, 0.03, . . . , 1.0`—and measure them (to high enough precision) to be certain we'd found a value very near the optimum. This would require many A/B tests. Running an MAB instead, using all the proposed `threshold` values as arms, would be more efficient but would still require a long experiment because of the large number of arms.

RSM measures only a small number of `threshold` values. The surrogate function estimates profitability at all in-between values, and then we find the `threshold` that maximizes the surrogate's estimated profit. Maximizing the surrogate makes it unnecessary to experimentally measure the many in-between threshold values, as we would have had to with A/B testing or MAB, saving us time and other experimentation costs.

In the sections that follow, you'll use RSM to optimize `threshold` to the value that maximizes profit. Before we begin, however, we'll write a simulator, a Python function, of the prop trading strategy. We'll apply the RSM procedure to this simulator. In practice, you'd apply the same procedure to your production trading system.

SIMULATE AN INDIVIDUAL MEASUREMENT OF PROFIT

The prop strategy's profit depends on (1) the signal that predicts the direction of the price, (2) the parameter `threshold`, and (3) the trading cost. We'll simulate these three features in a Python function that produces an individual measurement. Just as in previous chapters, we can run experiments on the simulator since we don't have a real trading system available. Then you'll learn how to optimize the simulator's `threshold` parameter with RSM to the value that maximizes profit.

When evaluating a prop strategy, quants sometimes track a metric called the *markout profit*. Markout profit is a measure of the profit of a single trade. It compares the traded price and the market price at some fixed time—say 1 minute—after the trade. For example, if we bought 100 shares at $5.00/share, then 1 minute later the market price was $6.50/share, we'd log a markout profit of

$$100 \text{ shares} * (\$6.50/\text{share} - \$5.00/\text{share}) = 100 \text{ shares} * \$.050/\text{share} = \$50$$

We'll take it one step further and subtract the cost, too. (If the cost was $0.01/share, then the markout profit would be 100 share * $.49/share = $49.)

Markout profit will serve as the business metric for your prop strategy. To construct a simulator in Python, we'll model markout profit, `profit`, like this:

$$profit = pps \times |signal| - cost + \varepsilon$$

The (expected) profit increases linearly with the signal at a rate of `pps`, the "profit per signal." The cost, `cost`, is the trading cost, and ε represents the unpredictable portion of the fluctuations of the market, which we model as normal (Gaussian). This just says that our signal predicts market moves and that trading in the direction of the signal (i.e., buying when the signal is positive or selling when it is negative) will tend to earn us some profit.

The vertical bars around `signal` are the absolute value notation. They make the point that since we're going to buy when the signal is positive and sell when the signal is negative, we're going to profit regardless of the sign of the signal. For example, if `signal` is `-1.3`, we'll sell and earn pps × 1.3 - cost + ε in profit.

We'll model the signal as a *unit normal*, a normal distribution with mean zero and standard deviation 1, which (I'll state here without justification) is not unreasonable for a quant's signal. The following listing puts all this together to simulate the mark-out profit of a single trade.

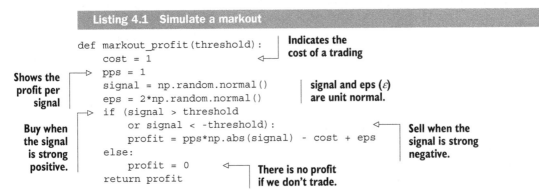

Listing 4.1   Simulate a markout

```
def markout_profit(threshold):        Indicates the
    cost = 1                          cost of a trading
    pps = 1
    signal = np.random.normal()       signal and eps (ε)
    eps = 2*np.random.normal()        are unit normal.
    if (signal > threshold
        or signal < -threshold):                        Sell when the
        profit = pps*np.abs(signal) - cost + eps         signal is strong
    else:                                                negative.
        profit = 0          There is no profit
    return profit           if we don't trade.
```

Shows the profit per signal

Buy when the signal is strong positive.

Note that cost, pps, and thus profit are dimensionless—not necessarily dollars or euros or yen. If it helps to think in terms of your favorite currency, that's fine.

You can imagine the prop strategy functioning as a sequence of events, where a single event is the arrival of new market data from the exchange. When that happens, the prop strategy recomputes the signal and decides whether to buy, sell, or, if the signal isn't strong, just do nothing. With each event, the strategy would log its decision (buy, sell, do nothing), the price at which it traded, and the market price 1 minute later. A single call to markout_profit() simulates one of these events and returns the mark-out profit computed from the logged values. In our usual terminology, the output of markout_profit() is an individual measurement.

To get a feel for the output of markout_profit() and build some "domain knowledge" of the simulator, I called markout_profit() 10,000 times with threshold=1 and found the following:

- With that threshold, 68% of the time markout_profit() didn't trade and returned profit=0. In other words, the strategy is usually waiting patiently for a trading opportunity to arise.
- The markout profit has mean = 0.17 and standard deviation = 1.2. Notice that the mean markout profit is less than the cost to trade (cost=1). This is not unrealistic for very short-term trading strategies.
- Of the calls to markout_profit() that resulted in a trade (100% – 68% = 32%), the mean markout profit was 0.53 and the standard deviation of markout profit was 2. A histogram of the markout profit for the 32% of calls that resulted in trades is shown in figure 4.3.

In the experiment we design in this chapter, markout_profit() will serve as the individual measurement. Figure 4.3 shows that markout_profit()'s output varies from call to call (characterized by the standard deviation) but that it has some expectation (estimated by the mean). The goal of RSM is to find the value of threshold that yields the highest expectation for markout_profit().

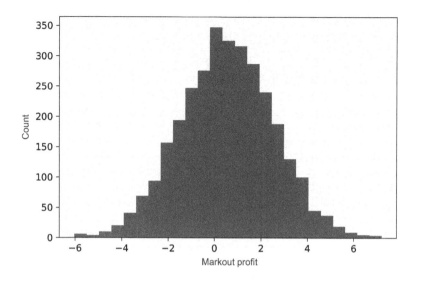

Figure 4.3 Histogram of markout profit of simulated trades. Sixty-eight percent of calls to `markout_profit(threshold=1)` **result in no trade, so** `markout profit=0`**. The other 32% of calls—about 3,200—do trade and have mean profit** `0.53` **and standard deviation 2. This figure shows a histogram of the 3,200 calls that traded.**

Now that we've defined the business metric, we need to choose which values of `threshold` to measure. First, we'll use domain knowledge to limit the range of threshold values. Afterward, we'll make sure we're measuring enough values of `threshold` to meet the needs of the analyze stage.

LIMIT THE RANGE OF PARAMETER VALUES WITH DOMAIN KNOWLEDGE

While you can't know which value of `threshold` is optimal (maximizes the business metric) before trading your strategy, as an experienced quant trader, you will have both general trading knowledge and information specific to your strategy that tell you what range of `threshold` values is reasonable. This domain knowledge sets bounds on the `threshold` values over which RSM will search for an optimum.

We already possess some knowledge of this prop trading system that we can use to limit the range of values of `threshold`. We know that `signal` is a standard normal— mean zero and standard deviation 1. (In a real system, you will know characteristics of your signal, such as mean and standard deviation, because they will be part of your system's design.) Knowing that the `signal` is unit normal and that it is used by the strategy in the statements

```
if signal > threshold: BUY
if signal < -threshold: SELL
```

we can draw a couple of useful conclusions.

First, we must have `threshold >= 0`. If we didn't, then both `BUY` and `SELL` actions could be valid at the same time. For example, if `threshold=-1` and `signal=0`, both `if` statements would evaluate to `True`. Our strategy must choose one action—buy, sell, or wait—at a time. See figure 4.4 for an illustration.

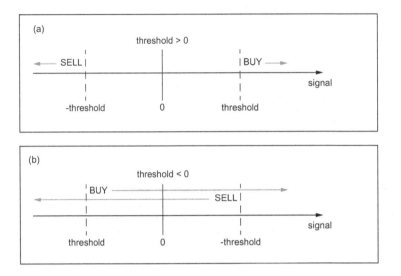

Figure 4.4   The strategy cannot function with `threshold < 0`. The horizonal axis represents signal value. (a) `threshold > 0`. The region of signal values where a `BUY` (resp. `SELL`) order is issued is far to the right (resp. left). In between, the strategy does not issue an order. (b) `threshold < 0`. The region of signal values where a `BUY` would be issued overlaps the region where a `SELL` would be issued. It is unclear which order should be issued in the center (overlap) region where `threshold < signal < -threshold`. (Note: `-threshold > 0` since `threshold` is negative.)

Second, since `signal` is normal with standard deviation of 1, it will very rarely take a value greater than 2 (5% of the time). Therefore, we can limit `threshold` to `threshold < 2`.

We just used domain knowledge to limit `threshold` to `0 < threshold < 2`. When *optimizing* a parameter of any system, you will typically be able to reason in a similar way to determine a range of values for the parameter.

We need to delve a little more deeply into the properties of continuous parameters in order to understand how the RSM analyze stage takes advantage of them. With that knowledge, you'll be able to choose exactly how many and which values of `threshold` to measure in the first run on your trading strategy.

CONTINUOUS PARAMETERS IN RSM

The analyze stage can make estimates of `markout_profit()` at unmeasured values of `threshold` because `threshold` is continuous. We'll take some time to understand how to make these estimates; then we'll use this new knowledge to choose values of `threshold` that will make the analyze stage's estimation process effective.

RSM's goal of finding the optimal `threshold` differs from the goal of the last two chapters. In chapter 2, our experiments were designed to learn whether a modified system, version B, was better than the current system, version A. Using A/B testing, we could, in principle, compare a system with `threshold=1` to a system with `threshold=2`, thus selecting from two possible values of `threshold`. We could even use multi-armed bandits from chapter 3 to compare multiple values—for example, `threshold=0.5`, `threshold=1`, `threshold=1.5`, and `threshold=2`—to see which would produce the highest markout profit. RSM takes things a step further and searches the full range of values, `0 < threshold < 2`, for the optimum.

RSM more precisely locates the optimal threshold than A/B testing or multi-armed bandits. To do this, we take advantage of the fact that `threshold` is a continuous parameter. The definition of a continuous parameter is best understood by contrasting it with the two other parameter types you might find in any engineered system.

- *Categorical parameter*—A parameter that takes one of a few arbitrary values. For example, a parameter `exchange` in a trading system could take a value `NASDAQ` or `NYSE` (two different exchanges). In an ad-serving system, a parameter `position` (of an ad on a web page) could take a value `top of page` or `side of page`.

- *Discrete (ordinal) parameter*—A parameter that takes an integer value. Unlike a categorical parameter, discrete parameter values are ordered—that is, it makes sense to say that one value is greater than or less than another. For example, a trading-system parameter `num_orders` might take a value `1`, `2`, or `3`. In a list of search results on a web page, a parameter `num_items` might determine how many items to display.

- *Continuous parameter*—A continuous parameter takes real (in the mathematical sense) values. It is ordered, like a discrete parameter, but, unlike a discrete parameter, between any two values of a continuous parameter there is another valid value: If `1` and `2` are valid parameter values, then `1.5` is also (as are `1.25`, and `1.333 . . .`, and, in fact, any other real value between `1` and `2`). We'll call these *interior values*. Another continuous parameter is `threshold`, as it can take any real value in the interval `0 < threshold < 2`. Another example of a continuous parameter is a weight in a linear combination of features in an ML model, like `w` in `x1 + w * x2`, which might take any value in the interval `[-1,1]`.

Table 4.1 summarizes the properties of the three types of parameters.

The metric `markout_profit` is also continuous. We say it varies continuously with `threshold`. This means that if `threshold_1` is close to `threshold_2`, then `markout_profit(threshold_1)` is close to `markout_profit(threshold_2)`. This property makes it possible to form reasonable estimates of `markout_profit` for unmeasured values of `threshold`—as long as those unmeasured `threshold` values are close to

Table 4.1 Properties of parameter types. Consider any two parameter values, a and b. If it makes sense to say a > b or a < b, then the parameter is ordered. If you can always find more parameter values between a and b, then the parameter has interior values. Continuous parameters are both ordered and have interior values. Discrete parameters are ordered but don't have interior values. Categorical parameters are unordered (and so cannot have interior values).

Parameter type	Ordered	Interior values
Categorical	X	X
Discrete	√	X
Continuous	√	√

measured ones. Forming estimates like this is called *interpolation*, and it is discussed in the next section.

Real-world business metrics tend to vary continuously with continuous parameters, so you can expect response surface methodology to be useful in *optimizing* a continuous parameter for almost any system you work on.

INTERPOLATION OVER CONTINUOUS PARAMETERS

First, we'll take a look at how a simple interpolation between two measurements works. Then we'll see that we need at least three measurements to create a surrogate function that has a maximum at an unmeasured threshold value. Finally, we'll decide how many aggregate measurements to take to be prepared for the analysis stage.

Assuming `markout_profit` varies continuously with `threshold`, then if we know `markout_profit` for both `threshold_1` and `threshold_2`, we could interpolate to make a reasonable approximation at some value between `threshold_1` and `threshold_2`. Let's say that

```
threshold_1 = 1
threshold_2 = 2
markout_profit(threshold_1) = 5
markout_profit(threshold_2) = 6
```

Since `markout_profit` varies continuously with `threshold`, we can estimate `markout_profit` at a nearby `threshold` value, `threshold_mid`

```
threshold_mid = (threshold_1 + threshold_2)/2
```

with an estimated markout profit of

```
(markout_profit(threshold_1) + markout_profit(threshold_2))/2 = 5.5
```

Figure 4.5 depicts this graphically.

Figure 4.5 shows a line segment interpolating `markout_profit(threshold)` between two measured values. Were you to take only these two measurements, you would conclude that the optimal parameter was `threshold_2`, because that is where `markout_profit(threshold)` is largest.

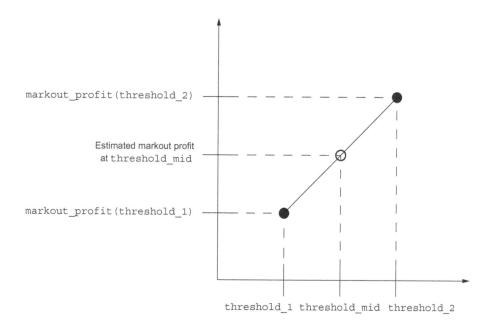

Figure 4.5 **Interpolation of a continuously varying business metric over a continuous parameter.**
If we know `markout_profit(threshold_1)` **and** `markout_profit(threshold_2)`, **the**
values at the solid dots, we can estimate profit at `threshold_mid = (threshold_1 +`
`threshold_2)/2` **as** `(markout_profit(threshold_1) +`
`markout_profit(threshold_2))/2`.

When interpolating between only two measurements, we should always just draw a line segment because it's the simplest way to "connect the dots." That means that the maximum `markout_profit(threshold)` will always be at one end (left or right) of the line segment as depicted in figures 4.6(a) and 4.6(b). This, in turn, means that we'll always choose one of the *measured* values—which are at the ends of the line segment—as our optimal `threshold`.

Choosing between measured values of `threshold` is something we could have done with A/B testing or MAB. The power of RSM's surrogate function (the model of the response surface) comes to the fore when we find an optimum at an unmeasured `threshold`, via interpolation. To find a maximum at an unmeasured `threshold`, we'll need to take a third measurement.

Adding a third measured value, as in figures 4.6(c) and 4.6(d), allows the surrogate to take a "hump" shape—a parabola. Figure 4.6(c) and 4.6(d) show measurements at the filled dots but have their maximum at the open dots—at unmeasured thresholds.

If we were to measure even more values of `markout_profit(threshold)`, we might find a way to refine the interpolation of the function `markout_profit(threshold)`, but three is the minimum number needed to model a parabola. Since experiments take time and cost money to run, we'll measure `markout_profit(threshold)` at not more than the minimum number necessary: three.

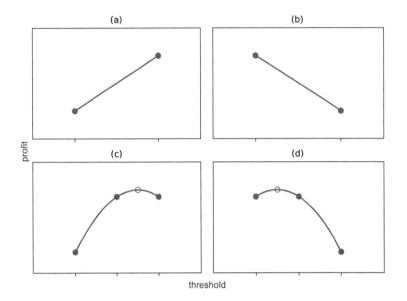

Figure 4.6 Measured values of `markout_profit(threshold)` **and interpolations between them. When we interpolate between only two measured values, shown as filled dots in (a) and (b), the maximum profit occurs at one of the measured values. When a third measured value is added, as in (c) and (d), the maximum profit may occur at an interpolated value, shown as an unfilled dot in (c) and (d). Thus, for interpolation to be useful in estimating an optimum at an unmeasured value of** `threshold`**, at least three points must be measured.**

Be aware that a parabola makes a good model only when you take measurements close to the optimal `threshold` value. Although the function `markout_profit(threshold)` may take an arbitrary shape, close to the maximum it will look something like a parabola, similar to figures, 4.6(c) and (d). The resemblance is simply because a maximum is the top of a hump in the function, and a parabola is a hump. If you go too far from the top, though, the resemblance will break down.

This caveat tells us that we need to keep the three `threshold` values close together. We say that we are interpolating *locally* (in a small range of thresholds) rather than *globally* (over a large range). How do you know if the range of thresholds is small enough to be considered "local"? Well, if approximating `markout_profit` as a parabola works well, then the range can be considered local. Yes, that's circular reasoning. No, I can't offer better reasoning. The point is simply that if the approximation doesn't give good results, you might have to shrink the range of threshold values.

Knowing that we need to measure three values in a small range of `threshold` and that domain knowledge limits the range to 0 < `threshold` < 2, let's measure `threshold` at values 0.5, 1.0, and 1.5. We'll stay clear of lower values at the outset, so we don't risk trading too quickly, thus losing money to trading costs (e.g., at `threshold` < 0.5).

In this section, we learned that continuous parameters are special in that they enable you to interpolate between measured values to find at which parameter value the business metric is maximized. To find an optimum at an unmeasured parameter value, we need to measure the business metric at three values of the parameter. We also need to keep those values in a small range so that the function (business metric versus parameter) is well-modeled by a parabola. In the next section, we'll discuss how many individual measurements to take at each of the three `threshold` values to get good estimates of `markout_profit(threshold)`.

DETERMINE THE NUMBER OF INDIVIDUAL MEASUREMENTS

You just learned that you need to measure profit at three or more threshold values to make it possible to use interpolation to find the optimal threshold. Before that, we used domain knowledge to limit the range of `threshold` to `0 < threshold < 2` and decided to measure `markout_profit(threshold)` at `threshold = 0.5, 1.0, 1.5`. Now you'll learn how to design an experiment to take those measurements. Next we'll discuss running the experiment. Analysis of the experiment will consist of interpolating and finding the optimal threshold and will be presented in the subsequent two sections.

Recall that A/B test design teaches us to use randomization to remove bias from our measurements. When A/B testing an agency execution system in chapter 2, you randomly assigned each incoming customer order to either version A or version B of the system's trading strategy. Similarly, when measuring `markout_profit(threshold)` at each of three values of threshold, you'll need to randomly assign each trading decision to `threshold=0.5`, `threshold=1.0`, or `threshold=1.5`.

A/B test design also teaches us to use replication to reduce the standard error, SE, of a measurement to an acceptably low value. We can apply the A/B approach for determining the number of replications to use by treating each value of `threshold` like a "B version" of the system.

First, we measure `sd_1_delta`, the standard deviation in an individual measurement using either previously logged measurements of the business metric or by running a pilot study to collect such measurements. We effectively did that when constructing the histogram shown in figure 4.3. The standard deviation of the 10,000 trades was `sd_1_delta = 1.2`.

Next, we specify a practical significance level, `prac_sig`, which is determined by business considerations for the system at hand. If we treat the construction of figure 4.3 as "prior business experience" with this system, we could take some percentage of the observed markout profit, `0.17`, as a practical significance. We'll use 20% of markout profit, `prac_sig = 20% × 0.17`, which is about `prac_sig = 0.03`.

In practice, you might be building a brand-new trading strategy and have no experience running the system in production and, thus, no data from which to estimate `sd_1_delta` or to get a sense for a meaningful `prac_sig`. In this case you could use values estimated from simulated trading, also called *backtesting*, to produce a distribution of markout profit. Simulation is a valuable tool used by quants to develop trading strategies, but it isn't a substitute for measurements from production trading.

Finally, we can calculate the number of individual measurements needed to take an aggregate measurement with

```
num_ind = (2.48 * sd_1_delta / prac_sig)**2
```

giving `num_ind = (2.48*1.2/.30)**2`, or about `N=10,000` individual measurements.

There's a difference between this experiment and an A/B test that's worth highlighting. In an A/B test, we only compare two different system versions. In this experiment, we're comparing three versions—that is, each threshold is a different version of the system. The analysis of false positives changes slightly when we compare multiple versions. We'll discuss the details in chapter 8, section 8.3, but for now suffice to say we need to increase `num_ind` to `(3.08 × 1.2/.03) 2 ≈ 15,000`.

If your proprietary trading strategy trades 1,000 stocks and makes an average of 10 trades/stock/day, it can take 50,000 individual measurements per week. To take `num_ind = 15,000` individual measurements for each of the three parameter values, you'd need 3 parameter values × 15,000 individual measurements per parameter value = 45,000 individual measurements. It would take about 5 days—one business week—to run the experiment.

This completes the design of the experiment. We know for which threshold values we want to measure profit, and we know how many individual measurements to take. In the next sections, we'll run the experiment using simulation and analyze the results.

4.1.2   Take the measurements

Now that we've chosen which settings of `threshold` to measure—`0.5`, `1.0`, and `1.5`— and calculated the number of individual measurements to take, `num_ind = 15,000`, we're ready to take the measurements. See figure 4.7.

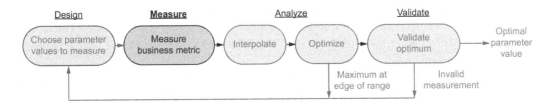

Figure 4.7   Measure stage. First, run an experiment to measure `markout_profit(threshold)` **at the** `threshold` **values chosen in the design stage.**

Now it's time to trade the prop strategy and take measurements. You'll run an experiment to measure the business metrics, `markout_profit(threshold)`, at each of the `threshold` values chosen in section 4.1.1, the design stage.

In this section, we'll simulate the experiment with the function `run_experiment()`, so we have something concrete to discuss. See the following listing 4.2.

Are we taking measurements?

You might look at `num_ind = 15,000` and be surprised that it is such a large number. After all, our goal is to keep the number of measurements small.

The resolution to this contradiction is that RSM is minimizing the number of *aggregate measurements*; N = 15,000 is the number of individual measurements. We take many individual measurements so that the SE of each aggregate measurement (the error bars in figure 4.8) is small enough.

Our goal is to take fewer aggregate measurements—that is, measure fewer `threshold` values—than we would have using A/B testing or MAB to achieve the same final markout profit.

Listing 4.2 Simulate the experiment

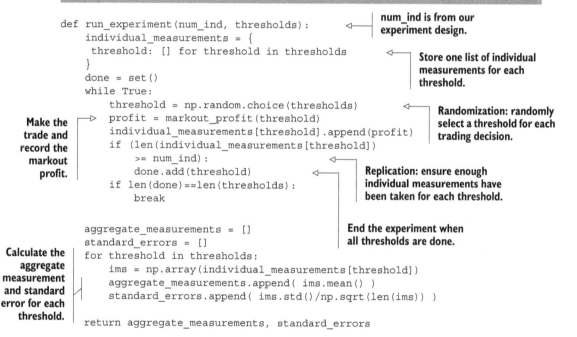

```
def run_experiment(num_ind, thresholds):          ←  num_ind is from our
    individual_measurements = {                       experiment design.
      threshold: [] for threshold in thresholds    ←
    }                                                 Store one list of individual
    done = set()                                      measurements for each
    while True:                                       threshold.
        threshold = np.random.choice(thresholds)   ←  Randomization: randomly
        profit = markout_profit(threshold)            select a threshold for each
        individual_measurements[threshold].append(profit)  trading decision.
        if (len(individual_measurements[threshold])
            >= num_ind):                           ←
            done.add(threshold)                    ←  Replication: ensure enough
        if len(done)==len(thresholds):                individual measurements have
            break                                     been taken for each threshold.

    aggregate_measurements = []                    End the experiment when
    standard_errors = []                           all thresholds are done.
    for threshold in thresholds:
        ims = np.array(individual_measurements[threshold])
        aggregate_measurements.append( ims.mean() )
        standard_errors.append( ims.std()/np.sqrt(len(ims)) )

    return aggregate_measurements, standard_errors
```

Make the trade and record the markout profit.

Calculate the aggregate measurement and standard error for each threshold.

The experiment runs similarly to an A/B test, in that we use randomization and replication. At each trading decision time, you randomly choose a `threshold` value to use for the decision. You run the strategy like this until `num_ind` individual measurements have been taken for each `threshold`. We can simulate the run of the first experiment with

```
np.random.seed(17)
thresholds = np.array([0.5, 1.0, 1.5])
aggregate_measurements, standard_errors = run_experiment(15000, thresholds)
```

Figure 4.8 plots the aggregate measurements and their standard errors.

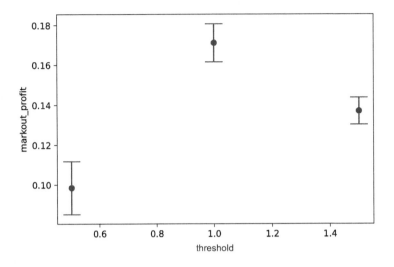

Figure 4.8 **Measurements of** `markout_profit` **at** `threshold=0.5,`
`1.0, 1.5,` **along with error bars showing ±SE**

There appears to be a maximum profit somewhere between `threshold = 0.5` and `threshold = 1.5`. While the best *measured* parameter value is `threshold = 1.0`, there might be an even better threshold among the *unmeasured* values elsewhere in the range `[0.5, 1.5]`. To find it, you'll interpolate. You'll estimate and plot the parabola—a model of the function `markout_profit(threshold)`—that fits the three points in figure 4.8; then find the value of `threshold` that maximizes that parabola.

4.1.3   *Analyze I: Interpolate between measurements*

In this stage, we'll build a model to interpolate between the measured values of `markout_profit(threshold)`. Also, we'll optimize to find the `threshold` that gives the highest interpolated value of `markout_profit(threshold)`. See figure 4.9.

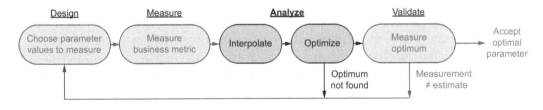

Figure 4.9 **Analyze stage. In this stage, you build a model to interpolate between the measured values of** `markout_profit(threshold)` **and find the value of** `threshold` **that optimizes (maximizes) the interpolated value of** `markout_profit(threshold)`.

The model, called the *surrogate function*, is a function of profit versus threshold. It estimates the true, underlying function from the aggregate measurements. The true, underlying function is called the *response surface*. Just like an aggregate measurement estimates the true expectation of a business metric, a surrogate function estimates the true response surface.

To find the equation for the parabola that passes through the three points in figure 4.8, we're going to use linear regression. (Please see appendix A for a short introduction to linear regression.) First, we'll specify this model, a parabola:

$$y = \beta_0 + \beta_1 x + \beta_2 x^2 + \varepsilon$$

where y is the aggregate measurement of profit, x is the threshold, and β_0, β_1, and β_2 are parameters of the model that need to be determined by linear regression. The final term, ε, is the approximation error, the difference between the interpolation estimate, $\hat{y} = \beta_0 + \beta_1 x + \beta_2 x^2$ and the measured value, y. (Note: The circumflex over a variable is usually read as "hat," so, $\hat{y}$, would be read as "y hat.")

Approximation error term

It so happens that when the number of aggregate measurements (three in this experiment) is equal to the number of parameters (three in this model), the model will fit the data exactly—that is, $\varepsilon = 0$. Later, in section 4.2, we'll take more measurements than we'll use in the surrogate function, and we'll find that $\varepsilon \neq 0$. The case $\varepsilon \neq 0$ is the usual one, so for now we'll just carry ε along in the calculations for the purpose of exposition.

Expressed in terms of the values from experiment two, y is the vector of aggregate measurements of profit:

$$y = [0.098, 0.0171, 0.137]^T$$

The right-hand side can be expressed compactly by writing

$$\beta = [\beta_0, \beta_1, \beta_2]^T$$

and a matrix, capital X

$$X = \begin{bmatrix} 1 & 0.5 & 0.5^2 \\ 1 & 1.0 & 1.0^2 \\ 1 & 1.5 & 1.5^2 \end{bmatrix}$$

Then the model becomes

$$y = X\beta + \varepsilon$$

which has a solution given by the normal equations (see appendix A):

$$\beta = \left(X^T X\right)^{-1} \left(X^T y\right)$$

We can calculate β using the normal equations as in the following listing.

Listing 4.3   Fit a one-parameter model using linear regression

```
def linear_regression(thresholds, aggregate_measurements):
    x = thresholds                                              Use familiar linear regression
    y = aggregate_measurements                                  variable names.
    X = np.array([np.ones(len(y)), x, x**2]).T
    beta = np.linalg.inv(X.T @ X) @ (X.T @ y)        Calculate beta vector
    return beta                                      using normal equation.
```

Compact form of model, capital X ⟶

The model is fit with `beta = linear_regression(thresholds, aggregate_measure-ments)`, which yields the vector of coefficients

$$\text{beta} = [\beta_0, \beta_1, \beta_2]$$

If you'd like a review of the matrix operations we'll use in this chapter (and in later chapters), please see the sidebar "Matrix operations in NumPy."

Matrix operations in NumPy

Matrix operations in NumPy mirror fairly well the mathematics they represent.

If we let `A` and `B` be matrices and `x` and `y` be vectors, then we can write

- Transpose—A^T as `A.T` and x^T as `x.T`
- Matrix product—AB as `A @ B`
- Matrix-vector product—Ax as `A @ x`
- Dot product—$x \cdot y$ or $x^T y$ as `x.T @ y`
- Matrix inverse: A^{-1} as `np.linalg.inv(A)`

For example, the normal equation $\beta = \left(X^T X\right)^{-1} \left(X^T y\right)$ is expressed in NumPy as `beta = np.linalg.inv(X.T @ X) @ (X.T @ y)`.

Finally, we get to the heart of RSM, the interpolation and optimization steps of the analyze stage. We use the model we just fit with linear regression to estimate values of profit, y, at thresholds, x, where we did not actually take measurements. Listing 4.4 contains the code that does that. The function, `interpolate()`, implements the surrogate function. It creates an array of `threshold` values between the minimum and maximum measured thresholds and estimates markout profit at each of those values. Following the model notation, the array of thresholds is called $\hat{x}$, or `xhat`. The interpolated values are computed with $\hat{y} = \hat{X}\beta$, or `yhat = XHat @ beta`.

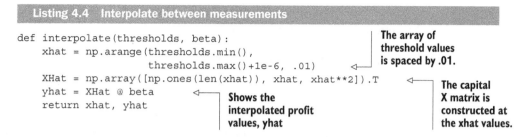

```
def interpolate(thresholds, beta):
    xhat = np.arange(thresholds.min(),
                thresholds.max()+1e-6, .01)
    XHat = np.array([np.ones(len(xhat)), xhat, xhat**2]).T
    yhat = XHat @ beta
    return xhat, yhat
```

The array of threshold values is spaced by .01.

The capital X matrix is constructed at the xhat values.

Shows the interpolated profit values, yhat

The extra +1e-6 in the expression for xhat just tells np.arange() to include the value thresholds.max() in the array as np.arange() creates an interval that is open on the right-hand side.

The output of interpolate() is plotted in the dashed line in figure 4.10, overlaid on the measured points from figure 4.9.

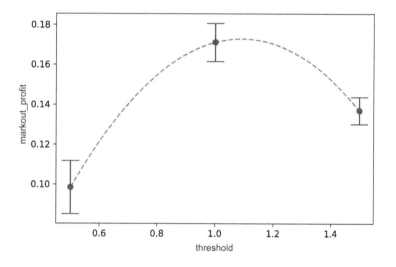

Figure 4.10 A surrogate function, an interpolation (dashed line) between measurements (dots) of profit. The curve, a parabola, estimated using linear regression, estimates the true response surface.

The results of this experiment, plotted in figure 4.10, suggest a maximum inside the measured threshold interval [0.5, 1.5]. Even more to the point, the maximum is between the measured values at threshold = 1.0 and threshold = 1.5.

Using the model of markout_profit(threshold), interpolate(), you can find the value of threshold that maximizes the estimated markout profit. We say you're *optimizing* the surrogate function.

Note that for some business metrics (e.g., the cost of execution from chapter 2), it's better to minimize than to maximize. All the reasoning in this chapter applies to minimization, too. The only differences are that for minimization, the parabola would be upside down and the optimal parameter would correspond to the smallest rather than the largest value of the business metric.

4.1.4   *Analyze II: Optimize the business metric*

Optimizing over the model you just fit is the highlight of RSM. Optimization quickly searches through many candidate values of threshold for the one that maximizes the estimate of the markout profit, estimated with `interpolate()`. This procedure will take a few milliseconds to evaluate hundreds of `threshold`s. Contrast this with the measure stage, which experimentally measured only three `threshold` values and would, on a real trading system, take about a week.

Optimization is straightforward for this experiment. In the language of `interpolate()`, we find the value of `xhat` at which `yhat` is a maximum. The following listing shows the code for this.

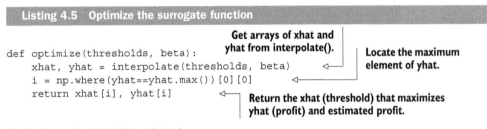

Listing 4.5 Optimize the surrogate function

```
def optimize(thresholds, beta):
    xhat, yhat = interpolate(thresholds, beta)
    i = np.where(yhat==yhat.max())[0][0]
    return xhat[i], yhat[i]
```

Get arrays of xhat and yhat from interpolate().

Locate the maximum element of yhat.

Return the xhat (threshold) that maximizes yhat (profit) and estimated profit.

Put into code, the full analysis is

```
beta = linear_regression(thresholds, aggregate_measurements)
threshold_opt, estimated_max_profit =
➥ optimize(thresholds, aggregate_measurements, beta)
```

The optimal value, `threshold_opt = 1.09`, is plotted as an X in figure 4.11. The `estimated_max_profit` at `threshold_opt` is `estimated_max_profit=.173`. Figure 4.11 visualizes the completed analysis of this RSM experiment: interpolation of `markout_profit(threshold)` via linear regression and optimization of `threshold` using the `interpolate()` function.

You just used an RSM procedure to design, measure, and analyze an experiment on your trading strategy. After choosing which parameter values to measure in the design stage, you then completed the measure and analyze stages:

1 *Measure stage*—Took aggregate measurements of the business metric at each parameter value.

2 *Analyze stage*

   a *Interpolate step*—Fit a model (a parabola) of the business metric as a function of the parameter—for example, `markout_profit(threshold)` using linear regression. The model estimates the business metric at parameter values at which you haven't taken any measurements.

   b *Optimize step*—Find the value of the parameter that maximizes the model's estimate of the business metric. This is called the *optimal parameter value.*

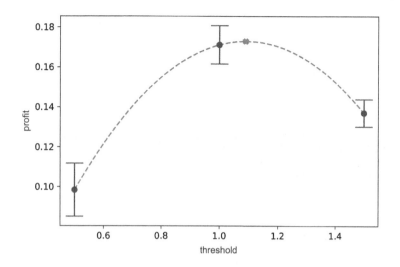

Figure 4.11 Visualization of full analysis of an RSM experiment. The experimental measurements with error bars are plotted as filled circles. The dashed curve is the surrogate function, fit by linear regression. The optimal threshold and associated estimated profit are plotted as an X.

You should think of the optimal parameter value as an estimate of the parameter at which the system will function at its best. It's an estimate because it is derived from the model rather than from a direct measurement of the production system. To have confidence that this parameter value is a good one, you need to take an experimental measurement. Consider the estimate produced by RSM to be an educated guess about where to set threshold for good performance. The only way to know for sure whether it works in production is to run it in production—that is, you need to take a measurement. The next section shows how.

4.1.5 Validate the optimal parameter value

You just saw how to estimate the optimal threshold at which to run the prop trading strategy. Before committing the production trading system to the new threshold, however, you'll take one final measurement to validate that the system works well when set to that value. See figure 4.12.

For the validation measurement, you'll set the threshold to the optimal value you estimated in the analyze stage. It was the first output of optimize(), called threshold_opt. Along with this output, you also got an estimate of the optimized profit at the optimal threshold, estimated_max_profit.

A SIMPLE VALIDATION MEASUREMENT

You take the validation measurement the same way as you took the measurements in the measure stage: You take num_ind = $(3.08 \times 1.2/.03)^2 \approx 15,000$ individual measurements of the production system with the threshold set to threshold_opt. Next,

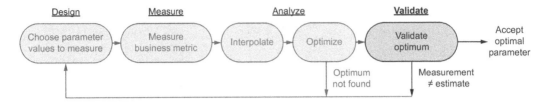

Figure 4.12   Validate stage. In this final stage, you'll run the production prop trading system at the optimal value of threshold **that you estimated in the analyze stage. If the measured markout profit at that** threshold **is close enough (see the next section for discussion) to the estimated** markout_profit (threshold), **then you may accept the optimal** threshold **as the result of the RSM process.**

compute the aggregate measurement (the mean of the individual measurements), call it a. m., and the standard error of the aggregate measurement

$$SE = \frac{\text{stddev(individual measurements)}}{\sqrt{N}}$$

You can consider the estimated optimal threshold, threshold_opt, valid if a. m. - 2 × SE < estimated_max_profit < a. m. + 2 × SE. Let's see why.

The aggregate measurement is well-approximated by a normal distribution with standard deviation SE It just so happens that 95% of the time a sample of a normal distribution lies within two standard deviations of the mean. This is roughly equivalent to saying, "If estimated_max_profit was outside the range a.m. ± 2 × SE, then there would be only a 5% chance that we were incorrectly declaring the interpolation invalid." This is a common criterion for declaring a single value (in this case, estimated_max_profit) as plausibly coming from a given distribution (in this case, the aggregate measurement).

We say that the value lies in the *95% confidence interval* of the distribution. The interval [a.m. - 2 × SE, a.m. + 2 × SE] is called the *95% confidence interval* of the aggregate measurement distribution. We can simulate the validation procedure like this:

```
np.random.seed(17)
aggregate_measurement, standard_error = run_experiment(15000,
    [threshold_opt])
print (aggregate_measurement[0]-2*standard_error[0],
    aggregate_measurement[0]+2*standard_error[0])
0.14048962175141153 0.17627270610659548
```

This code simulates an experiment of N = 15,000 individual measurements taken at threshold_opt. The value estimated_max_profit = 0.173 falls within two standard errors (i.e., standard deviations) of the aggregate measurement—that is, in the range [0.140,0.176], so we can say that the interpolation's estimate and the aggregate measurement agree.

If the estimate and measurement do not agree, then you need to investigate. It may be that a parabola was not a good approximation of the shape of `markout_profit(threshold)` in the interval of thresholds you chose. (Recall that the parabola was a model that was only expected to work over a limited range of parameters, and we couldn't be sure *a priori* what that range would be.) In that case, you need to shrink the interval and return to the measure stage on figure 4.12.

If the estimate and measurement do agree, then the result, `threshold_opt`, is valid. Sort of.

A MORE ROBUST VALIDATION MEASUREMENT

The short procedure I just described for validating the optimal `threshold` is sound in general, but for the system we're discussing (a prop trading system), as well as for the other systems discussed in this book (advertising, execution trading, recommender systems), you will generally find that the measurements can drift over time. This is called nonstationarity and will be discussed in more detail in chapter 8, section 8.1. That drift can make is so that noncontemporaneous measurements might not be comparable. In particular, the validation measurement of profit at `threshold_opt` might be higher or lower than it would have been had you measured it earlier, at the same time as you measured the profit at `threshold` = 0.5, 1.0, and 1.5.

Additionally, the RSM process is rather complicated compared to, say, an A/B test. It is, therefore, easier to make an error using RSM. We take on this risk of error because RSM holds the promise of reducing the number of experiments we need to run to find an optimal parameter value.

To cope with nonstationarity and the error risk induced by the added complexity of RSM, a better way to validate the optimal threshold would be to design an A/B test from scratch that compares the current, pre-RSM, production system (version A) to the system tuned to the optimal threshold estimated by RSM (version B). This A/B test will take contemporaneous measurements of profit for versions A and B and will be simpler to set up and run than RSM, so you will likely find that you have more confidence in the final answer.

When designing an A/B test, you need to specify `prac_sig`, the practical significance. Given a measurement of the markout profit for the current production system, `markout_profit_A`, a good value of `prac_sig` for this validation measurement would be `prac_sig = estimated_max_profit - markout_profit_A`. This says that you want to design an A/B test sensitive enough to detect the difference in profit the RSM process suggests you'll see. If the A/B test says you should accept B, then the RSM result is valid and you may run your production system at the optimal `threshold`.

We just saw all the steps of response surface methodology—design, measure, analyze, validate—applied to a system with a single continuous parameter. The procedure as depicted in figure 4.12 is the same when there are more parameters, but each step must be modified to account for the extra parameters. The next section will explore those modifications.

4.2 Optimizing two or more continuous parameters

In any real prop trading system—or any engineered system, for that matter—you will have more than one parameter to tune. RSM is capable of *optimizing* more than one parameter with the same stages described in the previous section; however, each stage must change in its details to handle the extra parameters.

As a first step, we'll expand the prop trading strategy to have two parameters. Then we'll proceed to modify each stage of the RSM process to handle those two parameters. The intent of each stage and the organization of the stages remains the same (figure 4.13). The modifications will apply to more than two parameters as well, although we'll see that RSM is best suited to *optimizing* three or fewer parameters.

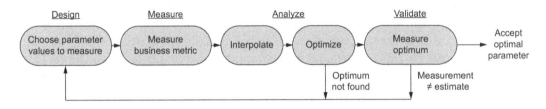

Figure 4.13 RSM for two or more parameters. The process remains the same, but some stages will change from their single-parameter version described in the previous section. Specifically, the design stage will introduce special parameter choices for two- and three-parameter systems. The interpolate stage will apply linear regression to models with more parameters. The optimize stage may use a more sophisticated numerical optimization technique.

The outline of the RSM procedure in figure 4.13 is familiar from section 4.1, where you optimized a single parameter. We'll need to modify some of the stages to deal with more parameters. Before we get into the details, though, let's see how your prop strategy can be improved by adding a second tunable parameter.

In the previous section, you optimized and traded a prop strategy with a single parameter, the `threshold`. The `threshold` determined how strong the trading signal needed to be for the strategy to send an order (BUY or SELL) to the exchange. Let's say you followed the single-parameter procedure in the previous section and found a good value of `threshold` at which to trade. Let's also say that you ran all those experiments sending orders to the market for $1,000 worth of stock each. (If a stock has price/share p, then $1,000 worth of stock is `1000/p` shares.) You chose $1,000 (a small size), say, because this is a new strategy, and you didn't want to take too much risk. But since you've proven in production that the strategy works, you're eager to take more risk for the possibility of generating more profit.

How much more risk should you take? One's initial intuition might be that raising the size of the orders to $2,000 would double the profit. Raising it to $3,000 would triple it, and so on. In practice, however, you'll find this problem: You won't always be able to trade at the size you ask for. You might ask to buy $3,000 worth of a stock but only actually get executed on $2,000 worth because there was no one willing to sell the extra $1,000 worth to you. In a situation like this, you would say that there isn't enough "liquidity." Generally speaking, you'll find more liquidity when the market is about to move against you. In other words, it's easier to trade when the trade will ultimately be unprofitable. This problem is called *adverse selection*, and the profit lost to it is called the *adverse selection cost*.

In summary, if you keep your order size too low, you'll miss out on the opportunity to make extra profit. If you make it too high, you'll face high adverse selection (lower profit, or even losses). Somewhere in between is the optimal, highest-profit order size. In this section, we'll see how to optimize both the order size and the trading threshold (which you optimized in section 4.1).

First, let's update the function `markout_profit()` to be a function of both threshold and order size. For simplicity, we'll express the order size in thousands of dollars. So a variable, `order_size = 1`, indicates that we're placing orders of size $1,000. We'll model the adverse selection cost, `asc`, as the function

$$asc = 0.001 \times e^{2 \times \text{ordersize}}$$

This expression for adverse selection cost is stylized—that is, based on a qualitative understanding rather than a model of data. It's based on a common quant trader observation that you can increase your order size a bit with a barely noticeable impact; then, as you continue to increase the size, adverse selection becomes severe. The coefficients `0.001` and `2` were chosen to make the values of `asc` compatible with the other values (e.g., `cost`, `pps`, `signal`) we have been using in `markout_profit()`.

What does asc look like?

If the function for `asc` seems a bit opaque, that's all right. When working with a real system, you can't observe its internal dynamics anyway. Instead, you develop techniques to get the answers you need *in spite* of that opacity. RSM is one of those techniques.

The updated version of `markout_profit()` is in listing 4.6. Sometimes the number of tunable parameters in an experiment or optimization is referred to as the number of *dimensions*. For example, if we're optimizing two parameters, we'll say there are two dimensions in the optimization or that the optimization is two-dimensional or "of dimension two."

Listing 4.6 Markout profit as a function of threshold and order size

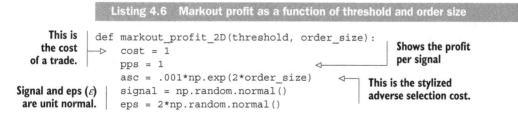

```
def markout_profit_2D(threshold, order_size):
    cost = 1
    pps = 1
    asc = .001*np.exp(2*order_size)
    signal = np.random.normal()
    eps = 2*np.random.normal()
```

This is the cost of a trade.

Signal and eps (ε) are unit normal.

Shows the profit per signal

This is the stylized adverse selection cost.

Buy when the signal is strong positive.

```
if (signal > threshold
    or signal < -threshold):
    profit = order_size*(pps*np.abs(signal) - cost + eps) - asc
else:
    profit = 0
    return profit
```

Sell when the signal is strong negative.

Profit is offset by adverse selection.

There is no profit if we don't trade.

Since we're *optimizing* two parameters in this example system, we'll say there are two dimensions and, where appropriate, append 2D—for *two-dimensional*—to function names to differentiate them from their (implicitly) 1D counterparts in the previous section.

In markout_profit_2D(), there is a tension between the profit (desirable) earned from the signal and the adverse selection cost (undesirable). They both increase with order_size but at different rates. This tension creates an optimal order_size at an "in-between" value—not too large or too small. You could potentially apply the 1D RSM procedure (described in the previous section) to locate this optimal order_size, just as you used it to locate the optimal threshold, but we want to know the optimum values of both order_size and threshold simultaneously. We'll use RSM to find the pair of values, threshold_opt and order_size_opt, that maximize markout_profit_2D(threshold, order_size).

You might be wondering whether you could just use the one-parameter procedure from the previous section to optimize threshold, then use it again to optimize order_size and consider the problem solved. You could. It's reasonably effective in some cases, but it's generally less effective than optimizing the two parameters simultaneously. In you're curious, see appendix B for a discussion. With the simulator in place, markout_profit_2D(), we'll now proceed to modify the design stage of figure 4.13 to optimize both parameters, threshold and order_size.

4.2.1 Design the two-parameter experiment

The RSM design stage (regardless of the number of parameters) consists of two parts: (1) using domain knowledge to decide which parameter values to measure, and (2) determining how many individual measurements (per parameter value), N, to take. We'll need to decide on values of both threshold and order_size. The number of individual measurements will be the same as in the 1D case.

In the previous section on 1D RSM, you measured threshold at three values, 0.5, 1.0, and 1.5. The domain-knowledge argument was that much lower values could lead to frequent, money-losing trades, and much higher values would prevent the strategy from trading very much at all.

All of your 1D experiments were run at order_size = 1. Although markout_profit() didn't specify order_size = 1 explicitly, the expression pps*np.abs(signal) - cost + eps from markout_profit() is replaced by order_size*(pps*np.abs(signal) - cost + eps) in markout_profit_2D(), and the two expressions are equivalent when order_size = 1. Since we're looking to increase profit, we'll try larger values of order_size.

It's not immediately obvious how large order_size can get. To be conservative, we'll at most double it.

We measured threshold at three values—0.5, 1.0, and 1.5—because we needed at least three values to interpolate (to fit a parabola) and find a maximum somewhere between 0.5 and 1.5. If we had only measured two values—0.5 and 1.5—our interpolation would have always been a straight line. The straight line could have estimated maximum profit at either threshold=0.5 or threshold=1.5 only. We paid the experimentation cost of measuring a third threshold to get the benefit of a more precise interpolation.

When deciding which threshold values to measure, we again need to consider the ability of the subsequent interpolation to locate the threshold that gives maximum profit and to be as frugal as we can with number of aggregate measurements to avoid increasing experimentation cost unnecessarily.

The same rationale applies in 2D that applied in 1D: We'll need three values of threshold in order to interpolate a maximum profit at a threshold value lying between the upper and lower limits. Similarly, we'll need to measure three values of order_size. See figure 4.14 for a visualization of the parameter values.

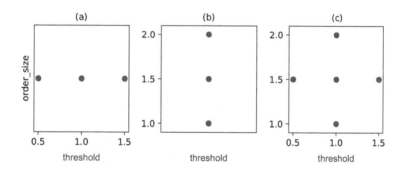

Figure 4.14 Design for a two-parameter (2D) experiment. (a) You need a minimum of three threshold values, (0.5, 1.0, and 1.5) to be able to interpolate the maximum markout_profit_2D(threshold, order_size) at a threshold between the left and right edges, threshold = 0.5 and threshold = 1.5. (b) Similarly, you'll measure three values of order_size (1, 1.5, and 2) to ensure that we can interpolate between the top and bottom edges. (c) In a single experiment, you can measure these five values simultaneously. When you analyze the experiment, you'll be able to interpolate markout_profit_2D(threshold, order_size) from the edges to center.

Figure 4.14(c) shows a design to measure five combinations of the parameters (threshold, order_size): (0.5, 1.5), (1.0, 1.5), (1.5, 1.5), (1.0, 1.0), and (1.0, 2). With measurements of markout_profit_2D(threshold, order_size) and each of those points, you'll be able to interpolate well near any of the four edges and near the center and use that interpolation to seek the optimize parameter combination (threshold_opt, order_size_opt).

You're not done yet, though. There's more space in the square in figure 4.14(c) to interpolate over than the edges and the middle. Since the optimum could be anywhere in this box, it's possible that the optimum you seek is in a corner. To be sure the interpolation is accurate near the corners, you should pay the extra experimentation cost and add four points in the corners of the design. The result is a *face-centered central composite design* (CCD), depicted in figure 4.15.

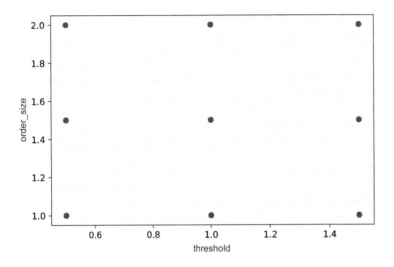

Figure 4.15   Central composite design (CCD), a design for a 2D RSM experiment. Adding four corner points enables the interpolation to work well across the full area of the square.

The kind of geometric reasoning we've used to devise the designs for our RSM experiments in this and the preceding section (the 1D case) is intuitive and useful for only these simplest cases. Designs may be made more efficient and can be extended to three or more dimensions. Such methods are beyond the scope of this book. (For additional reading, see NIST Engineering Statistics Handbook, section 5.3.3.6, www.itl .nist.gov/div898/handbook/pri/section3/pri336.htm.) The design of figure 4.15 is implemented in the following listing.

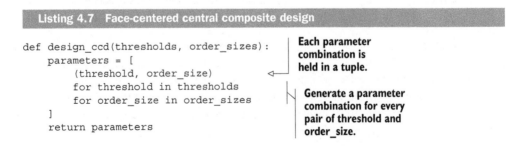

Listing 4.7   Face-centered central composite design

```
def design_ccd(thresholds, order_sizes):
    parameters = [
        (threshold, order_size)
        for threshold in thresholds
        for order_size in order_sizes
    ]
    return parameters
```

Each parameter combination is held in a tuple.

Generate a parameter combination for every pair of threshold and order_size.

You can generate a list of parameter combination tuples using

```
parameters = design_ccd(thresholds=[0.5, 1.0, 1.5], order_sizes=[1, 1.5, 2])
print (parameters)
[(0.5, 1), (0.5, 1.5), (0.5, 2), (1.0, 1), (1.0, 1.5), (1.0, 2), (1.5, 1),
    (1.5, 1.5), (1.5, 2)]
```

These nine tuples are the settings for which you'll measure markout profit in production. For example, the tuple `(1.0, 2.0)` represents setting `threshold` = 1.0 and `order_size` = 2.0.

You now know at which parameter combinations you will run your prop strategy to take aggregate measurements of markout profit. Next, you need to determine how many individual measurements to take for each aggregate measurement. In designing the 1D experiment in the previous section, we measured markout profit at `threshold` = 1.0 and `order_size` = 1.0 (`order_size` was not explicit in `markout_profit(threshold)` but was effectively 1) to have a mean of 0.17 and standard deviation of `sd_1_delta` = 1.2. We decided that domain knowledge (for the sake of presentation) of this prop strategy indicated that we should use 20% of the mean markout profit as a practical significance level, `prac_sig` = 0.20 * 0.17 ≈ 0.03. Combining `sd_1_delta` and `prac_sig` (with a slight modification to the standard formula for `num_ind`, which will be explained in chapter 8), the number of individual measurements is `num_ind` = (3.08×1.2/0.03) **2 ≈ 15,000.

This trading system can generate about 10 trading opportunities per day in each of 1,000 stocks, or about 10,000 individual measurements per day. In this 2D experiment, we need to measure N = 15,000 individual measurements for each of nine parameter combinations. This would take approximately 9×15,000 / 10,000 ≈ 14 days, or three business weeks. While this is not an unreasonable amount of time to spend on an experiment on a stock-trading system, there are ways to reduce the number of individual measurements required. (See, for example, P. Whitcomb and M. Anderson, "Right-sizing designs via fraction of design space plots," in *RSM Simplified: Optimizing Processes Using Response Surface Methods for Design of Experiments*. Boca Rotan, FL, USA: CRC Press, 2017.)

You now know how to design an RSM experiment to optimize two parameters by (1) creating a face-centered central composite design and (2) determining the number of individual measurements to take.

Note that it is possible to extend RSM to optimize more parameters (extend it to higher dimensions), but this book recommends you use Bayesian optimization for three or more parameters; we cover the topic in chapter 6. For now, let's see how to take measurements and analyze the 2D experiment we just designed.

4.2.2   *Measure, analyze, and validate the 2D experiment*

The procedure for taking measurements and analyzing a two-parameter (2D) RSM experiment follows the same steps as in the one-parameter case, except that the steps of the analyze stage—interpolation and optimization—are modified slightly to handle two parameters. Figure 4.16 reminds us where in this procedure the measure and analyze stages fall.

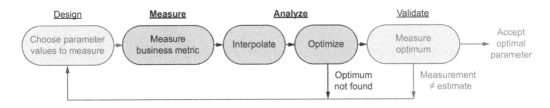

Figure 4.16   Measure and analyze a 2D RSM experiment. In the measure stage, you measure the business metric for each of the parameter values chosen in the design stage, just as you did for the 1D RSM. To execute the analyze stage, you need to use a more complex model for interpolation and search more parameter values during optimization.

First, let's run the experiment to collect the aggregate measurements.

TAKE THE MEASUREMENTS

The experiment will be simulated by run_experiment_2D(), shown in the following listing.

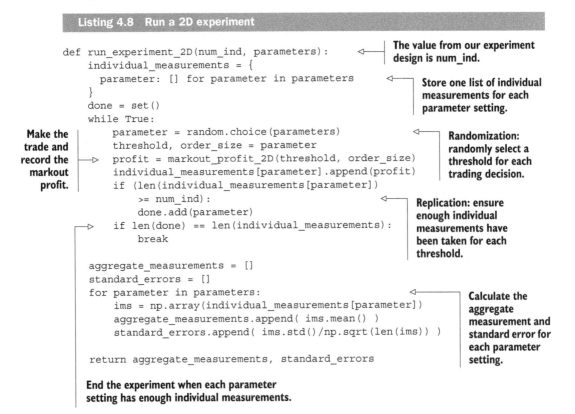

Listing 4.8   Run a 2D experiment

```
def run_experiment_2D(num_ind, parameters):          ◁─┐  The value from our experiment
    individual_measurements = {                            design is num_ind.
      parameter: [] for parameter in parameters    ◁─┐  Store one list of individual
    }                                                     measurements for each
    done = set()                                          parameter setting.
    while True:
        parameter = random.choice(parameters)       ◁─┐  Randomization:
        threshold, order_size = parameter                 randomly select a
        profit = markout_profit_2D(threshold, order_size) threshold for each
        individual_measurements[parameter].append(profit) trading decision.
        if (len(individual_measurements[parameter])
               >= num_ind):                          ◁─┐  Replication: ensure
            done.add(parameter)                           enough individual
        if len(done) == len(individual_measurements):     measurements have
            break                                         been taken for each
                                                          threshold.
    aggregate_measurements = []
    standard_errors = []
    for parameter in parameters:                     ◁─┐  Calculate the
        ims = np.array(individual_measurements[parameter]) aggregate
        aggregate_measurements.append( ims.mean() )       measurement and
        standard_errors.append( ims.std()/np.sqrt(len(ims)) ) standard error for
                                                          each parameter
    return aggregate_measurements, standard_errors        setting.
```

Make the trade and record the markout profit.

End the experiment when each parameter setting has enough individual measurements.

There is nothing fundamentally new in `run_experiment_2D()`. It takes an aggregate measurement consisting of `num_ind` individual measurements at each of the parameter settings supplied. We'll supply the nine parameter tuples returned by `design_ccd()`, and set `num_ind = 15000`, as determined in the previous section. You can design and run the simulated experiment with

```
np.random.seed(17)
parameters = design_ccd(thresholds=[1, 1.5, 2], order_sizes=[1, 1.5, 2])
aggregate_measurements, standard_errors = run_experiment_2D(
    15000, parameters)
```

The return values from `run_experiment_2D` contain aggregate measurements and SEs for each of the nine parameter tuples in `parameters`. It's useful to have them tabulated, but it can be easier to compare them visually, as in figure 4.17.

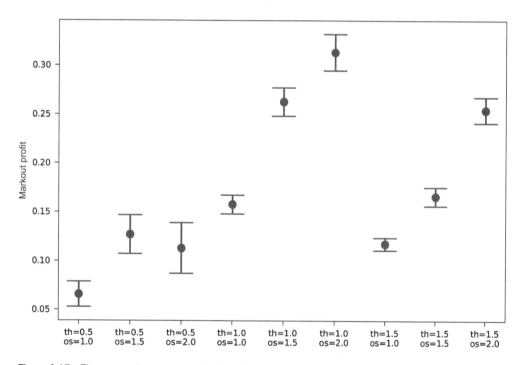

Figure 4.17 The aggregate measurements from the first 2D RSM experiment—th abbreviates `threshold`, and os abbreviates `order_size`. The nine parameter settings are along the x-axis. It is easy to visually compare the measured markout profits and their SEs. However, since the parameter settings on the x-axis are unordered, it is not possible to intuit where the optimal parameters setting might be.

Figure 4.17 is a good start. It shows us the aggregate measurements of markout profit and their SEs.

From this plot, we could tell which *measured* parameter setting is a good candidate for the optimal setting—`(1.0,2.0)` looks promising to me—but since the parameter settings in this plot along the *x*-axis are unordered, it's not possible to interpolate between them to unmeasured parameter settings. Indeed, since there are two parameters, there is no intuitive ordering along the x-axis. Therefore, it won't be possible to overlay the 2D interpolation of `markout_profit(threshold, order_size)` on top of figure 4.17 like we overlaid the 1D interpolation of `markout_profit(threshold)` on figure 4.8. Nevertheless, we'll see in the next section an alternative way to visualize the 2D interpolation.

We've taken the measurements and looked at the results. Now let's analyze the data by interpolating (via linear regression) between the measurements and optimizing over the surrogate function.

ANALYZE THE EXPERIMENT

Following the RSM procedure, we'll use linear regression to build a model of the (aggregate) measurements of markout profit we collected in the experiment we just ran. Then we'll find the parameter settings that yield the highest markout profit as estimated by that model.

The form of the model for a two-parameter system is a little more complex than that for a 1D system. In 1D, we modeled `markout_profit(threshold)` like this:

$$y = \beta_0 + \beta_1 x + \beta_2 x^2 + \varepsilon$$

where y was `markout_profit`, x was `threshold`, ε was approximation error, and the β_i were the coefficients that were found by linear regression.

In the present experiment, we have two parameters affecting `markout_profit_2D`, `threshold` and `order_size`. If we name `threshold` x_1 and `order_size` x_2, we can model `markout_profit_2D(threshold, order_size)` with

$$y = \beta_0 + \beta_1 x_1 + \beta_2 x_2 + \beta_3 x_1^2 + \beta_4 x_2^2 + \beta_5 x_1 x_2 + \varepsilon$$

It's helpful to compare the 2D model to the 1D model, as in table 4.2.

Table 4.2   **Comparison of terms in the 1D and 2D models. The linear and quadratic (univariate) terms translate to 2D simply by adding a second term for** x_2**. The cross term is new in 2D. It helps model behavior along the diagonals of the experiment design (CCD).**

Terms	1D model	2D model
Constant	β_0	β_0
Linear	$\beta_1 x_1$	$\beta_1 x_1 + \beta_2 x_2$
Quadratic (univariate)	$\beta_2 x_1^2$	$\beta_3 x_1^2 + \beta_4 x_2^2$
Quadratic (cross)	N/A	$\beta_5 x_1 x_2$

The term β_0 appears in both the 1D and 2D models. It is a constant offset to the mark-out profit, y. The linear term, β_1x, in the 1D model is expanded to two linear terms, one for each parameter: $\beta_1x_1 + \beta_2x_2$. The quadratic term, β_2x^2, is expanded even more. The first two quadratic terms in the 2D model, $\beta_3x_1^2$ and $\beta_4x_2^2$, enable interpolation of a maximum between the edges of the box containing the parameters. The final term, $\beta_5x_1x_2$, the *cross term*, enables interpolation in the areas between the center measurement and the corner measurements (along the diagonals) of the central-composite design.

The form of the model will be similar when there are three or more parameters—let's say d parameters. There will be one constant term (β_0) and d linear terms. There will be one quadratic term—of the form x_ix_j—for every *pair* of parameters. That's d(d - 1)/2 quadratic terms, a number that grows rather quickly with d. While it's certainly possible to manage the larger models that result from larger d in RSM (perhaps up to d = 5 is practical), in this book I'll stop at d = 2 and refer you to chapter 6 on Bayesian optimization for the handling of larger d in a more automated way. We'll find the β_i values that fit the aggregate measurements using the linear regression in the following listing.

Listing 4.9   Linear regression for two parameters

Shows the threshold settings ⊳

Shows the order_size settings ⊳

```
def linear_regression_2D(parameters, aggregate_measurements):
    parameters = np.array(parameters)
    x0 = parameters[:,0]
    x1 = parameters[:,1]
    y = aggregate_measurements
    X = np.array([np.ones(len(y)), x0, x1, x0**2, x1**2, x0*x1]).T
    beta = np.linalg.inv(X.T @ X) @ (X.T @ y)
    return beta
```

◁ Create a NumPy array for use in calculations.

◁ This is the normal equation.

The function linear_regression_2D() uses the same normal equation to find the beta values that we used in the 1D case, but the form of the model has changed. The normal equations apply no matter what the form of the model or the number of parameters. You can compute the beta values with

```
beta = linear_regression_2D(parameters, aggregate_measurements)
```

With the betas in hand, we can now proceed to interpolate over the model, as shown in the following listing.

Listing 4.10   Surrogate function for two parameters

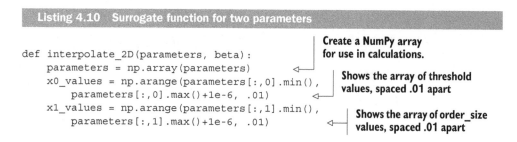

```
def interpolate_2D(parameters, beta):
    parameters = np.array(parameters)
    x0_values = np.arange(parameters[:,0].min(),
        parameters[:,0].max()+1e-6, .01)
    x1_values = np.arange(parameters[:,1].min(),
        parameters[:,1].max()+1e-6, .01)
```

Create a NumPy array for use in calculations.

◁ Shows the array of threshold values, spaced .01 apart

◁ Shows the array of order_size values, spaced .01 apart

```
x0hat_2d, x1hat_2d = np.meshgrid(x0_values, x1_values)
x0hat = x0hat_2d.flatten()
x1hat = x1hat_2d.flatten()
XHat = np.array([np.ones(len(x0hat)),
    x0hat, x1hat, x0hat**2, x1hat**2, x0hat*x1hat]).T
yhat = XHat @ beta
yhat_2d = np.reshape(yhat, (len(x1_values), len(x0_values)))
return x0hat_2d, x1hat_2d, yhat_2d
```

Represent the grid as an array.

Turns the array back into a grid

**Shows the estimated markout_profit
at each grid point**

**These are the model
terms at each grid point.**

**A 2D grid of all threshold,
order_size pairs**

Listing 4.10, `interpolate_2D()`, follows the same pattern as the 1D `interpolate()`. It computes the surrogate function's estimate of `markout_profit_2D()` at a bunch of parameter values. The NumPy code is a little more involved because of the extra dimension (the extra parameter). In particular, it generates a 2D grid of values over which to interpolate instead of just a 1D interval. The 2D grid is created by `np.mesh-grid()`, which generates pairs of `threshold`, `order_size` values covering the box defined by `0.5 < threshold < 2.0`, `1.0 < order_size < 2.0`. About 20,000 parameters pairs are generated in total.

Note that we can interpolate over many parameter pairs because interpolation is cheap—it takes less than 5 ms of computer time to generate all 20,000 estimates. In the design stage, we covered this same box with a grid of only nine parameter pairs (the CCD design), because each of those nine measurements incurred the high cost of an experiment. The disparity between the number of measurements and the number of estimates is what makes RSM so powerful: the more estimates we search through, the more precisely we can locate the maximum of `markout_profit_2D()`. Figure 4.18 visualizes the interpolation and highlights this disparity.

The nine dots in figure 4.18 mark the parameter settings where we measured markout profit. The rest of the box is filled with estimates from the interpolation. The power of RSM is the interpolation.

This procedure of interpolating a business metric between measured values is not unique to RSM. It finds use in other experimental optimization methods, such as Bayesian optimization (covered in chapter 6).

You can probably guess that the optimum parameter settings are near the top-middle just by looking at figure 4.18. Let's verify that by running an optimization. The optimization code is in the following listing.

Listing 4.11   Optimize the 2D surrogate function

**Locate the
maximum
element of
yhat.**

```
def optimize_2D(parameters, beta):
    x0hat, x1hat, yhat = interpolate_2D(parameters, beta)
    i = np.where(yhat==yhat.max())
    return x0hat[i][0], x1hat[i][0], yhat[i][0]
```

**Get grids of value from
interpolate_2D().**

**Return optimal parameters
and estimated markout profit.**

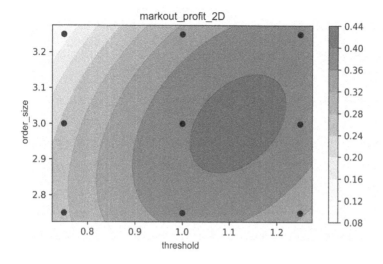

Figure 4.18 A two-dimensional surrogate function, an interpolation of
`markout_profit_2D` **over settings of** `threshold` **and** `order_size`. **The
filled dots mark the parameter settings where markout profit was measured in
the experiment. In this figure, there are many more estimates of markout profit
(around 20,000 interpolation estimates) than measurements (only nine).**

Putting it all together, the analyze stage is

```
beta = linear_regression_2D(parameters, aggregate_measurements)
threshold_opt, order_size_opt, estimated_max_profit = optimize_2D(parameters,
    beta)
```

The optimal parameters are `threshold_opt` = 1.15 and `order_size_opt` = 2.00, with
`estimated_max_profit` = 0.30. The optimum is, indeed, near the top-middle of figure 4.18.

Since the optimum is near the edge, you don't know whether the true optimum
could lie outside the box. The next step it to recenter the box on the optimum and
start again: design a new experiment, take measurements, then analyze them.

Notice that the range of estimated markout profits was large—from about 0.05 to
about 0.30. To recenter, let's choose the set of `threshold` values to measure to be 0.5,
1.0, 1.5, and the set of `order_size` values to be 2.5, 3.0, 3.5. First, we'll design the
experiment with

```
parameters = design_ccd(thresholds=[0.5, 1.0, 1.5], order_sizes=[2.5, 3.0, 3.5])
```

then run it:

```
aggregate_measurements, standard_errors = run_experiment_2D(15000, parameters)
```

Analyze the results:

```
beta = linear_regression_2D(parameters, aggregate_measurements)
threshold_opt, order_size_opt, estimated_max_profit = optimize_2D(parameters,
    beta)
```

The results of the experiment are shown in figure 4.19.

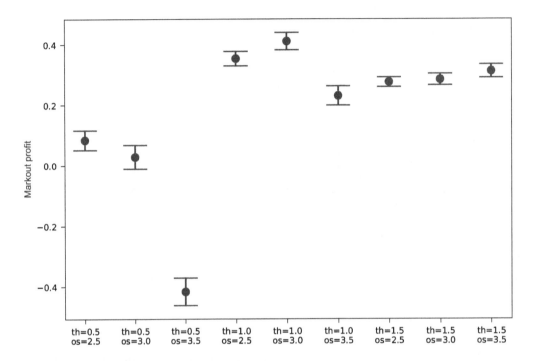

Figure 4.19   The results of the second iteration of the 2D RSM. Notice that one measurement, at `threshold=0.5, order_size=3.5`, has a markout profit far from the others. Outlying measurements like this violate our assumption that we're fitting a model near an optimum.

The measurements in figure 4.19 exhibit a strange feature, unlike any of the results we've looked at so far: The markout profit for `threshold = 0.5, order_size = 3.5` is much lower (`-0.40`) than that of all the other measurements. When one measurement is far from all the others, the shape of the function is likely too complex to be fit well by the simple (quadratic) model we proposed. (And we like using simple models because they require fewer measurements to fit and give more reliable estimates.) The solution is to shrink the parameter ranges while keeping the center in place and iterate. We'll use the `threshold` values $0.75, 1.0, 1.25$, and `order_size` values $2.75, 3.0, 3.25$.

```
parameters = design_ccd(thresholds=[.75,   1.0, 1.25], order_sizes=[2.75, 3.0,
    3.25])np.random.seed(17)
```

```
aggregate_measurements, standard_errors = run_experiment_2D(15000, parameters)
beta = linear_regression_2D(parameters, aggregate_measurements)
threshold_opt, order_size_opt, estimated_max_profit = optimize_2D(parameters,
    beta)
```

The results are shown in figure 4.20, along with the results of the previous iteration.

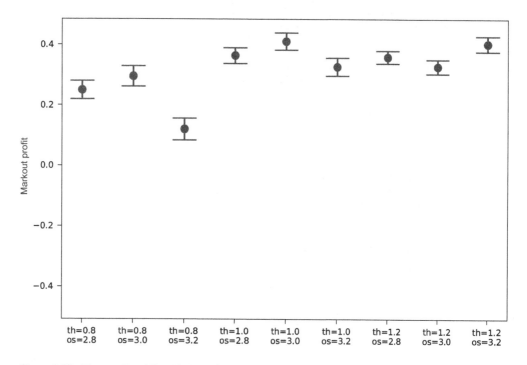

Figure 4.20   The results of the third, and final, iteration of the 2D experiment. There are no outlying measurements in this iteration, so we'll proceed to optimization.

This set of measurements looks much better: Figure 4.20 shows that there are no outliers this time. I would like to give you a hard-and-fast rule for identifying outliers, but there aren't any. Outlier rules exist, but they usually have a threshold that needs to be set by you. That being said, there are ways to automatically determine whether individual data points are "bad" for your regression, and such techniques would be useful here, but they are beyond the scope of this book. For now—and often in practice—judging by eye isn't so bad, especially when using a method like RSM, which is, overall, a manual (not automated) method. The final interpolation and optimization are shown in figure 4.21.

Our analysis is now complete. The optimal parameter settings suggested by RSM are `threshold_opt = 1.12` and `order_size_opt = 3.0`. The estimated markout profit at these settings is `0.41`. The next—and possibly final—step in the procedure is to validate this estimate by measuring markout profit at the optimal settings.

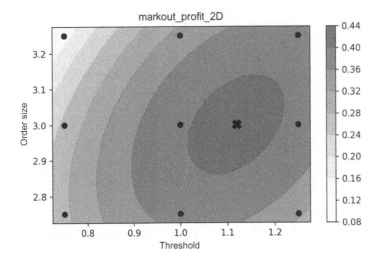

Figure 4.21   The third, and final, iteration of the 2D experiment. The optimum (X) is at `threshold_opt = 1.12`, `order_size_opt = 3.0` **and has an** `estimated_max_profit` **of** `0.41`.

VALIDATE THE INTERPOLATION ESTIMATE

This stage works the same as in 1D: we'll check to see whether the estimated maximum markout profit falls within the 95% confidence interval of the validation measurement.

```
aggregate_measurement, standard_error = run_experiment_2D(
    num_individual_measurements=15000,
    parameters=[(threshold_opt, order_size_opt)]
)
```

Figure 4.22 reminds us of where we are in the RSM procedure.

The validation measurement results are `aggregate_measurement = 0.37`, `standard_error = 0.026`. These values translate to a 95% confidence interval of `[aggregate_measurement - 2*standard_error, aggregate_measurement + 2*standard_error]` = `[0.32, 0.43]`.

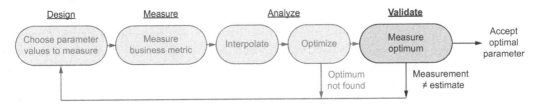

Figure 4.22   The validation stage in 2D is the same as in 1D. Measure the markout profit and its SE. If the estimate is not within the measurement's 95% confidence bounds, then return to the design stage; otherwise the RSM procedure is complete.

The estimated maximum markout profit of 0.41 falls within the 95% confidence interval from the validation measurement, so the result is validated.

Summary

- Business metrics generally vary continuously with continuous parameters, and this makes interpolation possible.
- Response surface methodology (RSM) reduces experimentation cost by interpolating—via a surrogate function—to estimate a business metric at unmeasured parameter settings.
- You optimize over the surrogate function to estimate both the optimal parameter settings and the business metric at those settings.
- RSM prescribes iteration over multiple measurements and analyses to locate a system's optimal parameter settings.
- Since RSM's output is an estimate of the optimal parameters, a final measurement is required to validate that estimate.

5

Contextual bandits: Making targeted decisions

This chapter covers

- Predicting the business metric outcome of a decision
- Exploring decisions to reduce model bias
- Exploring parameters to reduce model bias
- Validating with an A/B test

Thus far we've conducted experiments that compared two or more different versions of a system: A/B testing and multi-armed bandits evaluated arbitrary changes, and RSM optimized a small number of continuous parameters. Contextual bandits, in contrast, use experimentation to optimize multiple (potentially millions of) system parameters—but they can do so only for a narrowly defined type of system. Specifically, the system should consist of (1) a model that predicts the short-term, business-metric outcome of a decision and (2) a component that makes decisions based on the model's predictions. A contextual bandit is at the heart of any personalized service you might regularly use: news, social media, advertisements, music, movies, podcasts, and so on. Tuning these systems' parameters without experimentation can lead to suboptimal results and "feedback loops" (see section 5.2.1).

122

In this chapter, we'll develop an intuitive ("greedy") contextual bandit (CB) for a simplified social media recommender system (section 5.1). We'll see how the absence of information about the things we *didn't* recommend (missing counterfactuals) curses the greedy CB and how epsilon-greedy exploration of decisions (section 5.2 and from chapter 3, section 3.1) breaks that curse. Next, we'll optimize the system even more quickly by exploring the model parameters with Thompson sampling (section 5.3, and from chapter 3, section 3.3). Finally, since a CB is a relatively complex method, we'll take a step back and validate the whole thing with an A/B test (section 5.4), similar to how we validated our RSM results in chapter 4, section 4.1.5.

5.1 Model a business metric offline to make decisions online

As a first step toward understanding the contextual bandit, we'll build a simple one using a typical first-pass strategy: (1) fit a prediction model from logged data, and (2) make decisions in production based on the model's predictions. This is called a *greedy contextual bandit* (for reasons explained later). Before we start, let's get an overview of a contextual bandit system.

The contextual bandit (CB) is typified by a recommender system. A recommender system suggests content—for example, social media posts—to a user, and the user responds by engaging with or ignoring the content. A generic CB is shown schematically in figure 5.1.

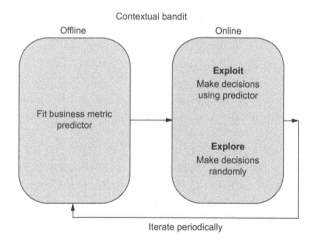

Figure 5.1   A generic contextual bandit (CB). A CB consists of offline and online parts. In the offline part, you fit a model that predicts the business metric. Online, the system usually makes prediction-based decisions that exploit the model to increase the business metric. Sometimes it makes decisions randomly—it "explores"—to collect novel data for the next offline fit.

The system logs the content shown and the user's response. That logged data then becomes the input to an offline routine that fits a prediction model. In a recommender system, the model would take (features representing) the user and the content as input and produce a prediction of whether or how much the user will engage with the content. Notice that the prediction depends on both the user and the content since we expect different users to prefer different content.

We'll set the notion of exploration (see "Explore" in figure 5.1) aside, but we'll come back to it in section 5.2. In the rest of section 5.1, we'll build a greedy contextual bandit—a simple, intuitive CB with no exploration. We observe that the logged data it generates is incomplete and then propose exploration as a way to expand the logged data.

5.1.1   *Model the business-metric outcome of a decision*

To have something concrete to discuss, let's imagine you're an ML engineer working on a small social media app. In the interest of starting simple, your app shows just a single piece of content—call it a "post", a short piece of text, possibly accompanied by an image—to a user when they open the app. That single post is selected from a larger set of available posts called the *inventory*. We won't concern ourselves with the origin of the posts but will take them as given by some other part of the company.

Our goal is to show posts that users would prefer to see. A typical way of measuring users' preferences is through engagement. Did they "like" the post by clicking a thumbs-up, heart, plus sign, or up arrow? Did they repost? Leave a comment? Share with a friend? As your new social media app possesses Zen-like simplicity, you'll eschew engagement buttons. Instead, you'll just measure how long it took for the user to close the app after seeing the post. In your app, users engage with a post simply by viewing it. Your assumption is that a user who likes a post more will take longer to close the app. Call this metric `viewing time`. Viewing time is the business metric outcome of your system's decision about which post to display.

The model we need to build, then, will output a prediction of `viewing time` given, as input, a `user`, and a `post`. The model is the function

$$viewing\ time = f(user,\ post)$$

The model will run on your server. When a user opens the app, it will connect to the server and download the content of a single post. We'll refer to the server and the app together as "the system."

In CB-speak, the user is called the *context*, the act of displaying the post is the *action*, and the viewing time is the *reward*. When the system displays a post, it has taken one of many possible actions because there are many posts from which to choose. The action the system takes depends on the context (i.e., different users prefer to see different posts). Finally, the system is "rewarded" for taking better actions with more viewing time. Next, as we have in previous chapters, we'll build a simulator of the system we're discussing and perform experiments on it.

SIMULATE THE VIEWING TIME

For the sake of exposition, we'll simulate the measurement of viewing time. Then we'll fit a prediction model to its output. See the following listing.

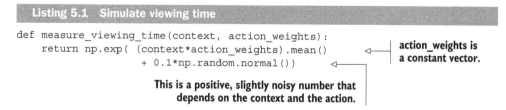

Listing 5.1   Simulate viewing time

```
def measure_viewing_time(context, action_weights):
    return np.exp( (context*action_weights).mean()
                 + 0.1*np.random.normal())
```

action_weights is
a constant vector.

This is a positive, slightly noisy number that
depends on the context and the action.

We simulate the viewing time as a random number with mean depending on both context and action_weights (described below). Beyond this, the details of the simulation aren't important to us since we'll be treating measure_viewing_time() as a black box and learning about it by taking measurements of it—just as we would with any real-life system.

The argument context is a vector containing the features that describe the user. These features might represent the user's demographic (age, zip code, etc.), reported interests (e.g., results of a survey they took when signing up for your app), how often they use the app, and so on. The context features were designed by you, the ML engineer, and they will be inputs to your reward-prediction model.

The argument action_weights are something completely different. They model how a user (the context) responds to different posts. We can't observe action_weights—they're part of the black box—and we won't try to measure them. They're just here to make a simulator on which we can practice our experimental method. As such, we set action_weights to the output of np.random.normal() and leave it unchanged for all of the examples in this chapter.

To get a feel for the output of measure_viewing_time(), see figure 5.2, which shows a histogram of output values for 1,000 randomly chosen context vectors.

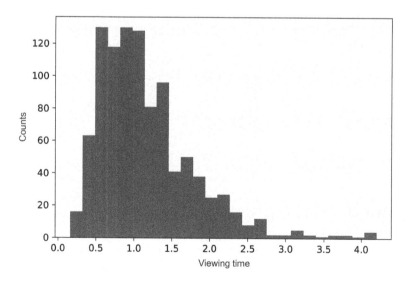

Figure 5.2   A histogram of 1,000 output values generated by
measure_viewing_time()**. Note that the values are all positive.**

These are the values your model will try to predict. The system will use the predictions to select posts that users will hopefully spend more time viewing. Let's fit a prediction model now.

FIT THE PREDICTION MODEL

You fit the prediction model offline, periodically (e.g., every day or every week) using logged data as the source. The logged data contains one sample for each user interaction event: When a user opens the app, the system displays a post, and the user views it for some amount of time. When that event completes, the system logs a sample containing three values: `context`, `action`, `reward`. We'll represent that with the structure in the following listing.

Listing 5.2   A logged sample

```
class Sample:
    def __init__(self, context, action, reward):
        self.context = context          ◁———  context is an ndarray (a vector)
        self.action = action                   of features describing a user.
        self.reward = reward            ◁———
```

action is an index to the displayed post. ⤷

reward is the viewing time.

The production system logs one `Sample` for every user interaction event. For a small app, there might be hundreds per day. For a large social media site, there might be hundreds of millions or even billions of such events per day.

We'll say that there are a fixed number of posts, `num_actions`, available in the system. Then `Sample.action` can take values 0, 1, 2, ... `num_actions-1`. In a real system, the number of posts might change with time, necessitating a more sophisticated model. Fixing the number of posts allows us to build one model for each post.

For each post, we'll model the reward—viewing time—as a linear function of the context vector, like so:

$$\text{reward} = \beta \times \text{context} + \varepsilon$$

or, if we write `y` = `reward` and `X=context`, then

$$y = X\beta + \varepsilon$$

Ultimately, you'll run a linear regression to find the vector β. In fact, you'll run one linear regression for each of the `num_actions` posts and, thus, calculate `num_actions` β vectors. But first you need to process the logs.

First, collect the logs for each action (post) from the log of the whole day, which consists of all events, regardless of the action. See the following listing. (Note: The logs for the day, `logs`, are a Python list of `Sample` objects.)

Listing 5.3   Collect logs for each action

```
def collect_logs_by_action(num_actions, logs):
    samples_y = [[] for _ in range(num_actions)]
    samples_x = [[] for _ in range(num_actions)]
    for sample in logs:
        samples_y[sample.action].append(sample.reward)
        samples_x[sample.action].append(sample.context)
    return samples_y, samples_x
```

Sort samples into buckets indexed by sample.action.

The values returned from `collect_logs_by_action()`—`samples_y` and `samples_x`—are each a list of `num_actions` lists (yes, that's a "list of lists") of samples for a single action (post). For example, `samples_x[3]` is a list of all the samples where the values of `action` is 3.

Also note that `collect_logs_by_action()` will take all of the logs collected by the system to date—not just the logs from the previous day. Logged data is valuable to the regression, so we'll make sure to use all the data we can get.

In the variable `Sample.context`, you'll find the features representing the user. Let's say there are `num_features` of them so that `len(context)==num_features`. The function `build_models()` in the following listing performs one linear regression on each of the `num_actions` sets of samples.

Listing 5.4   Build a model for each action

```
def build_models(num_features, samples_y, samples_x):
    betas = []
    for y, x in zip(samples_y, samples_x):
        y = np.array(y)
        x = np.array(x)
        if len(y) > 0:
            beta = np.linalg.pinv(x.T@x) @ x.T@y
        else:
            beta = np.zeros(shape=(num_features,))
        betas.append(beta)
    return betas
```

Transform lists to ndarrays.

We need some samples to fit.

Perform linear regression.

Collect num_actions betas.

Pseudoinverse

A keen observer might notice that the linear regression in `build_models()` uses `np.linalg.pinv()` instead of `np.linalg.inv()` (note the p before inv) to perform the matrix inverse. The p stands for "pseudo." The pseudoinverse (the Moore-Penrose pseudo-inverse) is a generalization of the matrix inverse that is defined for special cases where the inverse is undefined but is otherwise equal to the inverse. The inverse may not be defined when there are too few samples or the regressors are very similar to each other. You can think of pinv as a more "robust" inv for doing linear regression in practice.

Now you have the components needed to build a model for each post (`action`) that can predict the `viewing_time` (`reward`) for each user (`context`). The final piece of the contextual bandit puzzle is the online decision-maker that chooses posts for users.

5.1.2 Add the decision-making component

To complete the recommender system, you need to pair your prediction model with an online component, a decision-maker, that chooses the best post to display to a user (figure 5.3).

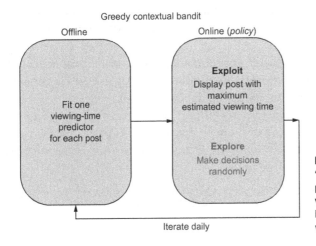

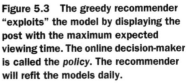

Figure 5.3   The greedy recommender "exploits" the model by displaying the post with the maximum expected viewing time. The online decision-maker is called the *policy*. The recommender will refit the models daily.

In CB lingo, the decision-making component is called a *policy*. For the social media app we're discussing, which shows only one post to a user, the policy should find the post that maximizes the model's prediction of viewing time. According to your company's marketing researchers, maximizing user's viewing time is the company's goal.

You'll refit the `viewing_time` models every day. The code for the policy is in the method `Recommender.policy()` in the following listing.

Listing 5.5   A greedy recommender

```
class RecommenderGreedy:
    def __init__(self, num_features, num_actions):
        self._num_features = num_features
        self._num_actions = num_actions

    def reset(self):                                     ◁——  Initialize betas to
        self._betas = [np.random.normal(size=(num_features, ))     random values.
            for _ in range(self._num_actions)]
                                                         ◁——  Fit the model offline
    def fit_offline(self, logs):                               to logged samples.
        samples_y, samples_x = collect_logs_by_post(num_actions, logs)
        self._betas = build_models(self._num_features, samples_y, samples_x)
```

**Decide,
online,
which
post to
display.**

```
def policy(self, context):
    viewing_max = -np.inf
    for action in range(self._num_actions):
        viewing_hat = context @ self._betas[action]
        if viewing_hat > viewing_max:
            action_best = action
            viewing_max = viewing_hat
    return action_best
```

**Estimate
viewing time.**

**Track post with
maximum estimated
viewing time.**

RecommenderGreedy is a complete contextual bandit. The method `fit_offline()` collects the logs by post and builds the models. The method `policy()` runs online (in production) and decides which post to display to a user (context). A real-world policy would likely be more complex. It could include safety checks or manually designed decision logic that works in tandem with the model's predictions.

There's one more method, `reset()`. This method solves a problem we haven't yet discussed, the "cold start" problem. A cold start is when the system hasn't yet run and, thus, no logged data exists. How can you fit a model with no samples? How can you run the policy to log samples without a model? It's a chicken-and-egg problem.

A common solution, in practice, is to create a manually designed policy. A manually designed policy can use domain knowledge to decide what to show users. Maybe you suspect users like to see the latest posts, so you'll show everyone the most recently created post, for example. Or maybe you'll just choose one at random, because you know that all the posts in your inventory have been vetted by in-house moderators and thus are good enough to show anyone without fear of discouraging them from coming back.

The solution we'll use here is to initialize the betas to random values. This is not quite the same as choosing a random post; instead you're picking a random model and then using it repeatedly to choose posts. Either way, the system will run and the policy will produce some samples in the logs. Now you're ready to run the greedy recommender system and evaluate its performance.

5.1.3   Run and evaluate the greedy recommender

Your greedy recommender is complete and ready to run. It'll start on day 1 with random betas just so that the policy has a model to work with. The policy will display posts to users and log samples consisting of context, action, reward.

Since with each action the recommend is trying to maximize the user's viewing time, a natural metric to evaluate the system each day is the mean viewing time per post. We're taking the mean over a day since that's the period over which we're refitting the model. This way the evaluation metric is produced once per model.

We'll run a simulation of the greedy recommender system for 30 days and see how it performs. The simulation uses num_features = 5 and num_actions = 30 and is shown in figure 5.4.

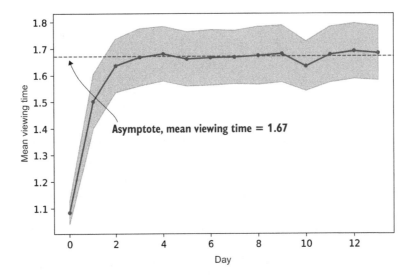

Figure 5.4   Performance of the greedy recommender. The system starts with random model parameters, achieves poor performance, then improves quickly—in 2 days— until it reaches its asymptotic performance level (dashed line) at around 4 days.

The first thing to notice in figure 5.4 is that the system starts, on day 1, with relatively poor performance. This is because the model was initialized with random betas. After the first day, the recommender builds a model from the collected data. That model runs on day 2 with much better performance. Finally, by day 4, the system has "learned" all it can and reaches maximum performance, around mean viewing time = 1.67.

Short-term rewards only

Contextual bandits work only in cases where the rewards are short-term. Short-term rewards are metrics that are caused by a single action. For example, a click on an ad is a reward for showing (the action) a relevant ad, and a user clicking play is a reward for suggesting (the action) a desirable song.

In contrast, a multistep metric, usually called a "return," is the sum of the rewards for a sequence of actions, each of which depends on the actions that came before it. For example, imagine this sequence:

1 The system suggests a horror movie to a user.
2 The user declines it.
3 The systems suggest another horror movie to a user.
4 The user declines it.
5 The system suggests a bland documentary.
6 The user watches—but *only* because they need some relief from the fright of seeing the trailers for the horror movies. Normally they would not watch a documentary.

The above interaction tells us that suggesting horror movies is a good setup for getting a user to watch a documentary. The whole sequence needs to play out to get the final reward, which is that the user watches the documentary.

Because a contextual bandit deals with only one-step rewards, it would, given this interaction with the user, log the three samples:

- `context=user, action=suggest horror movie, reward=0`
- `context=user, action=suggest horror movie, reward=0`
- `context=user, action=suggest documentary, reward=1`

From this data set, a CB would (1) learn not to suggest horror movies (since the reward was 0 when it suggested horror movies) and (2) learn *to* suggest documentaries (since the reward was 1 when it suggested a documentary).

It would be wrong on both counts. The right thing to do is to follow the full suggestion sequence: horror, horror, documentary. But the model builder (the regression) considers the samples independently, and so it misses the dependence between the three samples.

The greedy recommender works: it optimizes the model parameters via regression to logged data and, as a result, improves the business metric (the viewing time). This type of system works well with linear regression models, logistic regression models, deep neural networks, and so on. It is robust and has been proven in practice many times over.

It can be improved, however. A common problem that crops up with systems like this is that since no data is logged for the actions not taken by the policy, the model can't make a good prediction about them. For example, if the system never shows me a post about cooking, how will it learn that I like cooking? On the other hand, if it doesn't know that I like cooking, why would it show me a post about cooking? The next section discusses this problem in more detail and provides a solution: exploration.

5.2 Explore actions with epsilon-greedy

You've built a greedy recommender. It's been quite a bit of work already: You've had to build a supervised learning model (the linear regressions), deploy it to production in a policy, and log the decisions along with their rewards. The mean viewing times your system achieved weren't bad, but they could have been better. Let's take a moment to understand how, and then begin working on the fix, which is exploration.

When your system recommends a post to a user, it makes a tradeoff, if only implicitly. When it decides to display the post that it predicts will garner the most viewing time from the user, it is also deciding *not* to display any of the other posts. Would the user have viewed any of the other posts for a longer time than the one displayed? You'll never know. It's the *counterfactual*: the knowledge of what *would have happened* had the system made a different decision.

In this section, we'll see how missing counterfactual data can degrade a model's predictions. We'll also see how to systematically collect counterfactual data for the purpose of improving the model's predictions. We'll collect the data using epsilon-greedy exploration, a technique we first discussed in chapter 3, section 3.1.

We'll see later that exploration is a short-term cost (an experimentation cost) that pays off by creating a better prediction model in the future. The "greed" in the name RecommenderGreedy is that it takes a short-term view of reward and doesn't pay the cost of exploration. First, let's look more closely at the problem of missing counterfactuals.

5.2.1 *Missing counterfactuals degrade predictions*

To clearly see the effect of missing counterfactual data on a model, imagine the recommender system logged the following three samples from displaying post #1 three times, which we'll denote by action = 1:

```
contexts = [
    [1, 0, 0],
    [0, 1, 0],
    [0, 0, 1]
]
rewards = [
    0.6,
    0.9,
    1.3
]
```

In this example, there are three contexts (rows), each containing three features (columns). For each context sample, there is a corresponding reward. For example, the first sample can be described as this: the system received a reward = 0.6 (viewing time) when it showed post #1 to a user modeled by the feature vector context = [1,0,0].

We can fit a predictive model, just as we did in the previous section, using linear regression:

```
x = np.array(contexts)
y = np.array(rewards)
beta_1 = np.linalg.pinv(x.T @ x) @ (x.T@y)
```

In this case, beta_1 = [0.6, 0.9, 1.3], where the length of beta (three) matches the number of features (which is the number of columns in the context matrix).

Let's consider a user, call them User A, modeled by the context context_a = [0,0,1]. This happens to be the context of the third sample, earlier. When running with the model we just fit, the system would predict that the user's viewing time (reward) would be context_a @ beta_1 = 1.3. This matches the reward value in the third sample, making it a good prediction.

Imagine, instead, that the system hadn't shown post #1 to a user modeled by the third context, context = [0, 0, 1], but instead had shown the user, say, post #2. The samples for post #1 would be missing that counterfactual data—that is, the sample answering the question, "What would have happened if it had shown post #1?"

In short, the third sample would be missing

```
contexts = [
    [1, 0, 0],
    [0, 1, 0]
]
rewards = [
    0.6,
    0.9
]
```

and the model would have `beta_1m = [0.6, 0.9, 0]`. (I have appended m to the name of beta to indicate that it is derived from a sample with a missing counterfactual.)

This model, call it "Model 1m," predicts that User A would view post #1 at a level of `context_a @ beta_1m = 0.0`. This is a very strongly biased (read: bad) prediction, because we know from the earlier data set that User A would have viewed for a time of `1.3`. Of course, Model 1m didn't have a chance of making a good prediction because it didn't have any data about the case of User A viewing post #1 to fit on.

This is a stark example of how missing counterfactuals can create model bias. In practice, the biases induced by them may be milder. Also, the biases may span multiple features or combinations of features. In some cases, simply collecting more data can reduce the bias—if the new data happens to have the requisite samples. In other cases, the bias could remain or get worse, as explained next.

FEEDBACK LOOPS

Let's pause for a moment and think about what would happen if Model 1m ran in production. Since Model 1m predicts 0 reward (viewing time) for displaying post #1 to User A, the policy would always choose to show User A some other post. This would cause the logged data to, again, be missing a sample of "context=User A, action=post #1," which would in turn cause the next, refit model to predict a reward of 0 for displaying post #1 to User A.

This is a vicious cycle: the biased predictions prevent the policy from logging the very samples required to improve the predictions, leading to a suboptimal model and, thus, a suboptimal policy. Figure 5.5 depicts such a feedback loop.

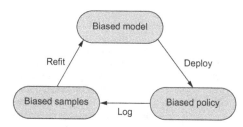

Figure 5.5   Feedback loop caused by refitting on logged samples. If the logged samples are biased, the fit will produce a biased model. If the model is biased, the policy will make biased decisions. The logs record samples of those biased decisions, and the bias is perpetuated.

Feedback loops may be more subtle in practice. Rather than missing all data for a specific combination of an action and a feature, logged samples might simply be biased to

- Include fewer samples of a certain feature.
- Contain fewer samples of some combination of features.
- Contain rewards that don't accurately represent the behavior of users modeled by certain features or combinations of features.

Feedback loops, and model bias in general, are insidious and thus difficult to intuit, so you should always proceed as if they are present. Did you happen to notice that the model in section 5.1 was biased? (Neither did I.) The next section shows how to use exploration to reduce prediction-model bias and break contextual bandit feedback loops.

5.2.2 *Explore with epsilon-greedy to collect counterfactuals*

Missing counterfactuals may bias model predictions, sometimes severely. The solution is to collect the counterfactual data by running some sort of experiment. A simple way to collect the counterfactual data would be to run a policy that showed *every* post to *every* user. Then you'd never have to ask, "What would have happened if I showed post P to user U?" because you'd have a sample in your logged data that told you. The problem is that users might not want to look at every post. In fact, the value your recommendation service promises to provide is to show users only the posts they will like. Put another way, the experimentation cost of showing every post to every user is too high. We need to lower that cost.

This section proposes a middle-ground solution between (1) showing all users all the posts and (2) showing only the posts your model predicts to be best—that is, to have maximum expected viewing time. The idea is to show users a few posts chosen at random interspersed among the predicted-best posts. This approach is called *epsilon-greedy*. It adds exploration to the greedy policy discussed in section 5.1 (figure 5.6).

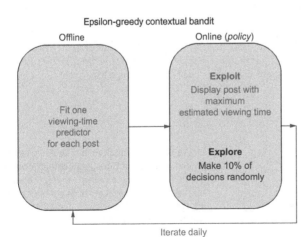

Figure 5.6   Epsilon-greedy adds exploration to the greedy recommender policy. Exploration collects counterfactual data by sometimes taking actions randomly instead of following the policy's prediction-based decision.

Epsilon-greedy is a straightforward modification that you can apply to any policy. Despite its simplicity, it's very effective. You choose a random action some small fraction of the time, say 10%, and use the original greedy policy the rest of the time (90%). The full policy, then, is 10% exploration and 90% exploitation.

Contextual bandit terminology

The contextual bandit may be understood from various perspectives. In this book, we view it as a powerful experimental method that may be used to optimize many (thousands, millions) parameters of a decision-making system, provided each decision can be directly associated with a short-term reward (see earlier sidebar, "Short-term rewards only").

Alternatively, you could describe a contextual bandit as an enhancement of a multi-armed bandit. The available decisions are the arms of the bandit. The enhancement is the addition of a context for each pull of an arm (each decision).

A contextual bandit can also be seen as a special case of reinforcement learning (RL). A reinforcement learning system makes a sequence of decisions. In an RL problem, the goal is to optimize the mean of all the rewards. In a full RL problem, it may be that each decision affects the context for the next decision. In the special case where each decision is independent (doesn't affect the next context), then the RL problem is the contextual bandit problem.

Finally, it's important to distinguish the contextual bandit problem from a pure supervised learning (SL) problem. In an SL problem, you are given samples of features (X, in this book's terms) and targets (y) that are assumed to be sampled at random. In the contextual bandit, the samples are *not* collected at random. They are collected by a policy that samples based on the output of the SL model—the SL model that was built on previous policy samples! In CB terms, X = (state, action) and y = reward, and the unsampled actions, the counterfactuals, are missing. When y has these properties, it is sometimes called *bandit feedback* to make it clear that you're not dealing with a pure SL data set.

We'll see below that the greedy recommender we constructed in section 5.1 was biased, and adding exploration with epsilon-greedy improves the average viewing time. See the following listing for the full epsilon-greedy recommender.

Listing 5.6 Epsilon-greedy recommender

```
class RecommenderEpsilonGreedy:
    def __init__(self, num_features, num_actions, epsilon=0.1):
        self._num_features = num_features
        self._num_actions = num_actions
        self._epsilon = epsilon

    def reset(self):
        self._betas = [np.random.normal(size=(num_features, )) for _ in
    range(self._num_actions)]
```

```
def fit_offline(self, logs):
    samples_y, samples_x = collect_logs_by_action(num_actions, logs)
    self._betas = build_models(self._num_features, samples_y, samples_x)

def policy(self, context):
    viewing_max = -np.inf
    if np.random.uniform(0,1) < self._epsilon:
        action_best = np.random.randint(
            0, self._num_actions
        )
    else:
        for action in range(self._num_actions):
            viewing_hat = context @ self._betas[action]
            if viewing_hat > viewing_max:
                action_best = action
                viewing_max = viewing_hat
    return i_post_best
```

Some fraction of the time (randomly)...

...choose an action at random.

Otherwise, use the original, greedy policy.

Very little of the original `RecommenderGreedy` needed to be modified to create `RecommenderEpsilonGreedy`. Nevertheless, the average viewing time increases, as shown in figure 5.7.

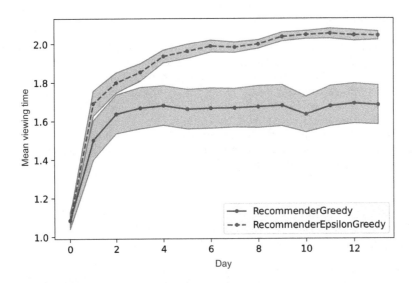

Figure 5.7   Epsilon-greedy exploration improves mean viewing time by showing posts to users that the original, greedy policy would not have. This counterfactual data reduces the bias of the prediction model. Better predictions make for a better policy.

It appears that adding exploration improved the recommender, but how exactly? The randomness in the actions—the exploration—cause the system to take actions (in contexts) the model would not have prescribed (i.e., the counterfactual data). The next time the model was fit, it had the data (in the logs) needed to make predictions about the rewards that would be received if those (previously counterfactual) actions were to be taken. The next day the system explored some more, further increasing the set of actions and contexts available in the logged data, refit again, and so on.

Over time, the logged data covered more and more actions and contexts, and the model became less and less biased. Thus, the predictions improved and so did the mean viewing time (the reward received).

Exploration is a tradeoff: invest some amount today and reap the benefits every day after. This begs the question of how much to invest—in other words, how large should epsilon be? It depends on how useful the unexplored actions are in improving the prediction model and how useful better predictions are in improving the selection of the best post. You, the engineer, need to tune the metaparameter epsilon to the system you're building. You might err on the side of caution and choose a small epsilon, knowing that the system will improve, if not at an optimal rate, or you might construct an A/B test where you compare two values of epsilon. The need to tune this parameter is a (minor) drawback of epsilon-greedy. That being said, epsilon-greedy is robust and simple to implement, so it's a good first choice for exploration.

It is known that epsilon-greedy has a regret of $O\left(T^{\frac{2}{3}}\right)$, where T is the number of periods (days for the recommender example in this chapter) the contextual bandit has been running (see J. Langford and T. Zhang, "The epoch-greedy algorithm for contextual multi-armed bandits." NIPS, 2007). It is also known that the optimal regret is $O\left(T^{\frac{1}{2}}\right)$, so epsilon-greedy is suboptimal. For reference, I'll repeat the definition of regret here. Recall, *regret* is the amount of business metric (e.g., viewing time) forfeited by not making the best possible decision every time.

One final thing to notice about epsilon-greedy is that it never stops exploring. It continues to pay the exploration cost even if there is no more business metric improvement to be had. You can see from figure 5.7 that at some point the average viewing time stops improving. If you had confidence that improvement had stopped, it would make sense to turn off exploration (i.e., switch to RecommenderGreedy, or, equivalently, set epsilon=0) to avoid paying the continued exploration cost.

Epsilon-greedy exploration reduces model bias, which in turn causes a contextual bandit to collect larger rewards. On the one hand, it is robust and simple to implement; on the other hand, it (1) has suboptimal regret, (2) has a tuning parameter, and (3) never stops exploring, even though it should. In the next section, we'll address all those objections with Thompson sampling, an exploration technique first introduced in chapter 3, section 3.3.

5.3   *Explore parameters with Thompson sampling*

Your users will appreciate the higher-quality posts that your system delivers after you add epsilon-greedy exploration. More precisely, they'll appreciate the posts that are displayed 90% of the time, when exploiting the predictions. They likely won't enjoy the exploratory posts that the system delivers the other 10% of the time. This section details Thompson sampling, which explores more efficiently than epsilon-greedy and steadily reduces the rate of exploration so that your users see fewer exploratory posts and more "exploitative" posts, making for an overall higher-quality experience on your social media app.

Epsilon-greedy is easy to implement and a great place to start with exploration, but with some added effort you can achieve optimal regret by using Thompson sampling. Unlike in the last section on epsilon-greedy, we won't apply Thompson sampling directly to the actions. Instead, we'll apply Thompson sampling to the parameters of the prediction model. Borrowing again from chapter 3, section 3.3, we'll use bootstrap sampling to make the implementation simple and usable across a wide range of model types. Thompson sampling is more complex than epsilon-greedy, in part because it requires changes to both the offline and online components of the system (figure 5.8).

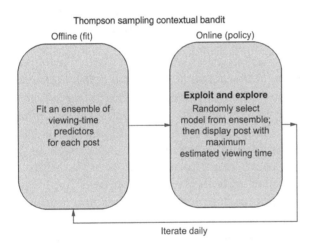

Figure 5.8   **Thompson sampling alters both the fit and the policy. You fit several models—called an** *ensemble*—**instead of just one. The policy uses a different, randomly selected model for each decision it makes.**

You integrate Thompson sampling into your recommender like this:

- Each day, build a varied set of models (say, 10), called an *ensemble*, instead of just one model (section 5.3.1 will discuss this in detail).
- Put the entire ensemble of models online.
- For each decision, the policy randomly selects a model (section 5.3.2) from the ensemble, then displays the post predicted by that model to have the highest viewing time.

Notice how, at decision time, a Thompson sampling policy randomly chooses a model rather than randomly choosing an action, as did the epsilon-greedy policy. For a single input, the set of all models' outputs forms a distribution of predictions. We'll see in the next section that the models in the ensemble differ only by their parameter values. Thus, we view Thompson sampling as exploration over parameters and epsilon-greedy as exploration over actions.

In the next section, we'll see how to generate multiple, varied models from a single set of logged samples using bootstrap sampling. Next, we'll see how the policy of randomly selecting a model is equivalent to a heuristic called *randomized probability matching*. Thompson sampling is randomized probability matching applied to a bandit problem, and it achieves optimal regret, $O\left(T^{\frac{1}{2}}\right)$, where T is the number of days the recommender has run (S. Agrawal, et al. "Thompson sampling for contextual bandits with linear payoffs," Proc. 30th ICML, 2013, pp. 127–135).

5.3.1   *Create an ensemble of prediction models*

If you run two fits using two different sets of samples, you will find different values of the betas, the parameters to the prediction model. In principle, if you wanted to create 10 different prediction models, all for the same recommender system, you could run the system for 10 days, put one day's worth of logged samples into each of 10 sample sets, then run one fit per set. The problem with that approach is that you'd need to wait 10 days before doing a fit. Fortunately, there's a cheat you can use: bootstrap sampling.

We first saw bootstrap sampling in chapter 3, section 3.3.1, where we applied it to individual measurements taken for each arm being evaluated by a multi-armed bandit. It's a great technique to have in your toolkit, and we'll be applying it differently here than we did in chapter 3, so let's take a minute to reintroduce it.

The idea behind bootstrap sampling is that of simulating an individual measurement by randomly sampling from real individual measurements that you already have on hand. You'll sample with replacement, meaning that if you simulate another individual measurement, you'll do it by sampling from the full set of real measurements.

For example, say you have num_ind = 4 individual measurements collected from an experiment, with business metric values {1, 3, 2.5, 1.5}. Taking a random sample from this set might yield the number 2.5. Another sample might yield 3. Since you're sampling with replacement, the next sample might be 2.5 again. Then, maybe, you sample 1.5. By this process, you have created a new set of four simulated individual measurements: {2.5, 3, 2.5, 1.5}. This set is called a *bootstrap sample*. A bootstrap sample will have roughly the same summary statistics—for example, mean, standard deviation—as the original measurements of which it is comprised.

As another example, imagine you measured the number of times each of a set of 100 users checked your app in a day. Say the measurements were uniformly distributed between 3 and 7 visits:

```
np.random.seed(17)
visits = np.array([3 + int(5*np.random.uniform()) for _ in range(100)])
```

You could simulate an individual measurement using

```
i = np.random.randint(len(visits))
visits[i]
```

where i is a random index to one of the entries of visits. To create a bootstrap sample with size equal to that of visits, generate len(visits) indices:

```
i = np.random.randint(len(visits), size=(len(visits,)))
bs_visits = visits[i]
```

Notice that each entry in i may take any value in 0 <= i < len(visits). Sampling this way is called *sampling with replacement*. Significant facts about this type of sampling are

1   The bootstrap data set may contain duplicate value from visits.

2   bs_visits may be any size—even larger than visits.

Figure 5.9 compares the distributions of visits and bs_visits.

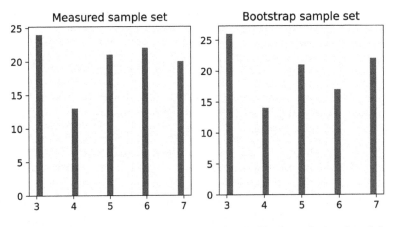

Figure 5.9   The measured and bootstrap sample sets. The two sets do not contain the same values, but their summary statistics are approximately the same. For example, their means are 5.01 (measured) and 4.95 (bootstrap). Their standard deviations are 1.45 and 1.49, respectively.

The two sample sets are similar but not precisely the same. For example, the measured sample set has mean 5.01 and standard deviation 1.45, but the bootstrap sample set has mean 4.95 and standard deviation 1.49. The values are close but not exact due to the randomness of bootstrap sampling.

   We can apply bootstrap sampling to the recommender's offline fitting routine to build an ensemble of models. To create a single model for the ensemble, take a bootstrap sample from the logged sample set; then run a linear regression on the bootstrap sample to find the beta values. Repeat this process for each model you'd like to add to the ensemble.

Ensembles and ensemble learning

We call a set of models an ensemble, especially if the models are designed for a similar purpose.

One way to make use of an ensemble of models is to average their predictions together to make a single, better prediction. That's not what we're going to do here.

Instead, we'll be randomly choosing a prediction from the collection of predictions of the models in the ensemble.

I mention this here for disambiguation only.

All the models in the ensemble will have similar beta values and give similar outputs, but there will be some variation between them. This variation will give rise to exploration in the Thompson sampling policy. The policy will choose one model at random, then take the action that model predicts to have the highest reward (viewing time). The following listing shows the full recommender with bootstrap sampling and the Thompson sampling policy.

Listing 5.7 Thompson sampling recommender

```
class RecommenderThompsonSampling:
    def __init__(
        self, num_features, num_actions,
        num_bs_samples
    ):
        self._num_features = num_features
        self._num_actions = num_actions
        self._num_bs_samples = num_bs_samples

    def reset(self):
        self._betas = []
        for _ in range(self._num_actions):
            self._betas.append([
                np.random.normal(size=(num_features,))
                for _ in range(self._num_actions)
            ])

    def _bs_sample(self, samples_y, samples_x):
        bs_samples_y = []
        bs_samples_x = []
        for action in range(self._num_actions):
            y = np.array(samples_y[action])
            x = np.array(samples_x[action])
            if len(y)>0:
                i = np.random.randint(0, len(y), size=(len(y),))
                y = y[i]
                x = x[i,:]
            bs_samples_y.append(y)
            bs_samples_x.append(x)
        return bs_samples_y, bs_samples_x

    def fit_offline(self, logs):
        fit_logs = logs
```

Create num_bs_ samples beta vectors for each action.

```
    samples_y, samples_x = collect_logs_by_action(
        num_actions, fit_logs
    )
    self._betas = []
    for _ in range(self._num_bs_samples):          ◁─┐   Create an ensemble
        bs_samples_y, bs_samples_x = self._bs_sample(        of models.
            samples_y, samples_x
        )
        self._betas.append(build_models(
            self._num_features, bs_samples_y, bs_samples_x
        ))

def policy(self, context):
    i_beta = np.random.randint(0, len(self._betas))    Randomly choose one model
    beta = self._betas[i_beta]                         from the ensemble...
    viewing_max = -np.inf
    for action in range(self._num_actions):       ◁─┐  ...then choose the best
        viewing_hat = context @ beta[action]             action according to
        if viewing_hat > viewing_max:                     that model.
            action_best = action
            viewing_max = viewing_hat
    return i_post_best
```

RecommenderThompsonSampling modifies fit_offline() to build an ensemble of num_bs_samples models. Also, policy() now randomly selects a model from the ensemble from which to take predictions. Figure 5.10 compares the performance of RecommenderThompsonSampling to the other two recommenders, greedy and epsilon-greedy. RecommenderThompsonSampling clearly outperforms the other two.

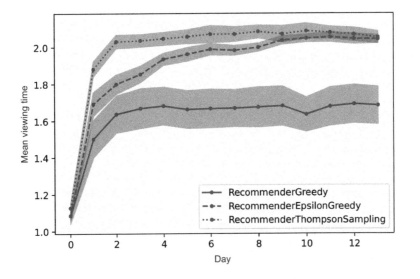

Figure 5.10 Thompson sampling achieves higher mean viewing time than the greedy or epsilon-greedy recommenders and does so sooner.

Thompson sampling not only outperforms epsilon-greedy on *this* problem but also outperforms it generally. Thompson sampling has proven-optimal regret (S. Agrawal, et al. "Thompson sampling for contextual bandits with linear payoffs," Proc. 30th ICML, 2013, pp. 127–135), whereas epsilon-greedy has suboptimal regret. In practice, bootstrap Thompson sampling is straightforward to implement, has excellent performance, and works with a wide variety of supervised learning (SL) methods. In this chapter, we used linear regression as the supervised learning method, but you could just as well use logistic regression, a deep neural network, or some other method.

In this section, we made the case that bootstrap sampling causes variation in the parameters of the models in the ensemble, and that variation, in turn, causes variation in the policy's choice of action. This approach produces a higher business metric than adding variation directly to the actions, as epsilon-greedy does. In the next section, we'll build some intuition for what makes Thompson sampling so effective in a contextual bandit problem.

5.3.2 Randomized probability matching

A Thompson sampling policy achieves higher viewing times (the business metric) than epsilon-greedy because its exploration method is more nuanced. Instead of always allocating 10% of its decisions to random, arbitrary exploration, it (1) biases decisions toward those more likely to improve viewing times, and (2) targets exploration toward decisions that will improve the models' predictions. It achieves both of these ends by making the probability of making a decision equal to the probability that the decision is best. This decision-making heuristic is called *randomized probability matching* (first discussed in chapter 3, section 3.3.2).

When the bootstrap Thompson sampling policy makes a decision, it first selects a model from the model ensemble completely at random, not preferring any one model over another. Then it displays the post that the selected model predicts will have the longest viewing time (figure 5.11).

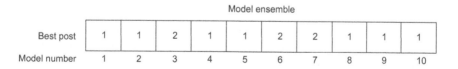

Figure 5.11 Each of 10 models in an ensemble predicts which post will result in the longest viewing time (i.e., recommending the post as the best one to display). Seven out of 10 models recommend post #1, and 3 out of 10 models recommend post #2.

Since each model in the ensemble was created in the same way (same sample set, same regression), each model is equally valid or equally "believable." Yet, the models may give different predictions about which post is best for the current user. Looking at figure 5.11, we see 7 models picked post #1 as best and 3 models picked post #2 as best. Since all the models are equally believable, we could interpret the disagreement probabilistically and say that the probability that post #1 is best is $7/10$, and the probability that post #2 is best is $3/10$. The probability a post (action, more generally) is best is proportional to the fraction of models in the ensemble that select it as best:

$$p_{\text{best}}(action) = \frac{(\text{number of models selecting action as best})}{(\text{total number of models in ensemble})}$$

Notice, also, that since a model is chosen at random from the ensemble by the policy, $7/10$ of the time the policy will decide to display post #1, and $3/10$ of the time to display post #2. In other words, the probability of taking an action, p(action), is equal to the probability that it is the best action:

$$p(action) = p_{best}(action)$$

This equality is the "probability matching" portion of the randomized probability matching heuristic. (*Randomized* just means that you draw a new model at random for each decision.) Thompson sampling is randomized probability matching applied to bandit (contextual or not) problems.

This heuristic says that if more models in the ensemble say a post is best, then that post is more likely to be displayed (exploitation). As a result, the system will be more likely to achieve higher viewing time. Nevertheless, the posts that are liked by fewer models will still get displayed sometimes (exploration). The heuristic, thus, balances exploration with exploitation.

Note that since users and posts are represented by features (e.g., user demographics, key words in a post), the model can generate a prediction of any user and any post—even ones that haven't been displayed before. The predictions won't necessarily be good (i.e., they might have high uncertainty, leading to disagreement across models in the ensemble). That disagreement drives exploration: some disagreeing models will predict a long viewing time, making a post more likely to be shown to a user. When that post is shown to that user, the actual viewing time will be measured and recorded in the log. The next time the models are refit, they will include that measurement, resulting in lower uncertainty about that same prediction (and about similar predictions, since the model will generalize to some extent). Less uncertainty in the predictions means less disagreement among the models, which means less exploration in the future.

Note that exploration depends upon disagreement *about a given context.* If there are many samples for User A (a frequent visitor), the sample set might show clearly that User A prefers gardening posts to posts about cooking. There's no need to explore User A further: just show them a gardening post. User B, however, might have generated fewer samples. Perhaps half the model ensemble suggests a gardening post and half suggests a cooking post. In this case the system will explore both options equally.

As time goes on, the system strategically collects samples to improve the model ensemble until disagreement disappears and exploration ceases. Let's rerun `RecommenderThompsonSampling` and monitor the disagreement between models in the ensemble. One way to do this is by plotting the average (over each day) of p_{best}(action) of the post the was displayed to the user (figure 5.12).

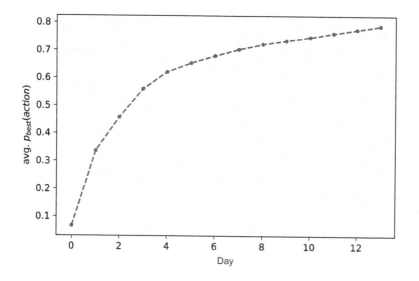

Figure 5.12   Average p_{best}(action) of the posts displayed to the user. Each day the Thompson sampling recommender becomes more certain of its decisions. As p_{best}(action) increases, exploration decreases.

At first, p_{best}(action) of the displayed posts are low. As the recommender progresses, p_{best}(action) increases. The models in the ensemble learn the preferences of the users and gradually come to a consensus about which post would be the best one to display to each user.

Bootstrap Thompson sampling applies the randomized probability matching heuristic to bandit problems. This heuristic balances the desire to make a decision that will achieve a good business metric (exploitation of the current models) with the desire to make a decision that will collect the samples needed to improve future models (exploration). Improved models lead to an even better future business metric. As always, an investment in experimentation in the short-term returns improved performance in the long-term.

5.4   Validate the contextual bandit

In chapters 2–4, we met experimental methods that could be used to optimize parameters of an engineered system. With A/B testing, for example, you could compare the performance of a system using two different values of a parameter. With multi-armed bandits, you could compare several values (each expressed as an "arm" of the MAB). With response surface methodology, you could optimize perhaps two to five continuous parameters simultaneously. A contextual bandit might seem like an amazing leap beyond these other methods because it can optimize thousands or even millions of parameters of the prediction model.

This amazing ability comes at a cost—complexity. A CB adds complexity to both the offline and online portions of the system:

- *Offline*—A CB requires you to fit a prediction model, or, in the case of bootstrap Thompson sampling (BTS), an ensemble of prediction models. You'll need to employ all your supervised learning skills here: feature engineering, feature selection, regularization, model selection, architecture design, and so on.
- *Online*—The policy will need to explore the space of decisions. For BTS, that will mean managing an ensemble of models—having them all "live" and ready to make a decision at any time. There will likely be other policy subcomponents that might interact with exploration, such as manually designed safety, business, or design constraints (whereby "manually designed" I mean code written to directly express domain knowledge or engineer preferences rather than code that is parameterized and optimized by experiment).

When you change any part of a complex system like this, it can be hard to tell what the effect will be. You should validate any changes to a CB system by running an A/B test to measure the effect of the change. Changes you might make while working with a contextual bandit include

- Switching from a manually designed policy to a prediction model-based policy
- Adding epsilon-greedy exploration
- Upgrading from epsilon-greedy to Thompson sampling
- Adding new features to the prediction model
- Adding or changing safety checks in a policy

It can take a new contextual bandit some time to "learn"—that is, to reach its maximal business metric. For example, see how in figure 5.10 it takes a few days for the average viewing time to rise to its maximum. Knowing that, you should discard the first few days from your A/B test. A fair comparison of the long-term performance of two CBs should compare them at "peak performance"—that is, after the performance has leveled off. How many days should you drop? That depends on your system. You'll need to monitor the performance over time to judge.

Summary

- You can experimentally optimize a very large number of parameters in a system where the business metric is a short-term reward.
- Exploration reduces model bias and breaks feedback loops that hamper performance improvement in contextual bandit systems.

- Epsilon-greedy exploration is simple and effective, but it requires the tuning of a metaparameter and achieves suboptimal regret.
- Bootstrap Thompson sampling has no metaparameter, achieves optimal regret, and may be used in conjunction with a broad range of supervised learning methods.
- Contextual bandits are complex, so changes to them should be validated with an A/B test.

Bayesian optimization: Automating experimental optimization

This chapter covers

- Combining ideas from RSM and MAB into one optimization method
- Automating response surface modeling with Gaussian process regression
- Automating experiment design by optimizing over an acquisition function

Before we begin, let's review:

- In chapter 2 (A/B testing), we talked about how to take a measurement of a business metric.
- In chapters 3 (multi-armed bandits) and 5 (contextual bandits), we saw that if you adapt your experiments based on uncertainty estimates, you can improve your business metric while your experiment is running. We said we were "balancing exploration with exploitation."
- In chapter 4 (response surface methodology), we showed how to use estimates of a business metric—a surrogate function—to reduce the number of measurements required to optimize parameters.

Bayesian optimization (BO) integrates all these ideas—taking measurements, building a surrogate, and balancing exploration with exploitation—into one optimization method that automatically designs a sequence of experiments that optimizes system parameters.

BO removes the subjectivity found in the RSM procedure. RSM designs are subjective because the choice of which parameter to measure is left to the engineer. RSM analysis is also subjective because the engineer chooses the form of the surrogate model. These manual steps can cause results to vary, depending on which engineer is executing the procedure. In addition, these steps take time. A better procedure (i.e., BO) executes the optimization procedure reliably (independent of the engineer) and quickly.

In this chapter, you will optimize the parameters of a source-code compiler. To get started, we'll walk through the entire procedure for a single parameter in a visual, intuitive way (section 6.1). Then we'll develop the components of the procedure in more detail: Gaussian process regression in section 6.2 and acquisition functions in section 6.3. Finally, section 6.4 will run a Bayesian optimization over all the compiler's parameters. We refer to the procedure as "automated" since the experiments are designed and analyzed by the Bayesian optimization algorithm without engineer intervention.

Bayesian optimization is a rich field with many applications, such as hyperparameter tuning of neural networks (http://mng.bz/gRzE). In this chapter, we'll explore an application to software engineering.

6.1   Optimizing a single compiler parameter, a visual explanation

Let's jump right in and apply Bayesian optimization to the problem of speeding up web server code compiled by a JIT (just-in-time) compiler. Your job is to make the resulting code execute as quickly as possible so that users don't get impatient and abandon the website while waiting for a page to load. To that end, we'll search for the JIT parameter values that minimize the CPU time it takes for the complied web server code to handle user requests (figure 6.1).

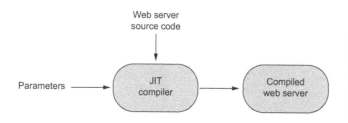

Figure 6.1   The JIT compiles web server source code. The speed (conversely, CPU time) of the compiled web server depends on the parameters used to configure the JIT.

The JIT compiler is configured with seven parameters. You'll use Bayesian optimization to find the parameter values that minimize the CPU time used by the compiled web server. The Bayesian optimizer will suggest a set of JIT parameters. You will configure the JIT with the suggested parameters, compile the web server code, then measure the CPU time used by the web server. The whole process will be repeated several times until you find the set of parameters that minimizes the CPU time.

The seven parameters control aspects of the JIT, such as how it lays out code in memory, how long it monitors the code (while executing in an uncompiled, interpreted way) before initiating the JIT compilation, and how aggressively it inlines (replaces a function call with a copy of function code). For presentation purposes, we'll simply represent the parameters as seven numbers, each between zero and one.

To find out how quickly the web server runs, you'll experimentally measure the CPU time offline by replaying user web requests that were logged by the production system. Since you'll use real requests and run the JIT and web server on the same hardware as is used in production, you'll get measurements of CPU time that faithfully reproduce their production values. Running such an experiment will take about an hour.

If you think this sounds like a problem to which we could apply RSM (chapter 4), you're right. The goal here is to optimize continuously valued parameters, just like we did with RSM. Unfortunately, RSM becomes cumbersome when optimizing more than three or four parameters, and this JIT has seven. Also, it can be difficult to define and fit the linear regression-based surrogate model of CPU time versus parameters when there are so many parameters. Finally, we like to visualize the surrogate function when manually designing the next iteration's experiment. Such visualization is difficult in dimensions greater than two or three. Bayesian optimization is not only capable of optimizing a system with seven parameters, but it also automates the entire procedure.

To get a feel for how Bayesian optimization works, let's walk through the optimization of a single JIT parameter. To build intuition, we'll visualize and discuss each step in this section, then in section 6.2 we'll delve into the details. The full procedure is depicted in figure 6.2.

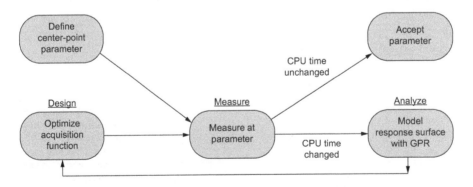

Figure 6.2 Bayesian optimization. After initialization at the center point, BO iterates through design, run, and analyze stages until the measured business metric stops changing. What makes BO so powerful is that the analyze and design stages are automated, freeing the engineer to devote more of their time to generating and implementing new ideas rather than to optimizing parameters.

The lower half of figure 6.2 shows the main loop: design, measure, analyze. To kickstart the process (upper-left bubble), we take a measurement at the center of the parameters' ranges. Since each parameter takes values in [0,1], each center value is at 0.5. This measurement will be used by the analyze stage to build the first surrogate model using something called Gaussian process regression (GPR; details in section 6.2).

The design stage runs a numerical optimization that seeks the parameter value that maximizes the acquisition function. This function determines how BO balances exploration and exploitation when designing an experiment (details in section 6.3).

On each iteration through the loop, the design stage chooses which parameter value to measure in the next measure stage. After some number of iterations, the measured CPU time stops changing. At that point, we say that BO has converged to an answer, the optimal parameter setting, and the process is complete. To get started, we'll build a Python simulation of the JIT + web server combination.

6.1.1 Simulate the compiler

As we've done in each of the chapters so far, we'll build a simulator (a Python function) of the system we're experimenting on. In this case, we'll simulate the offline CPU time measurement. The measurement works like this: You configure the JIT with a given set of parameters. Next, you compile the web server code. Then you send a battery of user requests to the web server, where the user requests are taken from production logs. Using the logs allows you to run this process offline and to repeat it for different parameter values.

The function simulating the entire process—the JIT plus the server running over the logs—takes a set of parameters as input and returns a single number, the average CPU time. The simulator is shown in the following listing.

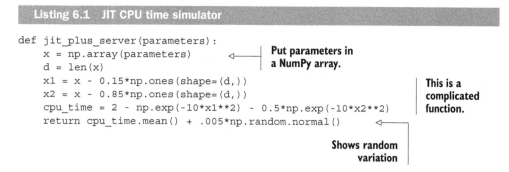

Listing 6.1 JIT CPU time simulator

```
def jit_plus_server(parameters):
    x = np.array(parameters)            ⟵   Put parameters in
    d = len(x)                               a NumPy array.
    x1 = x - 0.15*np.ones(shape=(d,))                    This is a
    x2 = x - 0.85*np.ones(shape=(d,))                    complicated
    cpu_time = 2 - np.exp(-10*x1**2) - 0.5*np.exp(-10*x2**2)   function.
    return cpu_time.mean() + .005*np.random.normal()   ⟵

                                         Shows random
                                         variation
```

The variable `cpu_time` is a complicated function of parameter values. Also, due to the presence of other processes (e.g., the operating system) running on the web server, fluctuations in caching, and possibly other factors, the CPU time may vary a bit from measurement to measurement. This variation is simulated in listing 6.1 by a random number.

As usual, we won't use any information about the simulator's internal workings when running our experiments. We'll just supply parameter values to it and accept the returned measurements. Let's get started and run the first experiment.

> **Black box optimization**
>
> Bayesian optimization is what is called a *black box optimizer*. This term refers to optimization algorithms that seek global optima of measurements of systems whose internal dynamics are unknown (or, at least, are not important). The term *black box* is meant to evoke the image of an object inside of which you cannot look. Thus, you cannot reason about its inner workings.
>
> A JIT compiler with many parameters may be treated as a black box, as all of the systems we have considered in this book may be, except perhaps the social media app of chapter 5, to which we applied the contextual bandit. In that case we understood that the policy took an action (to show a certain post) based on a known context (features representing the user and the post) and received a short-term reward as a direct result of the action taken. This extra information about the step-by-step workings of the system enabled us to optimize many (up to millions) parameters by combining offline supervised learning with online exploration.
>
> The JIT compiler is very different. All we know are the parameter values and the corresponding measurement (CPU times). We don't have a notion of actions or contexts or rewards to aid the optimization process.
>
> Note that A/B testing, RSM, and multi-armed bandits, while they can be applied to optimize black box systems, are generally not considered optimizers because they are not automated like Bayesian optimization is.

6.1.2   *Run the initial experiment*

Bayesian optimization will model the response surface from measurements of the CPU time. Then, based on the model, it prescribes a parameter value at which to take the next measurement. But what should you do when you start out and have no measurements? Without a measurement, BO can't build a model, and without a model, it can't prescribe a parameter value.

The answer is to just measure the CPU time at any parameter value you like. We'll start at the center parameter value. Each of the parameters lies in [0,1], so we'll measure at 0.5 (the center). For ease of presentation, in this section we'll just pretend the JIT has only one parameter. This will make it easier to visualize the BO procedure. In section 6.4, we'll optimize all seven parameters. Simulating the first measurement is straightforward:

```
np.random.seed(17)
jit_plus_server([0.5])
```

which produces a CPU time of

```
1.5607447789648075
```

(Note that we seed the random number generator, as usual, for reproducibility.) Now that we've completed the initialization experiment, let's move on to analyze it and design the second experiment.

6.1.3   *Analyze: Model the response surface*

To design an experiment, BO first builds a surrogate, a model of the response surface, the function CPU time versus parameter; then it searches for a "good" parameter value to measure next. We'll defer the definition of *good* until section 6.1.4. Here we'll focus on the response surface model.

Building a model from only one measurement seems like a lot to ask, but let's give it a try. First off, we know that (1) the parameter takes a value in [0,1], and (2) the CPU time is 1.56 when the parameter is 0.5. We can eke out a little more of a model by assuming that (3) our uncertainty in the value of the CPU time is smallest (let's just say 0) where we measured, at parameter 0.5, (4) increases to its largest value (let's call it 1) when the parameter is farthest from 0.5 (i.e., at 0 and 1), and (5) both CPU time and its uncertainty vary continuously (more on that in a minute) with the parameter.

That's actually quite a bit of information to work with—even though we only have a single measurement. Figure 6.3 combines all of these points into a sketch of the response surface.

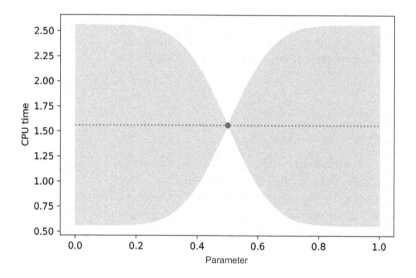

Figure 6.3   **A surrogate model coaxed from a single measurement. The measurement (black dot) is at parameter = 0.5, CPU time = 1.56. The uncertainty in CPU time, depicted by the gray areas, is 0 at the point of the measurement and one at the left and right edges.**

Since we know nothing more about CPU time than its value at `parameter = 0.5`, we can just assume it's constant across the parameter range. The assumption of continuity (point 4) means that we draw the dashed line and the boundaries of the gray area without any breaks or kinks.

Please take a careful look at the estimated response surface in figure 6.3. If it were your job to choose which point to measure next, which would you choose? That question is worth pondering for a bit before moving on to the next section, where we'll discuss how Bayesian optimization answers it.

6.1.4   Design: Select the parameter value to measure next

We've taken the initialization measurement at the central parameter value and modeled the response surface based on it. The next step is to use the information in that model to decide which parameter value should be measured next. Making that decision is what it means to design the next experiment.

One consideration that goes into that decision is what measurement would give us the most information about the shape of the response surface. Put another way, we should measure the parameter that would most reduce the uncertainty in our model. Thus, the right parameter value is the one where uncertainty is highest.

Because the surrogate function in figure 6.3 is symmetric about the center point, there are two parameter values where the uncertainty is maximized: 0 and 1 (i.e., the left and right edges). We could measure either. I'll arbitrarily choose the left edge, `parameter = 0`.

That's it. We just designed the next experiment by saying, "Measure `parameter = 0` since that's where the uncertainty in the model is maximized."

Running that experiment (that measurement) yields:

```
np.random.seed(17)
parameter = 0
cpu_time = jit_plus_server([parameter])
print (cpu_time)
1.2025010344211848
```

The CPU time of `parameter = 0` is `1.20`. We can estimate the response surface from the first two measurements, as shown in figure 6.4.

At this point we've completed most steps of the BO procedure, originally presented in figure 6.2 and shown again in figure 6.5, for reference.

The steps we've taken so far are

- Define an initial parameter value to measure, the center-point value.
- Run an experiment to measure its CPU time.
- Analyze the result by building a response surface model from one measurement.
- Design the second experiment based on that model.
- Run the second experiment, measuring CPU time at the second parameter.
- Analyze the second result by building a response surface model from two measurements.

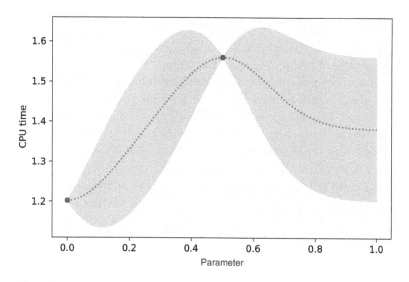

Figure 6.4   Response surface model based on two measurements. The uncertainty (gray area) in the estimate of CPU time is small at the measurement parameters (black dots). The CPU time (dashed line) varies smoothly across the parameter range and intersects the measured values.

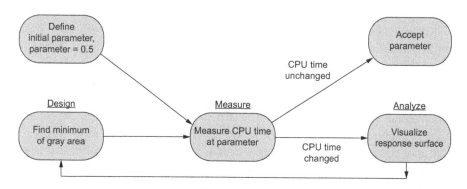

Figure 6.5   Bayesian optimization, as applied to JIT configuration in this section

We're going to design the next experiment, run it, analyze it, and keep repeating until the response surface model stops changing. Since our experiment design is based on the response surface model, our design will also stop changing from iteration to iteration. When that happens, we're done. The system is optimized.

There's one more point to discuss before we move on, though. The design of the third experiment is a little different from the design of the second. We'll talk about that next, in section 6.1.5. The good news is that every design afterward follows the same pattern as the third.

6.1.5   *Design: Balance exploration with exploitation*

When designing the second experiment, our goal was to improve the surrogate function, the model of the response surface, since, with only one measurement as its basis, it was a pretty poor model. We could continue to design experiments with this goal and always choose to measure the parameter where the model had the largest uncertainty. This would be a good strategy for building a high-quality surrogate. In fact, if we took that approach, once we were satisfied with the quality of the model, we could stop experimenting and ask, "At which JIT parameter value would the web server achieve the lowest CPU time?" We'd read the answer right off the plot of the surrogate (i.e., we'd look for where the dashed line had a minimum).

This approach is reminiscent of A/B testing in that we first collect all the measurements we need to be confident that we can make a good decision about how to configure the system; then we run the system with that configuration. In A/B testing we run a long experiment to determine whether version A or B is better; then we run the system with the better version. The way we just described Bayesian optimization, we'd repeatedly design and run experiments to produce a high-quality surrogate function, then run the system with the parameter value that would minimize CPU time.

When we discussed the multi-armed bandit (MAB) in chapter 4, we looked for ways to achieve a better business metric *while running the experiment.* The MAB does this by taking more measurements of the version (A or B) that it expects will give better performance. As its confidence in its measurements grows, it spends more and more time running the better version and less and less time on the worse version. We said that the MAB was balancing exploration (measuring the worse version to verify that it's genuinely worse) with exploitation—measuring the better version to capitalize on its higher business metric.

We can borrow this idea from MAB to improve the design of experiments in Bayesian optimization. When we chose the parameter that maximized the uncertainty of the model we were exploring, we were aiming to increase our confidence in the model. The "exploitation" of the model comes at the end, when we look for the parameter value that minimizes CPU time. Instead of separating these phases—first exploring, then exploiting—let's combine them into a single decision made during each experiment design at each iteration. Examine figure 6.6.

Given the model in figure 6.6, we could imagine designing an experiment purely to explore, as we did for the second experiment, or purely to exploit, as we expect to do when the optimization process is complete. Alternatively, we could balance these two competing objectives by looking for a parameter value that provides a "pretty good" CPU time and a "pretty uncertain" model estimate. In terms of the preceding plot, we want the dashed line to be low and the gray area to be large. A heuristic approach is to find the minimum of "CPU time minus model uncertainty." Graphically, that's the lowest point of the lower boundary of the gray area in figure 6.6. See figure 6.7.

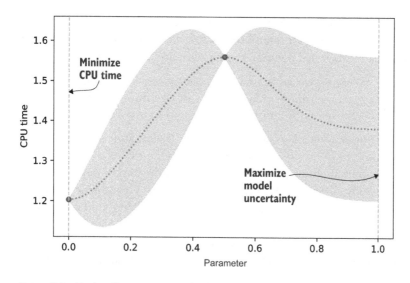

Figure 6.6 Exploration versus exploitation. To create a purely exploratory design, we would choose `parameter = 1.0`, **which maximizes model uncertainty. To create a purely exploitative design, we would choose** `parameter = 0.0`, **which minimizes CPU time.**

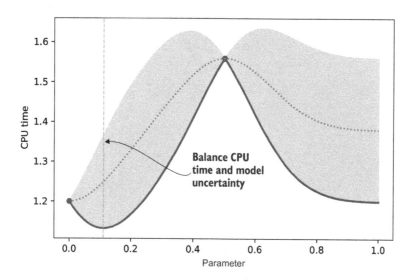

Figure 6.7 The parameter value around `0.11` **balances exploration (maximizing model uncertainty) with exploitation (minimizing CPU time)**

The lower boundary of the gray area is traced with a thick line in figure 6.7. Its minimum is around `parameter = 0.11`. This would be a good parameter value to measure next.

Notice that to design an experiment, we optimized over either the model uncertainty (previous section) or the CPU time—model uncertainty (this section). In Bayesian optimization, the function you optimize to design the next experiment is called an *acquisition function.* There are many forms for this function. They are all heuristics intended to strike a balance between exploration and exploitation.

DEFINITION   We optimize an *acquisition function* over the parameter values to design the next experiment. Many forms of this function have been proposed. Each balances exploration with exploitation in a slightly different way.

The practical implication of using one of these "balancing" acquisition functions is that we'll be more likely to run experiments that use less CPU time during the process of finding the optimal parameters. This means that the experiment will end sooner.

More generally, if we use Bayesian optimization in production, we'll achieve a higher business metric while running the experiment. That could mean you see more revenue, more clicks, or a better user experience while optimizing your system.

Continuing with our visual Bayesian optimization procedure, we'll keep picking the parameter that marks the lowest point of the gray area and run a few more experiments (figure 6.8).

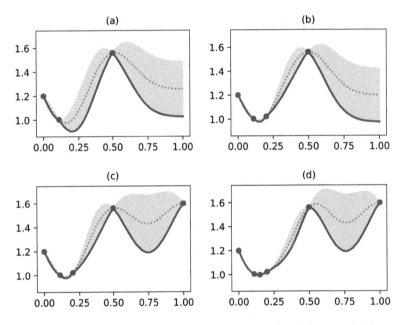

Figure 6.8   Four more iterations of a Bayesian optimization. In frames (a)–(d) we run four more iterations of the optimization. By frame (d), the parameter value (black dots) has stopped changing.

Figure 6.8 shows the surrogate after four more iterations. Notice how the parameter that minimizes the gray region settles down to a value around 0.15. We say that the optimization has converged at this point. We can stop designing new experiments and just keep the parameter set to 0.15, its optimal value.

We just took a short, visual tour of Bayesian optimization. We found the parameter of a JIT compiler that minimized the CPU time taken by a JIT-compiled web server using an intuitive visualization of Bayesian optimization.

In the next section, we'll look at Gaussian process regression, the procedure used to model the response surface. After that we'll examine acquisition functions in detail and write a simple routine to optimize them. Once that's complete, we'll have all the knowledge and code needed to run a Bayesian optimization completely automatically.

6.2 Model the response surface with Gaussian process regression

Our task in this section is to write the code that produced the response surface visualizations in section 6.1 (see, for example, figure 6.8). We'll write Gaussian process regression (GPR) code to both estimate the expected CPU time for a given parameter value and to report the uncertainty in that estimate. Then we'll query the GPR code at many values of the parameter to produce a visualization like in figure 6.9.

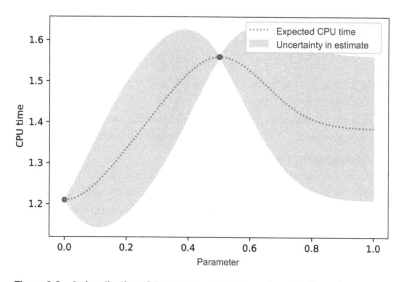

Figure 6.9 A visualization of the response surface produced by Gaussian process regression based on two measurements (black dots) at `parameter = 0.5` **and** `parameter = 0.0`

The CPU time estimates are visualized by the dashed line, and the reported uncertainty is the height of the gray area. Let's start by reproducing the dashed line in section 6.2.1; then we'll work on the gray area in section 6.2.2.

6.2.1 Estimate the expected CPU time

Let's say we've just completed the first two measurements of CPU time. Recall their values were 1.56, at parameter = 0.5, and 1.21 at parameter = 0.0. Now we want to create a function that will estimate CPU time at parameter values other than 0.0 and 0.5—at any value in the interval from 0.0 to 1.0. The function will take a parameter value as input and return a CPU time estimate. Let's start with a simple function and then refine it.

TAKE AN AVERAGE OF ALL MEASUREMENTS

The simplest way to generate an estimate of CPU time is just take the average (the mean) of the measurements taken so far: mean CPU time = (1.54 +1.21)/2 = 1.375. Let's start there; see the following listing.

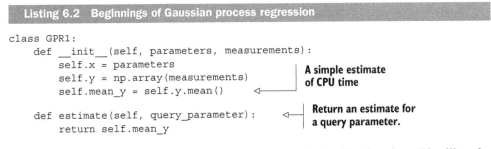

Listing 6.2 Beginnings of Gaussian process regression

```
class GPR1:
    def __init__(self, parameters, measurements):
        self.x = parameters
        self.y = np.array(measurements)          A simple estimate
        self.mean_y = self.y.mean()              of CPU time

    def estimate(self, query_parameter):         Return an estimate for
        return self.mean_y                       a query parameter.
```

We'll name the parameters and measurements x and y inside the class. That'll make the code a little cleaner in the long run.

In listing 6.2, the method estimate() returns self.mean_y for any value of the argument query_parameter. This is simple and reasonable, but we can do better.

WEIGHT NEARER MEASUREMENTS MORE

We can improve the estimates a bit with the intuition that if two parameters are closer to each other, then their CPU time measurements should be more similar. That would mean that if we wanted to estimate CPU time at, say, parameter = 0.4, we should form an estimate that's more similar to the measurement at parameter = 0.5 (i.e., CPU time = 1.56) than to the one as parameter = 0.0 (CPU time = 1.21).

One way to express that intuition is through a weighted average. In the preceding estimate, we used a simple average, which we could write as .5 × 1.54 + .5 × 1.21 = 1.365. A weighted average would replace the .5's with different numbers, which we call *weights*. The larger the weight, the more similar the estimate will be to the measurement. Forming an estimate for parameter = 0.4, we might use .8 × 1.54 + .2 × 1.21 = 1.458, which places more weight on the measurement at parameter = 0.5, the one nearer to parameter = 0.4.

Notice, by the way, that the weights add up to 1. In the first case, .5 + .5 = 1, and in the second case .8 + .2 = 1. This ensures that the resulting estimate has the correct scale. Imagine if we let the weights add up to 100 (to be extreme, to make the point): 50 + 50 = 100, then the estimate would be 100 times too large: 50 × 1.56 + 50 × 1.21 = 136.5.

In NumPy, we'd write the estimate as a weighted average like `weights @ y` and specify each weight as a function of the distance from the measured parameters (x) to the query parameter. A typical measure of distance between numbers is the absolute difference: `np.abs(x - parameter)`. We want the weight to decrease as this distance increases. There are many functions we could concoct that would do that, but the one typically used in GPR is

```
weight = np.exp(-np.abs(x-parameter)**2)=np.exp(-(x-parameter)**2)
```

This weight function is displayed in figure 6.10.

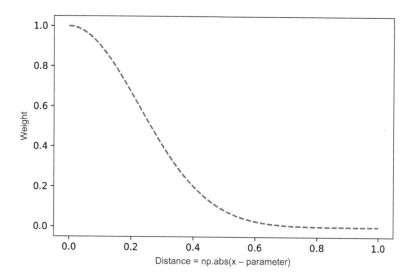

Figure 6.10   **The weight on a measurement decreases with the distance to the measurement.**

This function is called a *squared exponential kernel.* Other shapes—other kernel functions—may be used, but this one is the most common.

> **DEFINITION**   The kernel function tells how much to weight a measurement, as a function of distance to that measurement.

There's one more thing to mention about this kernel function. To use it well, you need to answer the question, "How far is far?" If two parameters differ by `0.1`, is that far? Maybe they need to differ by 100 to be far away. In our problem, the parameter only varies from `0` to `1`, but the kernel function doesn't "know" that. The way to deal with this is to divide the distance by a length scale, called `sigma`:

```
weight = np.exp(-((x - parameter)/(2*sigma))**2 )
```

Also, there's a `2` in there, by convention. The best choice of `sigma` can be determined from the measurements being modeled (see sidebar), but we'll just leave it as an argument to the class GPR for now.

Selecting the hyperparameter sigma

The argument to the class GPR, `sigma`, is a hyperparameter that controls how smooth the GPR surrogate function is. Larger `sigma` values yield smoother surfaces.

One way to select the best value for `sigma`, given a set of measurements, is leave-one-out cross validation (LOOCV). We won't cover this technique in depth, but suffice to say the procedure seeks the value of `sigma` that maximizes the accuracy of a prediction of each measured value when the prediction is derived from all *other* measurements.

The following listing shows GPR with the kernel-function-based weights.

Listing 6.3   GPR with a weighted average

```
class GPR2:
    def __init__(self, parameters, measurements, sigma):
        self.x = parameters
        self.y = np.array(measurements)
        self.sigma = sigma

        self.mean_y = self.y.mean()
        self.y -= self.mean_y

    def kernel(self, x1, x2):
        distance_squared = ((x1-x2)**2).sum()
        return np.exp( -distance_squared/(2*self.sigma**2) )

    def estimate(self, query_parameter):
        weights = [
            self.kernel(x, query_parameter)
            for x in self.x
        ]
        weights = np.array(weights)
        weights = weights / weights.sum()
        return self.mean_y + weights @ self.y
```

Remove average, model residuals.

Shows the squared exponential kernel function

There's one weight for each measurement.

Weights must sum to 1.

Combine mean and weighted residuals.

Listing 6.3 implements the weighted average we just discussed. The first thing we do is subtract the average (the mean) of all measurements (`self.y -= self.mean_y`). Since we decided in the previous section that the mean was a good start for a model, we just have to worry about modeling the residuals. Residuals are the parts of the data that a model doesn't explain, roughly "measurements minus estimates." We'll apply the weighting just to the residuals from the mean.

The weights are proportional to the kernel function. Notice that we divided weights by their sum, ensuring that they sum to 1. We can try it out with the sample measurements at 0.5 and 0.0:

```
parameters = [0.5, 0.0]
measurements = [1.52, 1.21]
gpr = GPR(parameters, measurements, sigma=0.25)
print (gpr.estimate(0.25))
print (gpr.estimate(0.4))
```

This yields

```
1.365
1.448
```

The first value matches the simple-average value just calculated because 0.25 is exactly halfway between 0.0 and 0.5, so the two weights are equal. The second value differs slightly from the value estimated above (1.458) because the weights used in the calculation in the text (0.8 and 0.2) were chosen by hand to make the presentation clear. The weights computed by GPR in listing 6.3 are 0.77 and 0.23.

To form estimates, GPR takes a weighted average of measurements and uses a kernel function for the weights. This is the core of GPR's approach to modeling, but there is one more point to make before we have the complete picture of GPR.

DON'T OVERWEIGHT CLUSTERED MEASUREMENTS

Since we know (or, more accurately, *require*) that neighboring measurements have similar values, it must be that taking a second measurement very near an existing measurement doesn't improve the quality of the estimates very much. To see what that means and why it matters, suppose we took a third measurement at parameter = 0.4, then tried to use all three measurements (at parameters 0.5, 0.0, and 0.4) to estimate CPU time at parameter = 0.25.

The simplest model would say to just average all three measurements together. The weighted-average model would weight the measurement at 0.4 a little more than the other two measurements because 0.4 is nearest to 0.25, like the triangle in figure 6.11.

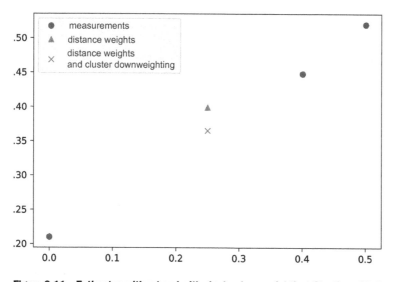

Figure 6.11 Estimates without and with cluster downweighting. Starting with the measurements (filled dots), we form an estimate (triangle) using GPR from listing 6.3, where a measurement's weight is based only on its distance to the estimate. A second estimate (x) reduces the weight of the two measurements on the right (at 0.4 and 0.5) since they are close to each other (clustered).

Our engineer's preference for simplicity (or Occam's razor, if you like) would put the estimate on a line passing through all three measurements. The triangle-marked estimate is above that line because the two measurements at parameters 0.4 and 0.5 have high CPU times, and each measurement is given the same weight by GPR in listing 6.3. We can compensate for clustering of measurements by reducing the weight on—call it "downweighting"—any measurement that has other measurements nearby.

In concrete terms, we'll downweight using the same kernel function that we used to downweight by distance, with two differences: (1) We'll apply it to the distance between pairs of measurements instead of the distance from a measurement to an estimate, and (2) we'll use it in the denominator since we want to *lower* the weight when measurements are nearer to each other. The whole procedure is shown in the following listing.

Listing 6.4   Full Gaussian process regression

```python
class GPR3:
    def __init__(self, parameters, measurements, sigma):
        self.x = parameters
        self.y = np.array(measurements)
        self.sigma = sigma

        self.mean_y = self.y.mean()
        self.y -= self.mean_y

    def kernel(self, x1, x2):
        distance_squared = ((x1-x2)**2).sum()
        return np.exp( -distance_squared/(2*self.sigma**2) )

    def estimate(self, query_parameter):
        kernels_x_query = np.array([          # kernels_x_query is a vector.
            self.kernel(x, query_parameter)
            for x in self.x
        ])
        kernels_x_x = np.array([              # kernels_x_x is a matrix.
            [
                self.kernel(x1, x2)
                for x1 in self.x
            ]
            for x2 in self.x
        ])
                                              # weights increases with
                                              # kernels_x_query and
                                              # decreases with kernels_x_x.
        weights = kernels_x_query.T @ np.linalg.inv(kernels_x_x)
        return self.mean_y + weights @ self.y
```

In listing 6.4, we moved the previous expression for weights to kernels_x_query. Recall that this term gives higher weight to measurements that are nearer to the estimate. A new expression, named kernels_x_x, appears in the "denominator" (okay, it's actually a matrix inverse, but let's wave our hands for a moment) of the weights and causes a weight on a measurement to decrease if the measurement has other measurements nearby. This is the cluster downweighting term. It serves a second purpose, too, in that it lets us skip the step of dividing by the sum of the weights.

Note, also, that since we need to compare all pairs of measurements, `kernels_x_x` is a matrix. Compare this to `kernels_x_query`, which is a vector because in it we compare each measurement to just a single number, `query_parameter`.

If you think of the `weights` elements as the relevance of each measurement, y, then you could say `weights @ self.y` is the relevance-adjusted estimate of CPU time at the query parameter.

At long last, we can reproduce the estimates (the dashed line) in the visualizations of the previous section. For example, to re-create figure 6.4, we do the following:

```
parameters = [0.5, 0.0]
measurements = [1.52, 1.21]
gpr3 = GPR3(parameters, measurements, sigma=.15)
x_hats = np.linspace(0,1,100)
y_hats = [gpr3.estimate(x_hat) for x_hat in x_hats]
```

Figure 6.12 shows the CPU time estimates, y_hats versus a range of parameter values, x_hats.

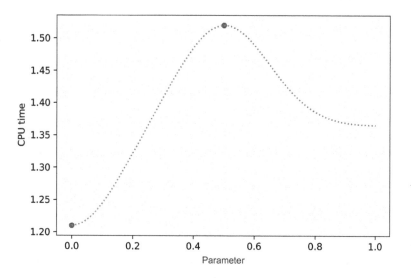

Figure 6.12   The CPU time estimates (dashed line) created with GPR3 from listing 6.4 using the measurements at parameters `0.5` **and** `0.0` **(black dots) as input**

The dashed line in figure 6.12 is the response surface, as estimated by GPR3. Other examples of GPR estimates are shown in figure 6.13 to give you a feel for how GPR3 estimates business metrics. As you look them over, keep in mind that the only input to GPR3 is the measurements (black dots) and the output is the entire dashed curve.

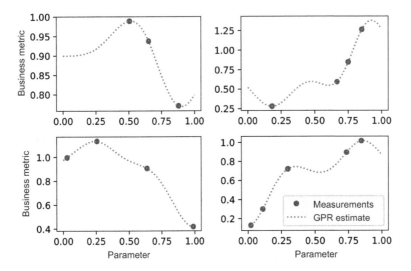

Figure 6.13   GPR estimates of various other business metric functions created with GPR3

COMPARE TO RSM

GPR differs from linear regression, used in RSM (chapter 4, section 4.1.3), in a couple important ways:

1   Linear regression requires the engineer to specify which terms to include in the model. GPR has a hyperparameter, `sigma`, instead.
2   Linear regression has a fitting step, where the beta values are determined. Once the betas are known, you may use the model to estimate the response surface. GPR estimates directly from data without a fitting step.

Point 1 removes the manual effort of selecting terms. A procedure (LOOCV, see earlier sidebar) for finding `sigma`, by contrast, may be simply and reliably automated. Point 2 may make GPR run more slowly, as estimating directly from data (rather than from a fitted, linear model) requires more computation. But the burden of this computation is generally dwarfed by the time taken to run an experiment that measures your business metric.

REVIEW

An estimate of a business metric (e.g., the CPU time), from measured values, consists of three parts:

- The mean of all measurements plus a relevance-weighted sum of measurement residuals, where relevance decreases with distance to a measurement
- The relevance decreases with clustering of measurements.

In the next section, we'll see how to get our GPR class to report how uncertain it is in its estimates of CPU time.

6.2.2   *Estimate uncertainty with GPR*

In the overview in section 6.1, we used both the expectation and the uncertainty of the surrogate to design an experiment when we looked for the lowest point of the gray area. In the previous section (6.2.1), we learned to model the expectation (i.e., to estimate the CPU time). Now we'll estimate the model uncertainty.

Before we begin, I want to distinguish between measurement uncertainty—that is, the standard error (as defined in chapter 2, section 2.2.1), and GPR's model uncertainty. Measurement uncertainty is a variation in the value of repeated measurements (e.g., many individual measurements of CPU time at the same parameter value). GPR estimates are uncertain because they are made at parameters where we haven't taken a measurement.

From that simple description—estimates are uncertain at parameters where we haven't taken a measurement—we can derive two features of GPR uncertainty: (1) It's zero at a measured parameter, and (2) it's maximized far from all measurements. If we, for a moment, think in terms of *certainty* instead of uncertainty, then these conditions might suggest a familiar functional form: Certainty is maximized at a measured parameter, and zero is far from all measurements. This is what the squared exponential kernel looks like (figure 6.14).

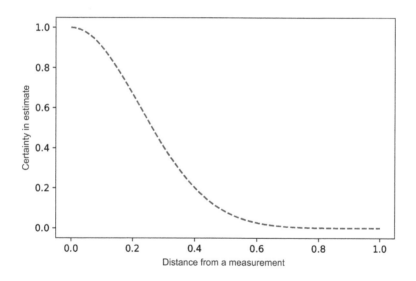

Figure 6.14   Certainty in a GPR estimate is maximized at a measured parameter and tends to zero as we move farther from a measurement.

Figure 6.14 makes the maximum certainty 1.0, which is as good a value as any. The model uncertainty is only a relative measure. We can ask it, "How much more certain are you of this estimate than of that estimate?" but we can't compare model uncertainty from one GPR regression to another. This is in contrast to standard error—that is, measurement uncertainty. Standard error has the same units (dimensions) as the measurement, and so you can compare SE from one experiment to SE from another.

Since model uncertainty is based on the same measurements as the estimates are, it is subject to the same considerations of "relevance" as the estimates were in the previous section. Namely, nearer measurements are more relevant, and clustered measurements are less relevant. We can express certainty as a weighted average and use the same weights as we used in listing 6.4:

```
weights = kernels_x_query.T @ np.linalg.inv(kernels_x_x).
```

For technical reasons (since variances add but standard deviations don't; see appendix C), we prefer to write an expression for squared certainty rather than certainty. We'll model the squared certainty associated with a single measurement by the kernel function, specifically, kernels_x_query. Then we'll combine the certainties contributed by each measurement using a relevance-weighted average:

```
certainty_squared = weights @ kernels_x_query
```

One more thing: we were looking to model *uncertainty*, not certainty. To do that, just write

```
uncertainty_squared = 1 - certainty_squared
```

or

```
uncertainty_squared = 1 - weights @ kernels_x_query
```

Since the maximal certainty is 1.0 (right on top of a measurement), the maximal squared certainty is also 1.0 (because $1.0^2 = 1.0$). The leading "1 -" in the equation transforms a maximal squared certainty of 1 into a minimal squared uncertainty of 0.

Finally, while the model uncertainty is only a relative measure, it is conventional to report the uncertainty on a scale that matches the overall scale of the residuals of the measurements. This rescaling will make it easier to construct a generic acquisition function (section 6.3) that works across business metrics of varying scales. The full GPR class, which reports estimated CPU time and estimated model uncertainty, is in the following listing.

Listing 6.5   Complete Gaussian process regression

```
class GPR4:
    def __init__(self, parameters, measurements, sigma):
        self.x = parameters
        self.y = np.array(measurements)
        self.sigma = sigma
```

```
    self.mean_y = self.y.mean()
    if len(self.y) > 1:
        self.std_y = self.y.std()
    else:
        self.std_y = 1

    self.y -= self.mean_y

def kernel(self, x1, x2):
    distance_squared = ((x1-x2)**2).sum()
    return np.exp( -distance_squared/(2*self.sigma**2) )

def estimate(self, query_parameter):
    kernels_x_query = np.array([
        self.kernel(x, query_parameter)
        for x in self.x
    ])
    kernels_x_x = np.array([
        [
            self.kernel(x1, x2)
            for x1 in self.x
        ]
        for x2 in self.x
    ])

    weights = kernels_x_query.T @ np.linalg.inv(kernels_x_x)
    expectation = self.mean_y + self.std_y*weights @ self.y
    uncertainty_squared = 1 - weights @ kernels_x_query
    uncertainty = np.sqrt(uncertainty_squared)

    return expectation, self.std_y*uncertainty
```

Need at least 2 y's to compute std dev.

Shows relevance-weighted squared uncertainty

We want uncertainty, not squared uncertainty.

Scale uncertainty to match measurements.

The standard deviation of the measurements (the y's) is stored in the class constructor for use later, in the return line of the `estimate()` method. That line rescales the uncertainty to match the scale of the measurements. Note also that `estimate()` returns uncertainty rather than its square.

You can re-create the visualization of the response surface, complete with uncertainty estimates, using

```
parameters = [0.5, 0.0]
measurements = [1.52, 1.21]
gpr4 = GPR4(parameters, measurements, sigma=.15)
x_hats = np.linspace(0,1,100)
y_hats, sigma_y_hats = zip(*[gpr4.estimate(x_hat) for x_hat in x_hats])
```

The variable `sigma_y_hats` holds the uncertainty estimates. Figure 6.15 plots `y_hats` versus `x_hats` with a dashed line and shows `sigma_y_hats` with a gray area. To further develop an intuition for GPR, please see some examples of GPR4 in action in figure 6.16.

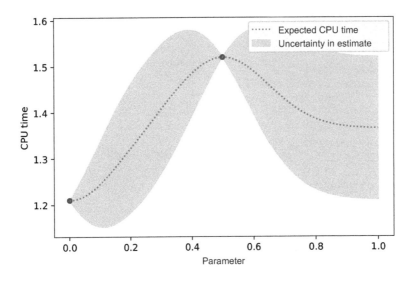

Figure 6.15   The estimates of expectation and uncertainty produced by GPR4 from listing 6.5

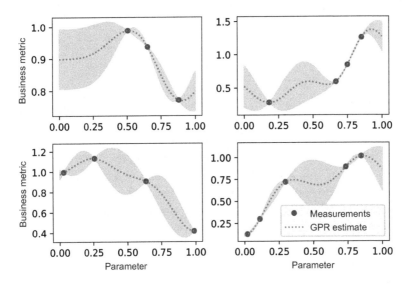

Figure 6.16   Four independent examples of GPR4 regressions. The measurements (black dots) in each panel are the input to GPR4.

The uncertainty in the CPU time estimates produced by a GPR regression

- Is distinct from measurement uncertainty (standard error)
- Is a relative measure of uncertainty
- Increases with distance from a measurement, and increases with clustering of measurements

We'll see in section 6.3 how the GPR output is used with the acquisition function to design an experiment.

6.3   Optimize over an acquisition function

Section 6.2 showed us how to create a surrogate function from measurements of CPU time at different parameter values. The next step in Bayesian optimization is to design an experiment by finding the parameter value that corresponds to the lowest point of the gray area, as in figure 6.17.

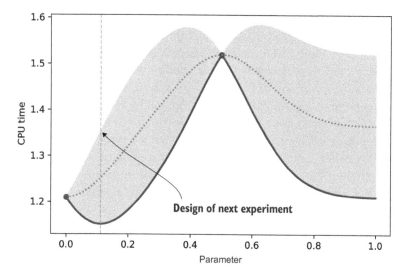

Figure 6.17   Design an experiment—that is, decide which parameter to measure next. The parameter minimizes the lower boundary of the gray area.

The minimum of the gray area is determined by both the expectation (the dashed line) and the model uncertainty (the height of the gray area). The lower black curve in figure 6.17 is expectation minus uncertainty, as returned by GPR4, from section 6.2.2.

The lower black curve is the acquisition function. Let's look a little more closely at it in the next section, then move on to minimize it.

6.3.1   Minimize the acquisition function

In Bayesian optimization parlance, "expectation minus uncertainty" is a specific acquisition function called the *lower confidence bound* (LCB). The function is given some flexibility by adding a parameter, k, like this: LCB = expectation – k × uncertainty.

In concrete terms, we could compute LCB, the lower black curve in figure 6.17, with

```
parameters = [0.5, 0.0]
measurements = [1.52, 1.21]
gpr4 = GPR4(parameters, measurements, sigma=.15)
x_hats = np.linspace(0,1,100)
```

```
y_hats, sigma_y_hats = zip(*[gpr4.estimate(x_hat) for x_hat in x_hats])
k = 1
lcb = np.array(y_hats) - k*np.array(sigma_y_hats)
```

Recall from section 6.2.2 that in GPR4, we multiplied the uncertainty by std_y before returning it. This gives the uncertainty the same scale as the measurements. Because of this, we can compare uncertainty to measurements in lcb and make k a number around 1.

By minimizing lcb, you're trading off (1) exploitation, a desire to compile web server to have the lowest CPU time (the y_hats term), with (2) exploration, the desire to take a measurement at a parameter where the model is uncertain (the sigma_y_hats term). You want (1) because that's the point of optimizing—to minimize CPU time. You want (2) because your model, as it stands, may not be giving you very good estimates.

Recall that model uncertainty is zero at parameter values that were measured. When you take a measurement at a parameter where model uncertainty is high, you know that the next time you run GPR, uncertainty will be zero at that parameter. Also, uncertainty will be reduced at nearby parameters.

If we used a large value of k, we'd be saying that we cared more about reducing uncertainty. A smaller value of k would say we cared more about reducing CPU time. The coefficient k is a metaparameter, like epsilon in the epsilon-greedy bandit (chapter 3, section 3.1.2). In fact, it serves the same purpose: to quantify the tradeoff between exploration and exploitation. Finding a good value requires experience with many optimizations. Unfortunately, there is no straightforward way to choose it. Fortunately, the overall experimental method seems to be robust to your choice of it. For now, we'll stick with k = 1. Several other acquisition functions have been studied (see the following sidebar). We're using LCB because it offers a good balance of simplicity and performance.

Acquisition function forms

There is no ideal acquisition function, only heuristics. Because of that, there are several acquisition functions in general use. Two interesting ones are expected improvement and Thompson sampling.

Expected improvement (EI) asks, which parameter would be expected to reduce the CPU time the most, compared to the so-far-best measured value? EI is convenient because it does not have a metaparameter. This is a commonly used acquisition function.

Thompson sampling takes a novel approach. Instead of looking at the surrogate function in terms of expectation and uncertainty, it treats it as a distribution of functions. In other words, the gray area contains many possible realizations of the function CPU time versus parameter. To design an experiment, you draw a single function from the distribution and minimize it. The advantage of Thompson sampling is that if you draw multiple realizations, you get multiple experiment designs. This is helpful if your system permits you to take measurements at multiple parameters simultaneously.

Now that we have the code for the acquisition function, optimization of it is straight-forward:

```
i = np.where(lcb == lcb.min())
print (x_hats[i])
[0.11111111]
```

You can verify by looking at figure 6.17 that parameter 0.11 is the minimum of the black curve. We've now developed the components needed to run a Bayesian optimization:

- Gaussian process regression (section 6.2) for modeling the response surface
- An acquisition function (section 6.3) to balance exploration and exploitation
- A method of optimizing the acquisition function (np.linspace and np.where)

This works fine when optimizing a single parameter but will need a little revising to extend to all seven JIT parameters. The good news is that only the final point—the optimization of the acquisition function (AF)—needs to change. We'll see how in the next section.

6.4 *Optimize all seven compiler parameters*

To find the AF-minimizing parameter, we evaluated the surrogate function at 100 parameter values and chose the parameter value where lcb==lcb.min(). This simple technique works great with only one parameter but generates too many evaluations for larger numbers of parameters. Let's see why (hint: it's the curse of dimensionality again).

Say we generated 100 values of the first parameter, parameter_1. If we added a second parameter, parameter_2, we'd want to know which pair of values parameter_1, parameter_2 was best. For each of the 100 values of parameter_1, we'd generate 100 values of parameter_2, leading to 100 x 100 = 100^2 = 10,000 parameter pairs and, thus, 100^2 evaluations of the surrogate function. Extending that reasoning to seven parameters implies we'd need 100^7, or 100 million million surrogate evaluations. That's too many. There's a simple and efficient way to find the AF-minimizing parameter.

6.4.1 *Random search*

The simplest way to optimize over multiple parameters without doing impossible amounts of computation is a technique called *random search*. Random search first evaluates some random set of seven parameters—call it the "current parameter vector." Then it does the following:

1 Generates a new parameter vector by adding a small random number to each element of the vector to create a new parameter vector.
2 Evaluates the new parameter vector.
3 If the new parameter vector has a lower LCB than the current one, it makes the new parameter vector the current parameter vector; otherwise, the current vector stays current.

The following listing shows the code.

Listing 6.6   Random search

```
def evaluate(gpr, x):
    x = np.mod(x, 1)                            Ensure the parameter
    y, sigma_y = gpr.estimate(x)                values are in [0,1].
    lcb = y - sigma_y                           Evaluate a
    return x, lcb                               parameter vector.

def random_search(gpr, num_parameters, num_iterations=1000):
    step_size = 0.1
    x_current = np.random.normal(size=num_parameters)       Initialize the current
    x_current, lcb_current = evaluate(gpr, x_current)       parameter vector.
    for _ in range(num_iterations):
        x_test = (
            x_current
            + step_size*np.random.normal(size=num_parameters)
        )
        x_test, lcb_test = evaluate(gpr, x_test)            If the test vector
        if lcb_test < lcb_current:                          has better lcb...
            lcb_current = lcb_test              ...make it the new
            x_current = x_test                  current vector.
    return x_current
```

Generate a new, test vector.

After repeating these three steps many times, it halts and returns the current parameter vector. Because of step (3), the LCB can only improve or stay the same from
iteration to iteration. Although it's simple, random search is rather (perhaps surprisingly) effective.

You can try out `random_search()` on the single-parameter surrogate we've been
studying for the past few sections:

```
np.random.seed(17)
parameters = [ np.array([0.5]), np.array([0.0]) ]
measurements = [1.52, 1.21]
gpr4 = GPR4(parameters, measurements, sigma=.15)
random_search(gpr4, num_parameters=1)
[0.11096591]
```

It reports `0.11096591` as the LCB-minimizing parameter, the same value (to three dec-
imal places) we found in section 6.3.1 using `np.linspace` and `np.where`. Figure 6.18
plots the variable `lcb_current` versus the iteration number. The function `random_
search()` finds the minimizing parameter value in just under 200 iterations. (Okay, so
it's not better than `np.linspace` when optimizing one parameter—but for seven
parameters it's incomprehensibly faster.)

The final component needed to write a Bayesian optimization routine for the full
seven-parameter JIT optimization problem is `random_search()`. In the next section,
we'll use `random_search()` to design experiments that we'll run on the JIT simulator.

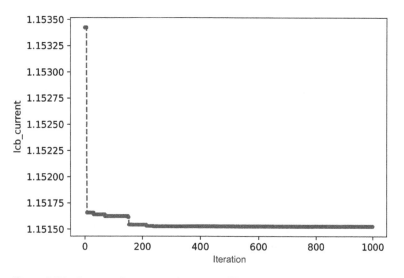

Figure 6.18   One run of `random_search()`. **The parameter value that minimizes** `lcb_current` **is found in under 200 iterations.**

6.4.2   A complete Bayesian optimization

The "inner loop" of a complete Bayesian optimization consists of the design, run, and analyze steps:

1   *Design*—Minimize LCB over the surrogate function to find the next parameter value to measure by `random_search()`.
2   *Run*—Measure the CPU time using `jit_plus_server()`, the JIT and web server simulator.
3   *Analyze*—Build a surrogate using `GPR4`.

These steps are depicted in the diagram redisplayed, for reference, in figure 6.19.

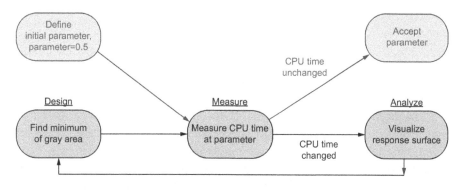

Figure 6.19   The inner loop of Bayesian optimization—design, run, analyze—is repeated until the measured CPU time stops changing.

Iterations through this inner loop will form the bulk of the work of optimizing the parameters. The other two stages—defining the initial parameter and accepting the final one—occur only once. See the following listing for the code.

Listing 6.7 Bayesian optimizer

```
class BayesianOptimizer:
    def __init__(self, num_parameters):
        self.num_parameters = num_parameters
        self.parameters = []
        self.measurements = []
        self.x0 = np.array([0.5]*num_parameters)

    def ask(self):
        if len(self.measurements)==0:
            return self.x0
        return self.new_parameter()

    def new_parameter(self):
        gpr = GPR4(
            self.parameters,
            self.measurements,
            sigma=0.15,
        )
        return random_search(gpr, self.num_parameters)[0]

    def tell(self, parameter, measurement):
        self.parameters.append(parameter)
        self.measurements.append(measurement)
```

Initialize at the center parameter.

Get the next experiment parameter to measure.

Search for the LCB-minimizing parameter.

Add the latest measurement.

To make use of `BayesianOptimizer`, you'd call `ask()`, then take a measurement, then call `tell()`. You'd repeat this process several times:

```
np.random.seed(7)
bo = BayesianOptimizer(num_parameters=7)
for _ in range(48):
    parameter = bo.ask()
    cpu_time = jit_plus_server(parameter)
    bo.tell(parameter, cpu_time)
```

You'd stop when the measurements of CPU time stop changing. You could judge whether they'd stopped changing by monitoring a plot of CPU time versus iteration through this loop. See figure 6.20.

You may recall from section 6.1 that a single measurement of the CPU time was expected to take about an hour. The optimization procedure in figure 6.20, then, would have taken about 2 days to complete using `BayesianOptimizer`.

You just completed the optimization of seven parameters using experiments that each took an hour to run. All the work of experiment design and analysis was handled by Bayesian optimization.

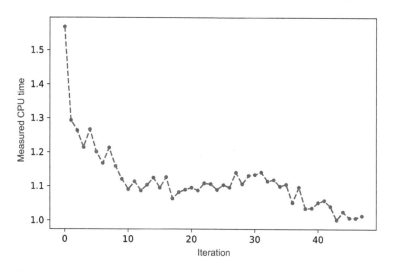

Figure 6.20 CPU time measured by `jit_plus_server()` **at parameters suggested by** `BayesianOptimizer`

Summary

- Bayesian optimization automates the design and analysis stages of experimental optimization.
- Gaussian process regression creates a surrogate function that models a response surface without requiring the engineer to specify the form of the model.
- Bayesian optimization designs experiments by running an optimizer, such as random search, relieving the engineer of the task of manually choosing parameters to measure.
- By optimizing over an acquisition function, you balance exploration (the desire to collect data to improve the surrogate) with exploitation (the desire to improve the business metric).

Managing
business metrics

7

This chapter covers

- Identifying metrics that directly impact your business
- Growing a collection of company-specific business metrics
- Engaging stakeholders when developing metrics
- Conducting experiments using multiple metrics

Up to this point in the book, we have described experimental methods that you can use to improve your business metrics. Since the decision to accept or reject a change to your system ultimately hinges on the values of those metrics, it is worth spending some time discussing how to define and employ them effectively. This is the subject of the present chapter.

Section 7.1 starts us out by contrasting metrics that are directly relevant to a business with other, more technical metrics. In section 7.2, we'll see how business metrics are derived and how they evolve, and we'll see how metrics have an inherent timescale that affects your ability to measure them. Finally, in section 7.3, we'll talk about how to use multiple business metrics to evaluate and experiment.

7.1 *Focus on the business*

We have used the term *business metrics* many times throughout this book without getting into detail about how they are defined. We'll do that in this chapter. Most importantly, the metrics should be directly relevant to your business. This may sound trivial, so to help make the point clear, let's contrast business metrics with other metrics that engineers use. This section warns of a trap for engineers: It is very easy to become focused on optimizing technical, engineering metrics (prediction quality, goodness-of-fit, etc.) and lose sight of the business in which you are engaged. Let's discuss this problem in the context of you as an engineer at a startup developing a new app-based product.

7.1.1 *Don't evaluate a model*

You are an engineer at a startup company that is developing an app that shows short videos to users. To survive at this stage, your company needs operating capital, which it intends to raise from investors. Your company has found that investors are very interested in how many daily active users (DAU) a product like yours has. Higher DAU implies a higher probability of investment. It seems like DAU is the right metric to optimize (at least for now).

You instrument your system to measure DAU. You find that your DAU is not bad, but it needs to be better for you to persuade investors. Currently, when a user opens the app, they see the most recently uploaded video. You surmise that if you could identify which videos a user likes and show those, then the user would be more likely to use the app again tomorrow, which would increase your DAU.

How can you tell whether a user likes a video? Well, at any point while the video is playing, a user can swipe up and the app will switch to the next video. You presume that if a user is swiping up, they probably aren't interested in the video. Bingo! You scan the production logs and see which videos each user swipes up on. You build an ML model that predicts the probability of an up-swipe, P{swipe}, based on features of the video like the video's author, the length of the video, and some other summary statistics you happen to already have computed for each video.

You now run your first A/B test. In the "B" version, you use your ML model to generate an estimate of P{swipe} for each video and show the video with the lowest P{swipe} first, the next-lowest P{swipe} second, and so on. The A/B test is a smashing success. DAU is dramatically better for version B than for version A.

Inspired by that success, you create more features and improve the model's predictions. Your measure of prediction quality is out-of-sample cross-entropy (an ML measure derived from the log data). You run another A/B test. Success. You get some investment capital, hire a small team of engineers, and task them with improving out-of-sample cross-entropy as much as possible.

After a few more rounds of model improvement, you find something surprising—and disappointing. Even though the cross-entropy keeps improving with each new model version, the DAU has improved by less and less (figure 7.1) and, in the last A/B test, hasn't improved at all. What happened?

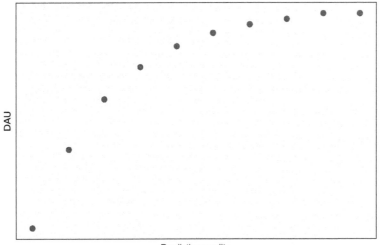

Figure 7.1   As the quality of the predictions, `P{swipe}`, produced by your ML model increases, the DAU increases, too, but at an ever-slower rate.

The short answer is that your team was focused on the wrong metric. They were improving cross-entropy, a generic, technical measure of model quality, rather than the specific, business metric—DAU. The connection between the two was hypothesized by you at the start, but there was no guarantee of a connection between them. You can reason this way: there are many possible business metrics (DAU, time spent/session, number of videos watched/session, etc.), and there are many possible prediction targets (probability of a swipe, probability of tapping "like," probability of sharing a video, etc.). Why should an improvement in predictions of any of those targets guarantee improvement in any one of the business metrics?

In practice, your intuition about a correlation between improvements in a certain model and improvements in a certain business metric might be right (if you are knowledgeable about the domain), but it's very hard to guess how strong that correlation will be. There are many aspects of your system that influence the value of a business metric—the code, the models, the hardware, the users (each of whom is complex on their own!), competitors, and so on. You can't hope to predict, measure, or even identify every one. Your prediction of `P{swipe}`—even if very good—is only one determinant of the DAU.

A useful analogy might be one of optimizing the running time of computer code. The tried-and-true approach is (1) profile the code to find the "hot spot" (i.e., where the code spends most of its time), (2) speed up the hot spot, and (3) repeat. If the speed of the code is analogous to a business metric, then improving the P{swipe} model is like removing a hot spot: once it's good enough, it's no longer the hot spot. Improving it further doesn't impact overall performance.

Also, it is common to find that as a system matures, the correlation decreases—that is, further improvements in a technical metric like P{swipe} don't lead to as large improvements in the business metric (e.g., DAU). Perhaps it's the case that no matter how good your predictions are, there will be other limits to users' behavior. Perhaps you have an excellent prediction of P{swipe}, but the best video you have has P{swipe} = 0.75. In other words, just because you can predict whether a user will watch a video doesn't mean you'll have watchable videos in your inventory. Even if you did, a user might not swipe. They might instead just close the app to go do something else. There are many factors that affect DAU that are independent of P{swipe} and cannot be controlled by improving the prediction.

However, this doesn't mean that you shouldn't have built the P{swipe} model. It's valuable, but optimizing it shouldn't have taken the focus away from improving the DAU. In the next section, we'll discuss a better approach.

7.1.2 Evaluate the product

We saw how it is easy to have one's focus drawn to a technical, nonbusiness, metric. The fix for this is simple to prescribe but requires some diligence to execute: With each pass through the engineer's workflow (see chapter 1, figure 1.1, and figure 7.2 here), you must return your attention to the business metric when you run your experiment, restart and consider all the ways you could improve the business metric, and choose the most promising thing to work on. It's what engineers call a *context switch*: you need to stop thinking about the last thing you worked on and refocus on the business needs.

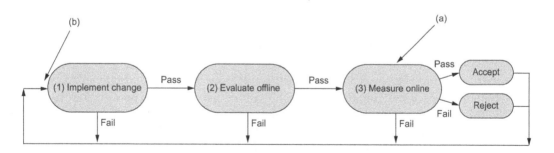

Figure 7.2 The engineer's workflow. (a) Return your attention to the business metric when you run an experiment, and (b) consider all the ways you could increase the business metric.

You might consider predicting targets other than P{swipe}. Maybe you could predict the probability that the user will click "like" or will share the video. Maybe you could combine multiple predictions into a single ranking system.

Maybe users get bored because the lowest-P{swipe} videos are all very similar. For example, maybe a user opens the app and sees several videos containing guacamole recipes. Even if the user likes guacamole and wants to make some to have with dinner, they might not want to watch several videos in a row about it. Maybe you need to find a way to add variety.

Maybe users appreciate the good videos only when they can contrast them with bad ones. (Or, at least, videos of moderate quality. You don't want to drive users away with bad videos.) Perhaps you save the very lowest P{swipe} videos to show only occasionally and intermittently.

There are infinite possible ways to modify your product beyond simply improving the quality of a prediction. If you take the time to consider the whole product and the business metric with each pass through your workflow, you may see a steadier improvement over time.

In this section, the business metric, DAU, was motivated by the demands of investors. In the next section, we'll look more deeply into the process of defining business metrics.

7.2   *Define business metrics*

Just as DAU was specific to the needs of the startup in the last section, business metrics will always be tailored to the business you are in and to the environment in which you are using the metric. You need to consider the broader goals of the business, the current market for your product, and the interests of all stakeholders—investors, employees, and so on. You should also consider how difficult it will be to measure the business metric, and this will determine how quickly and reliably you can improve your system using the experimental optimization methods presented in this book.

7.2.1   *Be specific to your business*

Your business is unique. Even if you have competitors, their businesses are only similar to yours. They're not the same. Your uniqueness should be reflected in your business metrics.

All short-video social media startups might be interested in higher DAU. After all, they are each building their product to attract users. But maybe your startup wants to foster positive interactions between users and so encourages commenting on videos that users enjoy. A business metric that measures "sentiment and quantity of comments per video" might be appropriate. Another short-video startup—a competitor—might just want people glued to their phones with their app open, and so it uses "time spent per day" as a business metric. Yet another competitor might cater to advertisers, and so it might use ad revenue as a business metric. Whatever your business metric is, it should measure your business's goals as specifically as possible.

To determine these goals, you will need the input of all stakeholders. That includes (but is not limited to)

- *Investors*—Those who want to profit in the long run and (increasingly) might want to avoid businesses that adversely affect society or the environment.
- *Users*—Those who want a product that serves them well. That could mean that the product is easy to use, cheap, conveys status, and so on.
- *Your team members*—Those who know what kind of objectives are possible to achieve and know well what problems the system is currently facing.
- *Other teams*—Those whose work might depend on changes that your team makes to the system.
- *Regulators*—Those who represent the public's interest in safety and the usage of public resources.
- *Advertisers*—Those who want users to see and respond to their ads.

Let's say that your company's business has matured a bit; DAU is high and stable. You are now ready to show advertisements. This pleases investors, who see an opportunity to earn a return on their investments. It also pleases advertisers, because they would like to sell products to your users. Users aren't happy about it, though, because they feel that the ads will detract from the videos and degrade the overall experience. The team responsible for the design of the app see an ad as a blemish of the thing of beauty they have created.

Each of the stakeholders might ideally optimize a different business metric—one that represents their interests. Your job is to find a metric, or a set of metrics (see section 7.3), that offers a good compromise. You might consider, for example, measuring both ad revenue and DAU. If, in your next A/B test, you can both increase revenue without decreasing DAU, that might indicate that users aren't unhappy, and neither are the advertisers or investors. If the designers can incorporate the ads into the app to their satisfaction without causing a decrease in DAU or revenue, then perhaps everyone will be satisfied.

Notice how the business metric shifted when your company graduated from "startup" mode and wanted to run ads. This won't be the last time it changes.

7.2.2 Update business metrics periodically

As your business evolves, so will your business metrics. You should reevaluate your business metrics periodically and update them to reflect changes in your business.

Your company changes. Employees turn over. Investors come and go. Users' tastes change. Users get older, and their needs change. Societal norms change. The economy changes. Since stakeholder interests determine your business metrics, your business metrics will change as your stakeholders do.

In the last section, you started showing ads and needed to update your business metrics correspondingly. Let's say your app gets very popular, and many people start paying attention to your business as a result. You find that parents are writing angry letters and blog posts complaining that their children are spending too much time on your app. Your app seems addictive. Regulators are calling you, asking you to defend your business. Advertisers are getting uncomfortable about being associated with your app because of the bad press. How can you adapt your app to help improve the situation? There might be many changes you could make, but first you need to define the objective of those changes—that is, the business metric. You could, for instance, measure the amount of time spent per user per session, or time spent per user per day. When you evaluate an A/B test, you could aim to *decrease* these metrics to below some reasonable threshold. By reducing the average time spent using your app, you might please your stakeholders: advertisers, investors . . . and society at large.

It is common to reevaluate business metrics quarterly. All stakeholders within the company weigh in to decide whether and how to change the metrics.

When considering a business metric update, in addition to stakeholder input, you should consider how hard it would be to measure a business metric. The main determinant of difficulty is the metric timescale, which we'll discuss next.

7.2.3 *Business metric timescales*

It would be fruitless to choose a business metric that you cannot measure via experiment. While it's possible that a business metric can be unmeasurable simply because it's poorly defined (e.g., "average beauty of the videos," "average charm of the posters"), more commonly a metric will be more difficult to measure because it takes longer to measure.

Recall that when we run an A/B test, we take an aggregate measurement, which is an average over `num_ind` individual measurements, given by `num_ind >= (2.48 * sd1_delta / prac_sig)**2` (see chapter 2, section 2.3.2). The key points here are

- The longer it takes to take a single individual measurement, the longer it will take to run an experiment.
- The larger `num_ind` is, the longer it will take to run an experiment.
- `Num_ind` increases with the standard deviation of the individual measurement (`sd1_delta`). The "noisier" the individual measurement, the longer the experiment takes.
- `Num_ind` increases as `prac_sig`, the practical significance level, decreases. If you need to take a more precise measurement, it will take longer.

These effects are best illustrated with examples.

TIMESCALE FOR AN INDIVIDUAL MEASUREMENT

Individual measurements come in many forms. You might, at a short timescale, record the latency of a web server's response, or at a long timescale, record how many unique users see your app in a month. Table 7.1 shows a variety of business metrics and their timescales.

Recall that each of the individual measurements would need to be taken many times to construct the aggregate measurement needed for an experiment. The metrics nearer to the bottom of the table would necessitate long experiments, potentially impractically long for rapid iteration on a product.

Table 7.1 Various business metrics ordered by timescale

Business	Individual measurement	Timescale
High-frequency trading (HFT)	Time through an FPGA (field-programmable gate array; a highly configurable hardware device used for some HFT applications)	10s of nanoseconds
HFT	Time through a trading engine	Microseconds
HFT	Time through a trading message processor	10s of microseconds
HFT	Long-haul microwave transmission	Milliseconds
Web/app product	Response time of a web server	10s of milliseconds
Website	Page load time	Seconds
Advertising	CTR	10s of seconds (e.g., from time of page load)
HF market-making	Holding time of a trade	Minutes
Social media	Time spent per session	10s of minutes
Social media	Time spent per day	Hours (no, really: http://mng.bz/09e6)
Web/app product	Daily active users	Day
Trading	Daily profit	Day
Advertising	Purchase of product seen in ad	Weeks
Web/app product	Monthly active users	Month
Web/app product	Results of a survey of users	Months

EFFECT OF NOISE IN THE INDIVIDUAL MEASUREMENT

The number of individual measurements, N, required by an A/B test increases with the square of sd1_delta. If sd1_delta doubles, N quadruples. Qualitative, we can say that num_ind is sensitive to the noise level.

The noise level of an individual measurement depends on many factors. All the following can introduce noise into a measurement:

- Thermal noise (a cold computing device operates more reliably than a warm one)
- Dependence on network communication
- Dependence on a human being's actions
- Dependence on financial instrument dynamics

You would expect the noise level of, say, a cold FPGA to be lower than that of a user's decision about whether to click on an ad, and it is.

EFFECT OF THE PRACTICAL SIGNIFICANCE

More precise measurement requirements (i.e., smaller practical significance) will make for longer experiments. N is sensitive to decreases in PS the same way it is sensitive to increases in sd1_delta.

You will typically require smaller and smaller PS as your business matures and you find it harder to find ways to make big improvements to your system. Also, as your business grows to a large user base, the impact of small changes to metrics like "time spent on our app" can have a large long-term impact on other metrics like ad revenue. Therefore, it might be worth taking a precise measurement of "time spent on our app" and be careful not to inadvertently decrease it.

You might also find that you require smaller PS values when you face strong competition. In high-frequency trading, for example, very small changes in latency can translate into large changes in profit as you outrun your competitors. In online advertising, click-through rates are typically measured in single-digit percentages, so even changes of less than 0.1% could be enough to get a meaningfully better ad response for your advertisers.

Now you know how to define a business metric that is specific to your business, satisfies stakeholders, and is measurable in a reasonable amount of time. Now it's time to use your metrics—likely multiple, simultaneously—in experiments. The next section tells how.

7.3   *Trade off multiple business metrics*

This book has presented experiments designed to optimize a single business metric. This is an idealization. In practice, you will need to make tradeoffs between multiple, competing metrics. This might be to satisfy multiple stakeholders or to address safety or ethical concerns, or simply because it is difficult to describe your business's objective with a single metric. You may even forgo some improvement due to the high cost of experimentation—some things are better done than perfect. Next we'll motivate these tradeoffs and present pragmatic ways to implement them.

7.3.1   *Reduce negative side effects*

There's a saying, "Be careful what you wish for because you just might get it." In engineering terms, optimization of a single, simple metric often causes negative side effects. Using multiple metrics to evaluate experiments can alleviate these side effects.

Engineering lore is filled with examples of unexpected behaviors of systems that have been optimized for a single objective. A paper by J. Lehman et al. (https://arxiv.org/abs/1803.03453) collects many amusing examples from reinforcement learning. Here are some more mundane examples.

In trading, a good first guess at a business metric is "profit"—that is, you should engineer a trading system to maximize profit. If you pursue this objective, you will likely (and quickly) find that you are taking on too much risk. So, really, you want to maximize profit but also minimize risk. If you are trading at high frequency, you might also find that if you send orders to an exchange too quickly, they ask you to stop trading. Thus, orders/second becomes another metric. There are many more metrics you'd likely want to monitor.

When you run an ad-serving system, you might start out using revenue as your business metric. You are running a business, after all. If you show ads more often, you might find that revenue increases, at least in the short-term. Over the long-term, users might dislike using the product because it contains too many ads and spend their time elsewhere. This would result in lower revenue. Thus, you should also monitor DAU, or time spent/user/day, or other similar metrics to take care that you're not annoying users with your attempts to increase ad revenue.

If you're engineering a social media ranking system, you might use "posts viewed/session" as a business metric. In your attempts to increase that metric, you might build a complex, difficult-to-interpret ML model to drive the ranking algorithm. What if the model downranks posts about suicide? This might increase "posts viewed/session" because seeing posts about suicide might be so unpleasant as to cause users to close the app. A friend who sees the post might reach out to the poster and offer help. If those posts get downranked, could an opportunity to help a suicidal person be missed?

Another good metric for social media is "number of likes/user/day." If users are clicking "like" (or "up" or "+" or "heart" etc.) more often, then they must be seeing more likeable content, right? Maybe. Instead, maybe they are clicking "like" on posts that shock them or express a strong, emotion-based opinion. Upranking this kind of content (via an ML model that simply notices what kind of content gets liked) might increase your business metric—"number of likes/user/day"—but it could fill your product with anger and outrage, making for a genuinely unpleasant experience for users. You might also consider metrics such as "interactions with remote social connections," "percentage of harsh/profane words in comments," and so on.

In general, increasing any one metric will decrease some other metric. You may please one stakeholder but displease another. A solution is to measure multiple business metrics and use them all for evaluating each experiment. In the next section, we show how to perform a multiple-metric evaluation in practice.

7.3.2   *Evaluate with multiple metrics*

At the analysis stage of your experiment, you will have measured multiple metrics. Now you need to combine them to make a single decision: Accept the new version of the system (e.g., "B" in an A/B test, or the best parameter set in a Bayesian optimization) or reject it and stay with the current version of the system.

One way to approach this decision is to make one business metric the optimizing metric and all the others constraining metrics (or "guardrails"). For example, choose revenue as the optimizing metric and DAU and time spent/day as the constraining metrics for an ad-server A/B test. If version B has higher revenue than version A but does not have lower DAU or time spent/day, then you can accept B. In general, if you can improve the optimizing metric without disimproving the constraint metrics, then you should accept the new version of the system.

An alternative—but difficult-to-use—approach is to combine multiple metrics into a single ubermetric by making a linear combination, like C1 x revenue + C2 x DAU + C3 x [time spent/day], where C1, C2, and C3 are constants that determine the relative importance of each of the metrics. It is *very* hard to figure out good values for the constants. The values will depend on all stakeholders' opinions and are completely subjective. You need to answer questions like "Is it worth losing 1 user per day if I receive C1/C2 dollars more per day?" and it just gets harder as you combine more metrics. Moreover, you are again optimizing a single metric (the ubermetric) and thus are open to negative side effects.

Needless to say, I don't recommend optimizing a linear combination of metrics. In fact, I don't really recommend *optimizing* at all. Instead, specify a threshold for each metric. For example, you could say that your goal is to increase revenue by $1,000/day and to get that you're willing to lose 5m of time spent/day but not willing to lose any DAU. You specify the decision criteria like this:

- revenue/day >= $1000
- time spent/day >= current value - 5m
- DAU >= current value

Then, if B meets all the criteria, you accept it.

Notice that you must specify just as many numbers—the three thresholds—as you did when creating the ubermetric, where you specified C1, C2, and C3. Thresholds are much easier to specify, however. That's because each threshold applies to only a single metric, whereas the C's compare each metric to all the others. It's easy to answer a question about a single metric, like, "Do I want revenue to increase by $1,000/day?" It is hard to compare metrics. For example, it would be hard to determine how many dollars/day you'd pay to gain 1 DAU plus 30s of time spent/day.

Finally, thresholds let you know when you're done. If, for example, you've found a version of the system that improves revenue/day by $1,000, you can stop this task and spend your time on something else. If your task was specified as "make revenue/day as high as possible" (i.e., to optimize), then even when you improved revenue/day by $1,000, you'd keep working on improving revenue.

This idea of improving until "good enough" instead of improving until optimal is called *satisficing*. The idea behind satisficing is that when you make your decision (accept/reject B), you're acknowledging both the value of your business metric and the cost of measuring it.

Summary

- Focus on business metrics instead of technical metrics.
- Create bespoke metrics for your business.
- Update your business metrics periodically, accounting for all stakeholders' interests.
- Define and use multiple business metrics.
- Specify thresholds for all business metrics as criteria to accept a new version of your system.

Practical considerations 8

This chapter covers

- Dealing with data that does not match statistical assumptions
- Identifying biases that may creep into experiments
- Avoiding behaviors that generate false positives
- Replicating experiments to validate that their results are robust

The experimentation methods presented in this book are powerful tools that you can use to improve your engineered system. They are powerful but not foolproof. We can make subtle or simple mistakes that can cause these methods to fail.

This chapter discusses various ways in which your author—and colleagues kind enough to sit for interviews for this book—has seen these methods fail. You could read this chapter as a set of warning labels for experimental optimization.

Section 8.1 shows how the analysis of an experiment can fail if the measurements do not meet the assumptions of the analysis. Perhaps you've heard the phrase "garbage in, garbage out." This is that. In sections 8.2 and 8.3, we look at early stopping and family-wise error, both sources of increased false positives. Section 8.4

discusses common psychological and methodological biases of which you should beware. Finally, section 8.5 explains how replicating experiments boosts confidence in their results.

Experimentation requires nothing if not humility. Chapter 1 (section 1.3.1) pointed out that most experiments will demonstrate that your new idea isn't any good. This chapter tells us that if you're not careful, your experimental results won't be any good, either. Take heart. If you're aware of these problems and use sound methods to deal with them, then when you finally put a new idea into production, you will be confident that it belongs there.

8.1 Violations of statistical assumptions

A common assumption in any statistical procedure is that measurements are independent and identically distributed, usually referred to as *iid*. Indeed, we implicitly assumed iid when developing the design and analysis stages for A/B testing. A second assumption, *stationarity*, is that the process that is generating the measurement does not change over time. This allows us to claim that the results of the experiment we're running *right now* will be applicable later on. Both of these assumptions—iid and stationarity—are routinely violated in practice. This section discusses ways to detect and cope with violations of these assumptions. First, let's dig into the iid assumption.

8.1.1 Violation of the iid assumption

The design and analysis stages of an A/B test (see chapter 2) rely on an estimate of the standard error of the aggregate measurement: `se_delta = sd/np.sqrt(N)`, where `sd = np.sqrt(sd_A**2 + sd_B**2)` is the (effective) standard deviation of an individual measurement (and `sd_A` and `sd_B` are the standard deviations of the individual measurements of A and B, respectively).

They also rely on the z score, `z = delta/se_delta`, following a normal distribution. For the estimate of `se_delta` to be valid and for z to be normal, the individual measurements must be iid. The term *iid* is two conditions: independent and identically distributed. We'll address them separately.

INDEPENDENT

When individual measurements are not independent, our estimate of the standard error of the aggregate measurement, `se_delta`, is too small. If we're unaware of this, then we'll overestimate the magnitude of z, because `z = delta/se_delta`. A larger-magnitude z will be more likely to cross the threshold for acceptance—`z > 1.64`—and make us more likely to accept the B version being tested. Thus, underestimating `se_delta` leads us to more often incorrectly accept B versions (i.e., to generate a false positive).

Let's see how the SE is too small by looking at the most extreme example of nonindependence. Say you intend to collect some individual measurements, but you inadvertently collect the same measurement multiple times. The standard deviation of these measurements would be zero, thus the standard error of the mean of these measurements would be zero. Put concretely

```
ind_meas = np.array([1.5]*10)
print (ind_meas)
print (ind_meas.mean())                      Collect the same
print (ind_meas.std())                       value multiple times.
[1.5 1.5 1.5 1.5 1.5 1.5 1.5 1.5 1.5 1.5]
1.5
0.0          SE is 0.
```

How could this happen? Perhaps there was a bug in the measurement code. Alternatively, there could be a flaw in the measurement methodology. Imagine the methodology was implemented as "Periodically wake up, pull the latest value (of a measurement) from a server, and save it to a file." If the period was small enough that no new values were yet generated on the server, you could get repeated values, similar to ind_meas earlier.

In a less extreme (and, in fact, totally realistic) case, you might see an occasional run of repeats resulting from sampling too quickly, like

```
ind_meas = np.array([1.5]*8 + [2.3, 3.1])
print (ind_meas)
print (ind_meas.mean())                          Shows a run of
print (ind_meas.std() / np.sqrt(10))             repeats of 1.5
[1.5 1.5 1.5 1.5 1.5 1.5 1.5 1.5 2.3 3.1]
1.74          SE is still
0.16          too small.
```

This time we compute the standard error—ind_meas.std() / np.sqrt(10)—and find that it's 0.16. If you were to sample correctly (i.e., only once per independent measurement), you'd collect the values 1.5, 2.3, 3.1, which has a standard error of 0.38, which is higher than the estimate of 0.16, earlier. The run of 1.5's is an example of nonindependence, and it caused the estimate of standard error to be too low.

Apart from measurement errors, this kind of *serial dependence* can arise in any measurements due to the dynamics of the system, unrelated to how you take your measurement. For example:

- The cost of executing a trade in a stock market might be correlated to the last executed trade if customers tend to send batches of similar orders (e.g., "buy $10,000 of each of these three energy stocks").
- The click indicator for an ad system might show runs of zeros when recording the behavior of a user who engages in long sessions (thus seeing many ads) but is generally disinclined to click on any ads.
- A music streaming service might see runs of "skips" as a user uses the skip button to search for a song or a run with no skips as a user listens to music while engaged in another activity.

Whenever you can predict the value of an individual measurement—even partially, even if they're not sequential—from other individual measurements, your measurements are not independent.

A simple mitigation for serial dependence, which is also called *auto-correlation*, is to take measurements less frequently. By doing that you'll be more likely to avoid collecting the same measurement (or correlated measurements) more than once. For example, if it takes 3 seconds for the serial dependence to decay away, you should sample less often than every 3 seconds. The downside is that you'll throw away some potentially useful measurements. A more refined approach would be to build a model of the serial dependence.

Generally speaking, if your measurements are dependent (i.e., not independent), you can effectively remove the dependence by building a model of it. That, however, is beyond the scope of this book. See, for example, *Time Series Analysis: Forecasting and Control* (Wiley, 2015) by Box et al.

IDENTICALLY DISTRIBUTED

Two individual measurements are identically distributed if they can be viewed as being drawn from the same distribution—same shape, same mean, same variance, and so on. Generally speaking, your individual measurements will not be identically distributed.

Individual measurements might take different means or variances on different days, for different users, for different stocks, for different advertisers, and so on. The differences might be large, or they might be small enough not to matter. Rather than taking a black-and-white, matters-or-doesn't-matter approach, you can take an iterative approach. (This is good advice for experimentation, modeling, and engineering in general.)

Start out by acting as if your individual measurements are identically distributed. Then see if you can find cases where that's untrue. Test hypotheses like

- "The click-through rate is much higher in the evening."
- "Revenue has higher variance on Saturday mornings."
- "Trading profit has lower variance for more liquid stocks."
- "Users from location X click 'like' more than users from location Y."

If a hypothesis proves useful, you can use an experimental design technique called *blocking* to account for the effect at measurement time. You can also use *ANOVA* to account for the effect at analysis time. It might also be helpful to build a linear model of all the relevant effects at analysis time. Such methods are beyond the scope of this book. See, for example, *Design and Analysis of Experiments* (Springer, 2017) by Dean et. al.

The iid assumption is a powerful simplifier of experiment design and analysis. Alas, it is usually violated to some extent. Techniques are available to deal with violations of this assumption.

8.1.2 Nonstationarity

A *stationary* system is one whose dynamics do not change over time. When we run an experiment (e.g., an A/B test or a Bayesian optimization), we implicitly assume stationarity of our engineered system. It's what gives us confidence that the result of our experiment will hold into the future, that the optimal parameters today will be the optimal parameters tomorrow.

In practice, everything's changing all the time—it's nonstationary. A trading system capitalizes on small predictive correlations, but in the process decreases the magnitude of those same correlations. The more companies that compete, the faster the correlations decay away.

An ad-serving system will see new products and services being created and advertised. It will also see users' tastes and tolerances (e.g., for ad types) change over time. Additionally, the products on which the ads are being run will deliberately be changed (through normal engineering) over time.

Some aspects of most systems change slowly enough that we can capitalize on our experimental results for some amount of time into the future. Maybe for weeks, maybe for months, maybe for quarters. It depends on the system and on what you're measuring.

The way engineers cope with these changes is to keep updating. Periodically update models with recent data (e.g., in a contextual bandit), periodically retune parameters (e.g., with Bayesian optimization), and continually generate new ideas to A/B test into the system.

TRANSIENT EFFECTS

It's possible that the act of starting a new experiment impacts the system in a temporary way. For example, if you run an A/B test on new feature of your web app, users might initially be intrigued. Many might try out the new feature. But after a few days, the novelty wears off and users ignore it. Permanently.

Remember that we run experiments with the hope that our results will hold in the future, that if we modify the system to get some benefit (e.g., high revenue), we'll realize that benefit for some time into the future.

In the preceding example, any benefit created by the new feature evaporated after a few days. So how should we interpret the measurements from this experiment? It would be wise to exclude all individual measurements taken in the first several days. You'll still collect the prescribed N individual measurements, but they'll all be taken after the first several days—after the *transient effect* has gone away.

The violations of statistical assumptions discussed in this section are well known, and we've seen that there are techniques available to cope with them. Because of this, in practice, any adverse impact (in this author's experience) seems to be mild. The next two sections, in contrast, cover what seem to be the worst two offenders in industrial experiments. Learning to avoid them might be the highest value-to-effort-ratio thing you could learn about experimentation.

8.2 *Don't stop early*

Imagine you're running an A/B test comparing the profit of two versions of a high-frequency trading strategy. You'll monitor the aggregate measurements of the profit of A and B. Likely you'll have a dashboard showing their current values, along with their standard errors, the z score, and guardrail metric values. If you see that B is losing a lot of money (compared to A), you'll probably want to halt the experiment for safety reasons. But what if B is only somewhat worse than A? Or maybe it's better than A (delta > PS) and the z score is larger than 1.64? Should you stop?

It's not unreasonable to answer yes. After all, the conditions for accepting B are z > 1.64 and delta > PS. The correct answer, however, is no. It is a harmful action that causes false positives, yet it's common enough that it has a name: *early stopping*.

Early stopping is an overloaded term

To avoid any confusion, I'll point out that the term *early stopping* is used in two ways:

- It refers to stopping an A/B test early and producing invalid results.
- It also refers to a regularization technique used in fitting neural networks, a type of machine learning model.

The two ideas are unrelated. The fact that they have the same name is a coincidence.

Sometimes early stopping is referred to as *peeking*, as in, "Don't peek at your A/B test while it's running." I prefer not to use that term. It's fine to monitor your A/B test while it's running. It's preferable, in fact. Monitoring will help you detect severe problems earlier. It's just a bad idea to *stop* the experiment based on the conditions z > 1.64 and delta > PS.

The z score is a function of measurements that have some variation over time. As a result, the z score has variation. That variation makes it possible for the z score to cross the threshold 1.64 during the A/B test and then cross back before the A/B test is done. In such a situation, if you stopped the A/B test when the t statistic crossed the threshold and accepted the system change, you would have generated a false positive. Had you waited until the A/B test completed and the z score crossed back to below 1.64, you would have instead rejected version B.

To see how this could be possible, let's simulate an A/B test and monitor the z score using the code in the following listing. For simplicity, we'll ignore the condition delta > PS in this discussion. Similar reasoning applies to it.

Listing 8.1 Simulate an A/B test and monitor the z score

```
def z_score_vs_n():
    def profit_A():
        return np.random.uniform(0,1)
    def profit_B():
        return np.random.uniform(0,1)

    z_scores = []
    ind_measurements_A = []
    ind_measurements_B = []
    for n in range(1, 100):
        ind_measurements_A.append(profit_A())
        ind_measurements_B.append(profit_B())
        a = np.array(ind_measurements_A)
```

Shows the individual measurements of profit

This is the aggregate measurement. ⌐→
```
        b = np.array(ind_measurements_B)
        delta = b.mean() - a.mean()
        se_delta = np.sqrt(a.std()**2 + b.std()**2) / np.sqrt(n)
        z_scores.append(delta / se_delta)        ←⌐ Calculate the z score after
    return np.array(z_scores)                       each ind. measurement.
```

We're simulating the individual profit measurements using profit_A() and profit_B(). Versions A and B produce the same profit, so this A/B test would ideally tell us not to switch from A to B.

The function z_score_vs_n() calculates the z score after each individual measurement based on all of the individual measurements collected so far. If we were to monitor this A/B test, we would see progressively computed z scores like those in figure 8.1.

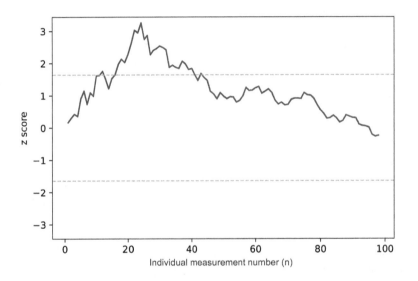

Figure 8.1   The z score of a monitored A/B test. The z score is recomputed at each individual measurement, n, from all measurements taken so far.

Notice how the z score rises above the threshold 1.64 when n is approximately in the range [10,40]. Had we stopped the A/B test early, in response to seeing z > 1.64, we would have switched to version B, generating a false positive. Had we waited until the end, we would have correctly rejected B. Figure 8.2 shows another simulation, where early stopping would have caused a false positive at individual measurement 30.

Early stopping will increase the rate of false positives—dramatically. Intuitively, this is because the more chances you have to make a mistake, the more likely you are to make one. In this case, the "mistake" is accepting B when z > 1.64. By allowing yourself to stop early, you give yourself many chances to make that mistake and generate a

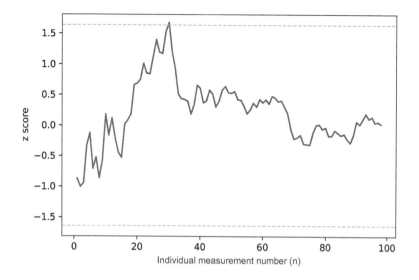

Figure 8.2 Early stopping would generate a false positive at `n=30`.

false positive. If you wait until the end of the A/B test, however, you only have one chance to generate a false positive. (Recall that you expect a 5% false-positive rate even when you wait until the end of the A/B test.)

Figure 8.3 plots the false-positive rate when running `z_score_vs_n()` for longer and longer A/B tests (i.e., larger `N`). You can imagine that each `N` corresponds to a different choice of `PS`. For smaller `PS`, you'd run a longer A/B test (use larger `N`).

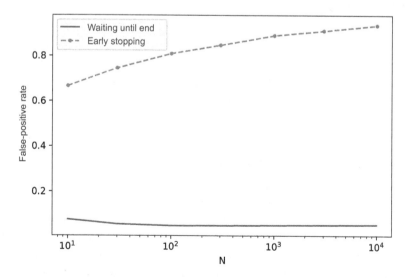

Figure 8.3 The false-positive rate increases dramatically when we allow early stopping. Note that the lower line is around 5% for all `N`. This is the designed-for false positive rate.

Early stopping is a common mistake. I have witnessed it multiple times. The scenario is usually like this: A team introduces A/B testing and appreciates having the measurements it produces to make their acceptance decisions. But system changes that need to be tested queue up, and they want to speed up the testing process. Early stopping seems like an intuitive solution until one or more performance-reducing changes are accepted into the system, and people start noticing the dip in business metrics in regular reports. The resolution is to back out all the suspect changes and start over. Early stopping results in a lot of wasted time.

Early stopping is one type of *p hacking*. If we were to measure, in an A/B test, that the business metric for version B was better than version A, then p would be the probability that we got a false positive. It's just a function of the z score: A higher z score means a lower p value. When we say, z > 1.64, we're equivalently saying p < .05. Anyway, that's the "p" in the phrase *p hacking*. The idea is that you're making a mistake that causes your result to look statistically significant (z > 1.64) when it isn't.

The use of the verb *hacking* seems to imply some malicious intent, or at least an experimenter bias. As in, you're either doing it on purpose or you're at least happy about it because you are able to report (albeit incorrectly) more positive results. But, in practice, p hacking seems (to this author) to mostly be due to the misuse of statistical methods.

If early stopping is p hacking in time—choosing a favorable time to stop an experiment and report the results as a "win"—then family-wise error is p hacking in space: at one point in time, you examine many business metrics to find one that you can report (albeit incorrectly) as statistically significant. Let's see how that works.

8.3   *Control family-wise error*

When you run an A/B test, you'll typically monitor more metrics than just the one you'll use for the final evaluation (see chapter 7, section 7.3.2). If we refer to this collection of metrics as a *family*, then a *family-wise error* is when you look over all the metrics to find one that has moved in a favorable direction by a statistically significant (z > 1.64) amount. In this section, we'll understand how family-wise errors increase the false-positive rate and how to control this kind of error. First, let's see how looking across many metrics for a "win"—called *cherry-picking*—increases the false-positive rate.

8.3.1   *Cherry-picking increases the false-positive rate*

Imagine you built a fancy new million-parameter neural network predictor to replace the old predictor in a social media recommender system. You run an A/B test comparing the system running with the old model (A) to the system running with the new model (B). The system shows to users short textual posts. Users may give the posts a thumbs-up—or mute the author, or scroll past it quickly, or linger for a while reading it, or write a comment, or even just close your app. There are many actions a user can take and, thus, many metrics to monitor and be concerned about.

Your team's main goal for this quarter is to increase the number of thumbs-ups users give out per day. Therefore, you run an A/B test with "thumbs-ups per user per day" as the business metric. At the same time, you monitor all the other metrics (muting rate, linger time, comment rate, etc.) to make sure you don't adversely affect them.

When the A/B test is complete, you find that the rate of thumbs-ups has not changed by a statistically significant amount. However, you notice that one of the other metrics—comment rate—has increased. You measure its z score as 2.1, which is greater than the significance threshold of 1.64. Now, even though comment rate isn't the focus for this quarter, your team is certainly not *unconcerned* with it. In some quarters, it actually is the focus. So, increasing comment rate is a good thing. Maybe your new model does add some value, even if it's not the value you'd originally intended. It would be a shame to throw away all your hard work just because you didn't improve the thumbs-up rate. You decide to change the business metric for your A/B test to "comment rate," and you recommend that your model be put into production.

This is seductive reasoning, but it's misguided. Here's why. Let's say you examine M metrics for statistical significance (i.e., for z > 1.64). The threshold 1.64 was chosen so that you'd have a 5% false-positive rate—for a single metric. But now you're examining M metrics and asking, "Are *any* of them statistically significant?" Let's compute the probability of a false positive with this new question. (Spoiler: It's a lot higher than 5%.)

For simplicity, let's say all the metric values are independent, and none of them truly are better for version B than for version A. We know that each one has a probability of 0.05 of showing a false positive, which equates to a probability of 0.95 of not showing a false positive. The probability of *any* one of them showing a false positive is "1 – probability of none of them showing a false positive":

$$p\_any = 1 - 0.95^M$$

To understand this intuitively, imagine rolling a single (six-sided) die, and asking the probability that you roll a 1. It's improbable—only 1/6. If rolling a die is analogous to running an experiment, then rolling a 1 is analogous to getting a false positive (although 1/6 is larger than 0.05, but let's not quibble about such details).

A family-wise comparison, then, is analogous to rolling many dice and asking whether *any one of them* comes up 1. That's highly probable.

In case that analogy is not intuitive, the probability of *any* die coming up 1 is 1-5/6)**D, where D is the number of dice, just like p_any. Figure 8.4 shows p_any for a range of M values.

You can see in figure 8.4 that when M=1 (i.e., for a single business metric), the probability of a false positive is p_any = 0.05, as expected. As M increases, however, the probability of a false positive increases dramatically.

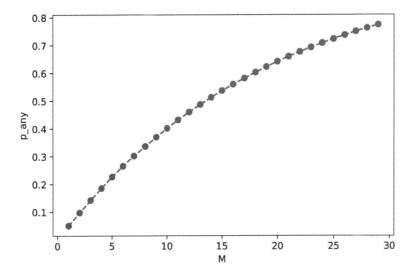

Figure 8.4   The probability of any one of a family of metrics generating a false positive versus the number of metrics, M, in the family

What's to be done about this? You can't avoid looking at other metrics altogether because you need to be sure you don't adversely affect them while trying to improve your main metric. There are two straightforward solutions: (1) Only accept B if your main metric is improved (according to the usual statistical and practical significance criteria), or (2) consider multiple metrics using a correctly computed false-positive rate. The next section shows how.

8.3.2   *Control false positives with the Bonferroni correction*

If you decide that you're willing to use your new model if any of M metrics are moved by a significant (statistical and practical) amount, then you'll need to modify your A/B test's design and analysis to accommodate that. The simplest way to do this is to use the *Bonferroni correction* to the false-positive rate.

In the A/B test design stage, we constrained the false-positive rate to 0.05 by choosing the threshold 1.64. We found 1.64 by looking up 0.05 in a z-score table. The Bonferroni correction says to look up 0.05/M instead and use whatever threshold the table reports. Call it z_table(0.05/M). As M increases, the threshold increases. Note also that you'll need to account for the false-negative rate (power analysis) and compute N for each of the metrics individually. For each metric, i, write

```
N_i >= ( (z_table(0.05/M) + .84) * sd1_delta_i / PS_i)**2
```

Note that each metric has its own sd1_delta_i and PS_i. Finally, you should run your A/B test with the largest N_i.

At analysis time, you'll again use the Bonferroni correction, `0.05/M`. For each metric, `i`, you'll compute the aggregate measurement, `delta_i`, and a z score, `z_i`. Then you'll check to see whether

```
z_i > ztable(0.05/M)
delta_i > PS_i
```

If any of the metrics meets these conditions, you can switch the production system to version B.

For more information about the Bonferroni correction, see https://mathworld .wolfram.com/BonferroniCorrection.html and references therein.

The Bonferroni correction keeps the false-positive rate for this kind of test—a family-wise test—under `0.05`. Figure 8.5 compares a corrected test to the uncorrected test from figure 8.4.

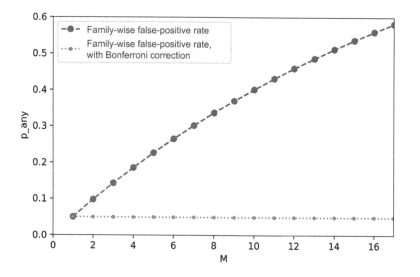

Figure 8.5 The Bonferroni correction controls the false-positive rate when comparing across a family of metrics.

Note that since this correction increases the z score threshold, it increases N, the number of individual measurements you'll need to take. The effect is, fortunately, not dramatic (figure 8.6).

Figure 8.6 shows that the number of individual measurements increases about twofold when the number of metrics increases from M=1 to M=15. The plot assumes, for simplicity, that all metrics have the same `sd1_delta` and `PS`.

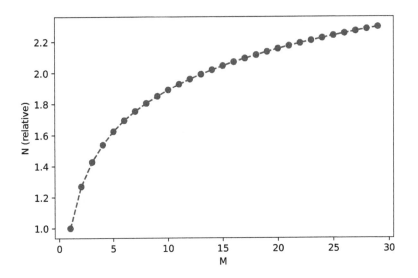

Figure 8.6   As the number of metrics in the family increases, the Bonferroni correction causes the number of individual measurements, N, in the A/B test to increase. The number N is plotted as relative to the uncorrected (single-metric) case. For M=15 metrics, about twice as many individual measurements will need to be collected.

The problems we've discussed so far in this chapter have been measurable and fairly correctable:

- Model any correlations.
- Update your models.
- Drop the transient.
- Don't stop early.
- Don't make uncorrected family-wise comparisons.

The next section looks at several biases that affect experiments. We know they're there; we can try to account for them, but we can never tell if we've made them go away.

8.4   *Be aware of common biases*

Biases can subtly guide your experiment toward one result or another without you being aware—even if you carefully design and conduct your experiment. Your best defense against these insidious troublemakers is to be aware of them and constantly be on the lookout for them. This section will discuss a few common biases, but many more (for an ever-expanding list, see catalogofbias.org) are known, and (presumably) even more are unknown.

We'll cover confounder bias, small-sample bias, optimism bias, and experimenter bias. I've chosen to highlight these biases out of the many possible biases because I've witnessed them in action enough to believe that you may, with high probability, encounter them.

8.4.1   Confounder bias

In chapter 2 we emphasized the point that confounders are removed by randomization. They are, indeed—assuming you really randomize over them.

Consider the following: You write some code implementing a version B. In the process you do some refactoring of existing code so that the new code cleanly interfaces with it. When you deploy that code, you're not just deploying version B. You're also deploying the refactored code.

It might be that your B code is some business logic that picks an ad from your ad inventory in a way that you think might be better than the existing A code. Let's say that it's not better, but the refactoring you did substantially decreased the time between a user request and the appearance of the ad. You might measure, in an A/B test, that the click-through rate on the ad increased significantly and attribute that improvement to the B code when, in fact, it was due to the speedup caused by the refactor.

The refactored code was a confounder that biased your result even though you randomized during the A/B test. The reason the confounder affected your result was that you were randomizing between the old A code and a new version that was "B + the refactored code."

You could encounter the same problem if you, say, configured B to connect to an alternate database. You might do this to protect the existing production system from any risk that B's database requests might interfere. But then you'd be comparing A to "B + alternate database." Examples like this are endless in large, complex engineered systems.

The mitigation is to simply watch out for confounders like this and keep A and B as similar as possible. Unfortunately, I can't tell you how to know for certain that you do *not* have such a confounder.

8.4.2   Small-sample bias

Small-sample bias is due to taking a small number of individual measurements. It causes the error in an aggregate measurement to be larger than you'd like. In that situation, you're more likely to incorrectly measure B being better than A or vice versa (i.e., to get a false positive or false negative).

We solved this with replication (chapter 2, section 2.2). When we design the A/B test, we calculate the minimum number of individual measurements, N, we'll need to limit the false-positive and false-negative rates to acceptable levels. The catch is there are different kinds of N. Allow me to explain.

You might say that each day users open your app and look at content items. It might be, if your business metric is "items viewed per day" that you calculate N in your A/B test in terms of the overall number of items served. But maybe, just by chance, your experiment interacts with only a small number of users. A result for a small number of users might not apply to the whole user base. Your experiment uses a large N for items but a "small N for users."

Alternatively, say you collect N individual measurements of items. It might be that some sessions consist of very many item views. If you collect them, then your collection of individual measurements could consist of a small number of sessions, even though it contains a large number of items. Your experiment is now "small N for sessions." You could imagine similar problems for other aspects of the system.

The mitigation is to randomly choose items to measure from all the possibilities available: across users, sessions, items, and so on. Again, there is no test to validate that you don't have this type of small-sample bias.

8.4.3   *Optimism bias*

"Optimism," in the sense of *optimism bias*, refers to a quality of a statistic, not of a person. Optimism happens whenever you apply a threshold to a statistic that has some variation.

Consider the rule that we use when analyzing an A/B test: "Switch to B if `delta >= PS`." Say the measured value, `delta`, is a distribution with expectation `delta_exp` and standard deviation `delta_se`. With high probability, `delta` will lie in the interval `[delta_exp - 2*delta_se, delta_exp + 2*delta_se]`. That means that values of `delta_exp` that may (not "must") meet the inequality `delta >= PS` are in the interval `[PS - 2*delta_se, infinity]`.

Put another way, the B versions that pass this test don't all have `delta_exp >= PS` because sometimes variation causes you to measure `delta` higher than `delta_exp`. The problem arises when, after the A/B test is done, over the long-term, you measure `delta` close to `delta_exp`, which may be less than `PS`.

Put yet another way, some B's just get lucky and pass your test, but they'll show poor performance over the long run.

This effect is called *regression to the mean*. For intuition, consider rolling a die as an analog of an experiment. In this experiment, the value on the die is analogous to `delta`. The expected value is `delta_exp = (1 + 2 + 3 + 4 + 5 + 6)/6 = 3.5`. You set `PS=5`.

You roll a die and get a 5 (i.e., `delta = 5`), so this die passes your test: `delta >= PS`. Then you roll it 100 more times—analogous to putting into production and letting it run for a long time—and on average you roll about 3.5. Randomness of the rolls means that sometimes you'll roll higher than expectation. Independence of the rolls means that rolling higher now doesn't mean you'll roll higher later.

When you apply a threshold acceptance rule to a noisy measurement, you should expect your future measurements to be worse, on average, than your thresholded measurements due to regression to the mean.

Regression to the mean is commonly reported by teams that use experimental optimization methods. Note that this effect may be induced by the rule `z > 1.64`, too, since `z` is proportional to `delta`.

There is no way to remove this effect. You could, in principle, decrease it by taking more precise (larger N) aggregate measurements, but that would come at the cost of running longer experiments.

8.4.4 *Experimenter bias*

The final bias we'll discuss is the experimenter. It's me. It's you. It's your teammate, your intern, your manager. While we may be aware of good experimental technique, we are only human. Our biggest flaw is that we want our new idea—our version B—to go into production. We want our idea to be right. Alas, recall from chapter 1, section 1.3.1 that we're usually wrong. Companies that use A/B tests at large scale consistently report that most A/B tests do not result in a switch to version B. The problem typically generated by experimenter bias, therefore, is a false positive. An experimenter accepts their version B even though it's not better than A.

Experimenters may express (or fall victim to?) their bias in many ways. If they are unaware of the problems presented in this chapter so far, they might

- Underestimate standard errors by using non-iid measurements and generate a false positive (section 8.1).
- Analyze a transient response and report it as the long-term expectation (section 8.1).
- Stop an experiment early because z looks good (section 8.2).
- Hunt around for a metric that makes their version B look good (section 8.3).
- Ignore any of the biases in this section when designing or analyzing their experiment.

There are two aspects to dealing with experimenter bias. One is combating your own, by relentlessly trying to prove yourself wrong, being perversely comfortable with usually being wrong, and cultivating the stubborn optimism required to keep trying.

The other aspect is dealing with *other experimenters'* bias. People don't like being wrong. They don't like when "math" tells them their intuition is wrong. They don't like people who tell them that math said that their intuition was wrong. Most people are not comfortable expecting to be wrong. It's doesn't come naturally to anyone.

So how do you tell someone that their great new idea doesn't work? You don't. Instead, create an experimentation process that everyone has to follow. That way nothing feels personal, and no one gets assigned the task of "delivering the bad news." Also, run the process publicly so that everyone can see that everyone else gets defeated by the A/B tests at about the same rate.

In addition, group discussions—also called *peer review*—of experiment design and analysis will be very helpful in detecting and excising experimenter bias. It turns out that people often have an "inverse" bias about other people's experiments, especially in competitive environments. That inverse bias helps each person find the flaws in other people's experiments.

So far, this chapter may have felt like a lot of bad news. A Pandora's chapter. Fortunately, like Pandora's box, in the end you'll receive something to combat all the problems presented so far—independent replication.

8.5   *Replicate to validate results*

A common thread in the previous sections of this chapter has been that you can neither rid your experiments completely of flaws, nor can you often even detect them. Our recourse is independent replication. We take the results from our experiments, and we try to reproduce them in later experiments. This chapter discusses a few ways to implement replication: run an A/B test to validate a more complex experiment, run a reverse A/B test for a long period of time, and measure the net effect of several experiments with a holdout test. Let's talk about validation first.

8.5.1   *Validate complex experiments*

The idea of running an A/B test after a complex experiment was first discussed in chapter 4, section 4.1.5, when presenting response surface methodology (RSM). RSM can take multiple iterations to complete, and each iteration requires multiple steps (modeling, optimization, recentering). That's a lot of complexity. The more complex a procedure is, the more likely an error may creep in. The same applies to a Bayesian optimization or any other complex experimental procedure you might encounter.

To reduce errors, you can take the result of your complex procedure, label it "version B," and run an A/B test to compare it to the production version that was running before you started the complex experiment.

To increase the informativeness of a validation, you might consider running an experiment under conditions that differ from the ones under which the original experiment was run. That could mean

- A different set of users (web apps)
- A different set of stocks (trading)
- Different servers, databases, data center, and so on
- After some meaningful amount of time has passed (to address nonstationarity)

Once you're convinced that your new version B is ready, you can apply it to the entire production system. Or you could be a little cautious and run a reverse A/B test.

8.5.2   *Monitor changes with a reverse A/B test*

Experiments have the unfortunate characteristic that they are run in a small period of time. This is a virtue in that the faster an experiment runs, the less time and risk you spend on it and the more time you have to experiment on other ideas. The problem is nonstationarity. The dynamics of your system change over time. You'd like to measure and capitalize on dynamics effects that last a long time (so you can capitalize on them for longer). The shorter an experiment is, the less confidence you'll have that its result will apply for the long-term.

One way to deal with this is to run a "reverse A/B test." In a normal (not reverse) A/B test, you'll typically dedicate a small amount of *flow*—flow could be users, impression, trades, and so on—to version B. You don't want to dedicate more than necessary because of the risk of running new code, so B's flow is generally small compared to the entire flow.

In a reverse A/B test, you scale B up to almost all the flow, but dedicate a little to the old version, version A. Then you can monitor the difference in business metric between A and B over a longer period of time—which still capitalizes on the effect you think B has on the system.

The reverse A/B will give you confidence that you made the right decision in moving to B, or, occasionally, it will point out nonstationarity, where B is no longer better than A, and save you from the negative impact of B. If that occurs, you might consider designing and running another A/B test—since the small reverse A/B test might not have the statistical significance you desire—or just reverting to A.

A reverse A/B test is great, but when you're running experiments frequently, the Bs that need to be tracked might pile up, making their reverse A/B tests use up too much of the flow. In that case you might consider batching results by time (i.e., creating a holdout).

8.5.3 *Measure quarterly changes with holdouts*

When you run experiments at high throughput, you'll have many results that need to be monitored over time. Also, your team might be evaluated on a periodic (e.g., quarterly, yearly) basis. To address both of these needs, you can run a holdout measurement. It will tell you whether a set of system upgrades (version Bs from multiple experiments) is working, and it'll report their net improvement on one or more business metrics.

To run a holdout, at the beginning of a quarter (or other evaluation period), make a snapshot of the system code, and run a small amount of flow through it. As the quarter progresses, run your experiments on the rest of the flow, and deploy good B versions to all the flow except the holdout. As the quarter progresses—and especially at the end—you can compare the net effect of deploying all your good B versions to the A version from the beginning of the quarter. This will give you confidence that your deployments were good decisions (in aggregate, at least), and yield business metric improvement values for you to report when evaluating your team's work.

Note that a common observation is that the sum of all the measured business metric improvements over the quarter is less than the net improvement measured by the holdout. This may be due to optimism in the original measurements, nonstationarity, or other reasons.

8.6 *Wrapping up*

We're nearing the end of *Experimentation for Engineers*. Over the past eight chapters, we've discussed

- The need to measure business metrics
- Experimental methods to measure business metrics
- Tips to integrate experimentation into your organization

Business metric measurements should be the ultimate arbiter of system modification—not prediction quality, simulations, or domain knowledge. Chapter 1 made the case for this.

The experimental methods presented in chapters 2–6 were ordered to show how each method is built upon the previous ones. Additionally, they are all explained from the perspective of experimental optimization. My hope is that by presenting all of these methods as a single, coherent subject, you will have found it easier to learn them and will find it easier to apply them (than if you had studied them independently).

Finally, chapters 7 and 8 connected the methods to the "real world," where circumstances are not ideal and where people (not mathematical rules) are making the decisions.

I hope you've taken as much away from this as I've put into it. It's been my pleasure writing for you.

Summary

- Verify that the iid and nonstationarity assumptions apply to your measurements.
- Don't stop early or cherry-pick or you'll generate many false positives.
- Incomplete randomization may leave confounder bias in your measurements.
- Replicate broadly to remove small-sample bias.
- Expect regression to the mean because of the optimism bias in your decision rule.
- Apply a standardized process, including peer review, to combat experimenter bias.
- Validate experimental results using reverse A/B tests and holdouts.

appendix A
Linear regression
and the normal equations

Linear regression is used in chapter 4 in the RSM analyze stage, as well as in chapter 5 in the contextual bandit's map from context and action to reward. It appears in many contexts in experimentation, machine learning, and quantitative trading. In this appendix, you'll learn about the core component of the solution to a linear regression problem, the normal equation.

A.1 Univariate linear regression

In chapter 4, section 4.1.3 we sought a model that could interpolate a function of the business metric—which, in chapter 4, was `markout_profit(threshold)`—between three measured values of the system's parameter (which was `threshold`). While there are simpler linear algebraic methods tailored to the specific problem of finding a parabola passing through exactly three points, we used linear regression because it continues to work as the number of aggregate measurements grows and the number of system parameters grows.

Linear regression estimates the weights (i.e., the betas) of a linear model. We say it *fits* the model to some measurements. The model we use in chapter 4, section 4.1.2 for 1D RSM is $y = \beta_0 + \beta_1 x + \beta_2 x^2 + \varepsilon$. In this model y varies linearly in each of β_0, β_1, and β_2. (Linear dependence on the betas gives rise to the name *linear model*. It doesn't matter that there's an x^2 term, which makes y nonlinear in x. Linear regression means "linear in the betas".)

For the moment, though, let's focus on a simpler model with one beta, called a *univariate model*: $y = \beta_x + \varepsilon$. We'll show how to find β, then come back to the more complex model afterward.

The first term in the model, β_x, is an estimate of y, and $\varepsilon = y - \hat{y}$ is the error in the estimate. We want to choose the value of β that results in the best fit. A fit is considered better if it has smaller-sized errors.

While ε may be positive or negative, and $\varepsilon = 0$ would be ideal, we could say that we want the size of the errors, $|\varepsilon|$, to be as small as possible. It turns out, for technical reasons, that absolute values are inconvenient to work with, but ε^2 is not, so we work with ε^2. We seek the value of β that makes the sum of ε^2 as small as possible. Figure A.1 depicts the univariate linear regression problem for five measurements.

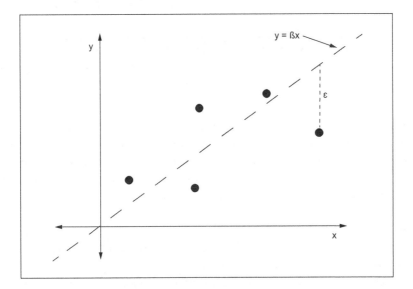

Figure A.1   Depiction of five measurements, filled dots, with values y_N taken at parameter values x_n. A model, $y = \beta_x + \varepsilon$, is shown as a dashed line. Each measurement's true value is the y value at its filled dot. The model's estimate of y, given beta β_x, is the point on the dashed line vertically nearest to it. The vertical distance is ε, the error.

Given a set of aggregate measurements indexed by n, y_n, each taken at a different parameter value, x_n, and some choice for β, would give an error $\varepsilon_n = y_n - \beta x_n$. If we took five measurements in an experiment, for example, we could tabulate all the information as in table A.1.

In other words, for every measurement $n = 1,2,3, \ldots$ we have a single value of ε, ε_n. In the notation of table A.1, the total error over the set of measurements is defined as $E = \sum_n \varepsilon_n^2 = \sum_n (y_n - \beta x_n)^2$. We want to find the value of β that minimizes E. This value is called the *ordinary least squares* (OLS) estimate of β. "Squares" because we're squaring the ε's, "least" because we're going to find the β that minimizes E, and "ordinary" to differentiate from the many variations of this procedure that have been invented.

Table A.1 Defining an error term, ε, for each of five measurements given a value for β

Index, n	Parameter, x	Measurement, y	Error, ε
1	x_1	y_1	$\varepsilon_1 = y_1 - \beta x_1$
2	x_2	y_2	$\varepsilon_2 = y_2 - \beta x_2$
3	x_3	y_3	$\varepsilon_3 = y_3 - \beta x_3$
4	x_4	y_4	$\varepsilon_4 = y_4 - \beta x_4$
5	x_5	y_5	$\varepsilon_5 = y_5 - \beta x_5$

The minimization of E can be performed analytically using a little calculus. Just differentiate E with respect to β, and set that expression equal to 0:

$$\frac{dE}{d\beta} = \sum_n 2(y_n - \beta x_n)x_n = 0$$

This is the normal equation. Equivalently,

$$\sum_n y_n x_n = \beta \sum_n x_n^2$$

or

$$\beta = \frac{\sum_n x_n y_n}{\sum_n x_n^2}$$

This is the OLS estimate of β. This result is significant because it can be expressed analytically. Often, in engineering, parameters for models or systems are found only approximately, using iterative guess-and-check-style optimization algorithms or laborious experimental methods (e.g., as taught in this book). Linear regression, by contrast, is fast and exact. Use it wherever you can! You can experiment with a small data set in Python:

```
x = np.array([1, 2, 3, 4])
y = np.array([.5, 1.1, 1.4, 2.1])
```

The solution for β is written in NumPy as

```
beta = (x*y).sum() / (x**2).sum()
```

You may write this more compactly using NumPy's @ (dot product) notation as

```
beta = (x@y) / (x@x)
```

Written either way, you should find that beta = 0.51.

A.2 *Multivariate linear regression*

Finding the β_i for the original multivariate (i.e., more than one β_i) model, $y = \beta_0 + \beta_1 x + \beta_2 x^2 + \varepsilon$, follows a similar path. To make the steps clear and concise, one typically uses matrix notation. Define a single vector, β, containing all of the β_i:

$$\beta = [\beta_0, \beta_1, \beta_2]^T$$

Define a matrix X where each row contains $[1, x_n, x_n^2]$, where n indexes the measurements:

$$X = \begin{bmatrix} 1 & x_1 & x_1^2 \\ 1 & x_2 & x_2^2 \\ 1 & x_3 & x_3^2 \\ & \vdots & \end{bmatrix}$$

You should convince yourself that if you multiply $X\beta$, each row of the resulting column vector is just $\beta_0 + \beta_1 x_n + \beta_2 x_n^2$. With this new notation, the multivariate model may be written to look very similar to the simpler, single-beta model we just worked with:

$$y = X\beta + \varepsilon$$

However, in this case, X is a matrix and β is a vector.

The solution—the best-fit value β—is the one that minimizes the error, $E = \sum_n \varepsilon_n^2 = \varepsilon^T \varepsilon$, where I've created a vector ε, the elements of which are ε_n, so that the error may be written compactly as $\varepsilon^T \varepsilon$, or $E = (y - X\beta)^T (y - X\beta) = y^T y - y^T X\beta - (X\beta)^T y + (X\beta)^T (X\beta) = y^T y - y^T X\beta - \beta^T X^T y + \beta^T X^T X\beta$.

Again, differentiate E with respect to β, and set that expression equal to 0 to get the normal equation:

$$\nabla_\beta E = 0$$

where the notation $\nabla_b f(b) = [df / db_1, df / db_2, df / db_3, \ldots]$. Going term by term,

$$\nabla_\beta y^T y = 0$$

$$\nabla_\beta y^T X\beta = (y^T X)^T = X^T y$$

using the identify $\nabla_b A^T b = A$,

$$\nabla_\beta \beta^T X^T y = X^T y$$

using $\nabla_b b^T A = A$, and

$$\nabla_\beta \beta^T X^T X \beta = 2X^T X \beta$$

using $\nabla_b b^T A^T A b = 2A^T A b$. Putting it all together you get

$$\nabla_\beta E = -2X^T y + 2X^T X \beta = 0$$

Whew. If that seems like a lot of notation, rest assured that it's all there to make the process of juggling multiple betas and all your measurements tidier. In the end, we get a nice, compact expression for β:

$$\beta = (X^T X)^{-1}(X^T y)$$

Please take a moment to convince yourself that if X was just a column vector of x_n and β was a scalar (a number), then this would be exactly the expression $\beta = \frac{\sum_n x_n y_n}{\sum_n x^2}$, the solution to the univariate model.

You can experiment with the multivariate model using a small data set:

```
x = np.array([1, 2, 3, 4])
y = np.array([.5, 1.1, 1.4, 1])
```

First construct X:

```
X = np.array([
   [1, x[0], x[0]**2],
   [1, x[1], x[1]**2],
   [1, x[2], x[2]**2],
   [1, x[3], x[3]**2]
])
```

Then write the solution for β in NumPy as

```
beta = np.linalg.inv(X.T @ X) @ (X.T @ y)
```

You should find that `beta = [-0.7 1.43 -0.25]`.

An excellent reference for linear regression in the ML context is chapter 3 of Hastie et al., *The Elements of Statistical Learning: Data Mining, Inference, and Prediction* (Springer, 2017).

appendix B
One factor at a time

An enticing approach to optimizing multiple parameters using RSM (see chapter 4, section 4.2) might be to use the 1D RSM procedure on each parameter in turn. For example, when optimizing two parameters, `threshold` and `order_size`, you could have first optimized only `threshold`, frozen its value, and then optimized only `order_size`.

This approach, called *one factor at a time* (OFAT), can be effective at improving the business metric of a system. In general, however, optimizing one parameter (aka, "factor") at a time will not find the optimal parameter settings. Let's walk through an example to see how that can be the case.

Suppose you have a system with two parameters x_0, and x_1 (these two parameters could represent `threshold` and `order_size`, for example). You want to find the settings of x_0 and x_1 that maximize y (the business metric, such as `markout_profit`). Also, imagine that you were handed the system already running with the settings tuned manually by an operator to $x_0 = -0.4$ and $x_1 = 0.8$. Let's say that at these settings $y = 6.84$.

First, you optimize x_0 with x_1 fixed at $x_1 = 0.8$. Figure B.1(a) depicts the horizontal line along which you run a 1D RSM. Figure B.1(b) shows how y varies with x_0. So y is maximized at $x_0^* = -0.18$, where $y^* = 4.08$. Returning to figure B.1(a), note that the X marks the value x_0^* that is optimal along that line.

Next, in OFAT style, we'll fix $x_0 = x_0^* = -0.18$ and vary just x_1 in a 1D RSM; see figure B.1(c). This 1D RSM finds that y is maximized at $x_1^* = 0.00$, where $y = 7.40$. Thus, the OFAT optimization suggests running the system at $x_0^* = -0.18$, $x_1^* = 0.00$, and estimates that the business metric will be $y = 7.40$. This is an improvement over the original, manually tuned parameters that ran at $y = 6.84$, but is it optimal?

Let's look at the full function $y(x_0, x_1)$. Figure B.2 shows that OFAT did not find the optimal settings.

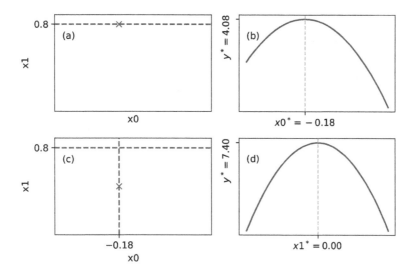

Figure B.1 Optimize a two-parameter system using OFAT. (a) First, optimize over x_0 at a fixed x_1. (b) A 1D RSM chooses $x_0{}^* = -0.18$, which maximizes y at $y = 4.08$. (c) Next, optimize over x_1 at the just-chosen optimum $x_0 = x_0{}^* = -0.18$. (d) (Note that the x-axis is now x_1.) A 1D RSM chooses $x_1{}^* = 0.00$, which maximizes y at $y = 7.40$.

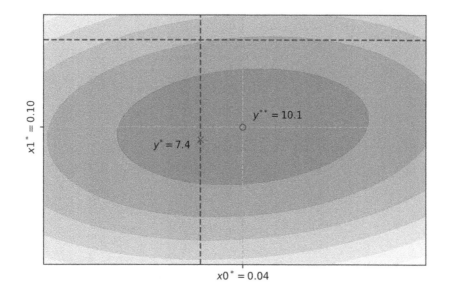

Figure B.2 The full function $y(x_0, x_1)$ reveals that the true maximal y is $y^{**} = 10.1$, which is significantly greater than the value found by OFAT, $y^* = 7.4$. The dark dashed lines show where we ran 1D RSM in OFAT—first on the horizonal line, then on the vertical line. OFAT suggested using the parameter settings marked with the X, even though the optimum is at the circle.

In a real system, you won't have access to the full function $y(x_0, x_1)$, but chapter 4 (specifically, section 4.2.1) shows how to estimate it with a 2D RSM procedure.

No discussion of OFAT would be complete without pointing out that in any real, sufficiently complex system you'll have many parameters available to set. You generally won't be able to optimize all of them at once. Even if you optimize two, or three, or more parameters, you'll still be leaving most of the system's parameters fixed. Maybe the best you can hope for (typically, in practice) is "a few factors at a time."

appendix C
Gaussian process regression

Gaussian process regression (GPR) is a method of estimating function values directly from a set of measurements. In the context of Bayesian optimization, we imagine there exists a true function, business metric versus parameter, from which we take a few measurements. GPR estimates the value of the business metric at parameters for which we haven't taken measurements. It forms these estimates from the measurements we have already taken.

Let's call the parameter x (a vector of all the system parameters) and the business metric y (a scalar, a number). Let's say we've already taken N measurements. We'll index them by i and call the measurements x_i, y_i. Note that each x_i is a vector.

Our task is to estimate the business metric at one or more parameter vectors for which we haven't taken measurements. Call these parameter vectors $\hat{x}_j$ and the estimates $\hat{y}_j$ and say there are M of them.

GPR is distinctly different from linear regression in that there is no fitting stage. GPR has no betas to estimate. Instead, it estimates the expectations of $\hat{y}_j$ directly from the y_i—as a weighted average of them. GPR goes further than that, though. It also estimates the covariance matrix of the $\hat{y}_j$. The covariance matrix tells us how uncertain GPR is about its own estimates, $\hat{y}_j$. It also tells us how similar any two estimates, say $\hat{y}_j$ and $\hat{y}_{j'}$, need to be to each other for them to be consistent with the set of measurements. This measure of similarity makes it so that the GPR estimates vary smoothly from parameter value to parameter value.

In what follows, we'll explain the GPR equations first presented in chapter 6, section 6.2 and summarized here:

$$\hat{y} = K(x, \hat{x})^T K(x, x)^{-1} y$$

$$S = K(\hat{x}, \hat{x}) - K(x, \hat{x})^T K(x, x)^{-1} K(x, \hat{x})$$

where $\hat{y}$ is a vector of all $\hat{y}_j$. $K(x, \hat{x})$ is a matrix whose i, j-th element is the kernel function

$$k(x_i, \hat{x}_j) = \exp\left(-\frac{\|x_i - \hat{x}_j\|^2}{2\sigma}\right)$$

$K(\hat{x}, \hat{x})$ and $K(x, x)$ are similarly defined. The model uncertainties of the $\hat{y}_j$ are the (square roots of) the diagonal entries of S, $\sigma_{\hat{y}}^2 = \text{diag}(S)$.

What makes GPR "Gaussian" is that we model each unmeasured y as a draw from a Gaussian distribution with mean $\hat{y}_j$ and variance $\sigma_{\hat{y}_j}^2$. Actually, we go further than that. We model all N measurements, y_i, and M estimates, $\hat{y}_j$, as a single, multivariate, $M + N$-dimensional Gaussian distribution, $p(\hat{y}|y)$. Treating this all as a single distribution means that

1 When we make a batch of estimates, $\hat{y}$, we'll preserve the property that nearby (in $\hat{x}$) estimates will have similar values.

2 We can state the estimation process as one of computing $p(\hat{y}|y)$, or, "What is the multivariate probability distribution of all of the $\hat{y}$ given that we know the exact values of the measurements y?"

Note that a Gaussian distribution is defined completely by its expectation and covariance. For a univariate Gaussian distribution—for a scalar z—we'd write

$$p(z) \propto \exp\left(\frac{-1}{2\sigma^2}(z - \mu)^2\right)$$

The probability is proportional to the exponential. If we wanted to compute the constant of proportionality, we could integrate over all values of z and insist that the integral equal 1 (i.e., the total probability possible is always 1). But we won't. We don't care about the constant here. We just want to know the expectation and variance. For a multivariate distribution—for a vector z—we write

$$p(z) \propto \exp\left(-\frac{1}{2}(z - \mu)^T S^{-1}(z - \mu)\right)$$

In the GPR estimation problem, we imagine a distribution over the collection of $N + M$ dimensions, the y and $\hat{y}$ together. To make it clear that we're dealing with two different sets of numbers, we'll write

$$z = \begin{bmatrix} \hat{y} \\ y \end{bmatrix}$$

and

$$S = \begin{bmatrix} K(\hat{x}, \hat{x}) & K(\hat{x}, x) \\ K(x, \hat{x}) & K(x, x) \end{bmatrix}$$

This is called *block matrix form*. The vector z comprises two column vectors stacked on top of each other. The matrix S comprises the four $K(\cdot,\cdot)$ matrices arranged as shown.

To simplify presentation, we'll assume the overall expectation is 0 ($\mu = 0$). Finally, to make this all easier to read (in my opinion), I'm going to define some working variables:

$$a = \hat{y}$$
$$b = y$$
$$A = K(\hat{x}, \hat{x})$$
$$B = K(x, x)$$
$$C = K(x, \hat{x})$$

Then we can write $z = \begin{bmatrix} a \\ b \end{bmatrix}$ and $S = \begin{bmatrix} A & C^T \\ C & B \end{bmatrix}$. Note that $K(x, \hat{x}) = K^T(\hat{x}, x)$.

The multivariate probability distribution becomes

$$p(a, b) \sim \exp\left(-\frac{1}{2} \begin{bmatrix} a & b \end{bmatrix} \begin{bmatrix} A & C^T \\ C & B \end{bmatrix}^{-1} \begin{bmatrix} a \\ b \end{bmatrix}\right)$$

and the task of estimation, "find $p(\hat{y}|y)$", is now "find $p(a|b)$".

Believe it or not, there's not much left to do. We need to invert the matrix, S (see sidebar), multiply out, and collect terms and we'll find that

$$p(a, b) \propto \exp\left(-\frac{1}{2}(a - C^T B^{-1} b)^T (A - C^T B^{-1} C)^{-1} (a - C^T B^{-1} b)\right) \exp\left(-\frac{1}{2} b^T B^{-1} b\right)$$

Inverting S

The inverse of

$$S = \begin{bmatrix} A & C^T \\ C & B \end{bmatrix}$$

is

$$S^{-1} = \begin{bmatrix} I & 0 \\ -B^{-1}C & I \end{bmatrix} \begin{bmatrix} (A - C^T B^{-1} C)^{-1} & 0 \\ 0 & B^{-1} \end{bmatrix} \begin{bmatrix} I & -C^T B^{-1} \\ 0 & I \end{bmatrix}$$

Where *I* is the identity matrix.

This is long and complicated, but at least it's already known. You can convince yourself that it's true by verifying that $SS^{-1} = S^{-1}S = I$, which is just the definition of the matrix inverse.

(continued)

For example:

$$SS^{-1} = \begin{bmatrix} A & C^T \\ C & B \end{bmatrix} \begin{bmatrix} I & 0 \\ -B^{-1}C & I \end{bmatrix} \begin{bmatrix} (A - C^T B^{-1} C)^{-1} & 0 \\ 0 & B^{-1} \end{bmatrix} \begin{bmatrix} I & -C^T B^{-1} \\ 0 & I \end{bmatrix}$$

$$= \begin{bmatrix} A - C^T B^{-1} C & C^T \\ 0 & B \end{bmatrix} \begin{bmatrix} (A - C^T B^{-1} C)^{-1} & 0 \\ 0 & B^{-1} \end{bmatrix} \begin{bmatrix} I & -C^T B^{-1} \\ 0 & I \end{bmatrix}$$

$$= \begin{bmatrix} I & C^T B^{-1} \\ 0 & I \end{bmatrix} \begin{bmatrix} I & -C^T B^{-1} \\ 0 & I \end{bmatrix}$$

$$= \begin{bmatrix} I & 0 \\ 0 & I \end{bmatrix}$$

Before we decipher this, note that $b = y$ is measured already, so they're constants. We said we don't care about constants because the real information is in the expectation and covariance, so we can simplify by dropping the second (constant) exponential, $\exp\left(-\frac{1}{2} b^T B^{-1} b\right)$:

$$p(a, b) \propto \exp\left(-\frac{1}{2}(a - C^T B^{-1} b)^T (A - C^T B^{-1} C)^{-1} (a - C^T B^{-1} b)\right)$$

This is also the distribution $p(a|b)$, since the b's are constant (fixed values), and we're only interested in how $a = \hat{y}$ varies.

From the form of the distribution above, we can read off the expectation of a,

$$\mu_a = C^T B^{-1} b$$

and the covariance:

$$S_a = A - C^T B^{-1} C$$

Translating these working variables back into the original ones yields

$$\mu_{\hat{y}} = K(x, \hat{x})^T K^{-1}(x, x) y$$

and

$$S_{\hat{y}} = K(\hat{x}, \hat{x}) - K(x, \hat{x})^T K^{-1}(x, x) K(x, \hat{x})$$

which are the GPR estimation formulae.

index